The M

Prion Lost Treasures

The Bourbons of Naples • Harold Acton

Disraeli • Robert Blake

Dylan Thomas in America • John Malcolm Brinnin

The River War • Winston S. Churchill

Doom • William Gerhardie

The Polyglots • William Gerhardie

Poets in a Landscape • Gilbert Highet

The Dilessi Murders • Romilly Jenkins

Mozart • Annette Kolb

Sardinian Brigade • Emilio Lussu

Napoleon and his Marshals • A G Macdonell

Kabul Catastrophe • Patrick Macrory

Byron — The Last Journey • Harold Nicolson

Verdun • Jules Romains

Conversations with Wellington • Earl Stanhope

Napoleon's Letters • J M Thompson

A King's Story • H. R. H. the Duke of Windsor

Memoirs Vol I • Duc de Saint-Simon

Memoirs Vol II• Duc de Saint-Simon

Memoirs Vol III• Duc de Saint-Simon

Century in Scarlet • Lajos Zilahy

The Dukays • Lajos Zilahy

Two Prisoners • Lajos Zilahy

The Case of Sergeant Grischa • Arnold Zweig

Text Acknowledgments

Several quotations are made in the text and the publishers wish to thank the following for permission to use them: Major-General E. L. Spears for permission to quote from *Liaison 1914* (Heinemann, 1930); and the Right Hon. The Earl of Ypres for permission to quote from *1914* by Field Marshal Sir John French (Constable, 1919).

Photograph Acknowledgments

Cover: Ullstein bild, Berlin

1, 2, 7, 8, 9, 10, 12 Roger-Viollet, Paris

3, 4, 5, 6, 11 Ullstein bild, Berlin

Contents

ACKNOWLEDGMENTS 5

LIST OF MAPS 9

LIST OF PHOTOGRAPHS 11

1. "THE PRUSSIANS ARE COMING!" 13

2. "NACH PARIS!" 26

3. TWO SONS OF THE PEOPLE 43

4. GENERAL CASSANDRA 56

5. "À OUTRANCE!" 71

6. TROUBLE ON OLYMPUS 83

7. GALLIENI'S FINEST HOUR 97

8. THE DEATH OF CHARLES PÉGUY 133

9. "AT THE OUTSET OF A BATTLE" 143

10. THE MARSHES OF SAINT-GOND 157

11. THE PARIS TAXIS 170

12. THE PRUSSIAN GUARD COMES TO A HALT 184

13. VON MOLTKE FEELS THE STRAIN 208

14. THE MESSENGER OF DEFEAT 220

15. "DECISIVE VICTORY 237

INDEX 252

List of Maps

	page
THE SCHLIEFFEN PLAN, 1905 AND 1914	31
THE GERMAN ADVANCE, AUGUST–SEPTEMBER 1914	59
THE BATTLE OF THE MARNE, 7–8 SEPTEMBER 1914	151
TAXIS TO THE FRONT	173
THE BATTLE OF THE MARNE, 9–13 SEPTEMBER 1914	227

List of Photographs

1. The Kaiser, Wilhelm II *(centre)*, with his Chief of Staff, Helmut von Moltke, during the initial German assault on France, 1914

2. General Joffre, the French Commander-in-chief.

3. General von Kluck, Commander of the German First Army, crossing the Marne, August 1914. Fresh artillery is being unloaded from railway carriages.

4. German forces marching through Belgium, August 1914.

5. German infantry taking a short rest on the way to the Marne front.

6. Dead horses and destroyed materiel on the road of the retreating British forces near Clery (Peronne).

7. General Galliéni, Military Governor of Paris, 1915, the year before he died.

8. General Franchet-d'Esperey, Commander of the French Fifth Army.

9. General Joffre talking to Field Marshal Sir John French, Commander of the British Expeditionary Force. General Wilson is on the right.

10. French troops from the Paris garrison arrive at the Marne front by taxi, September 1914. Some 1200 taxis were used to rush forces to the front line; some are visible in the background

11. German soldiers in postion, awaiting a counter attack.

12. French bayonet charge in the streets of Rembercourt (Meuse).

I

"THE PRUSSIANS ARE COMING!"

"THE SITUATION on our front, from the Somme to the Vosges, has remained unchanged during the past twenty-four hours. The speed of the German advance seems to have slackened." So read the communiqué of August 29, 1914.

I was eight years old at the time. I can still see the people in the street, still see them opening and reading their newspapers. They read the words again, then folded their papers and walked on, their faces frozen, lifeless. To our childish questions they made no answer.

The communiqué was read out in the village streets. As the garde-champêtre arrived in the square the villagers assembled at the sound of the drum, one, at least, from each family. The garde-champêtre read in a loud voice. But on that day, when he had finished, there were many among the listeners who hoped they had misunderstood; they made him repeat the incredible words: "From the Somme to the Vosges . . . "

Few countries have suffered so many invasions as France. Her cities and towns, her convents and villages have seen the coming of the Huns, the Normans, the Moors, the "Kaiserlicks", the Prussians and a host of others. The peasants of the north and east had become hardened to it; it was almost a matter of routine. They knew the drill. But this time they – and, indeed, all other Frenchmen – were stunned.

They looked back over the immediate past and tried to understand how it had all come about, "Surely we're not going to war over the Serbs," people had said. There were admittedly, some veterans of 1870 who still talked of La Revanche; but the sun shone, and life was good, there would be a bumper harvest. War would be an unthinkable folly. And yet, once the die was cast, the whole country went wild with enthusiam. Scrawled in chalk on all the troop-trains were the words: "Train de plaisir pour Berlin." A thousand soldiers leaving for the front would suddenly break into La Marseillaise at the top of their voices, their throats bursting, while the crowds cheered along the platform.

The four thousand three hundred trains carrying troops through the length and breadth of the country were gay with flags and flowers. Peasants in the fields would wave as these convoys went by. They drew into stations in a long, cheering, happy line to an uproarious welcome. The men in them were seized upon, embraced, loaded with gifts and flowers, with sausages and kisses, glasses of wine. Crowds gathered, even at the wayside halts, shouting, "Vive la France! Vive l'Armée!" The youngsters called out, "Come back soon!" and the soldiers answered, "We'll be back in two months' time!" Women held up their children like an offering to the gods. An entire population had taken leave of its senses.

The entry of the French troops into Alsace had stirred every heart. The frontier posts bearing the black eagle were torn up and thrown aside. The girls, with the great, black Alsatian bow in their hair, flung themselves into soldiers' arms. There was the triumphal entry into Mulhouse. But, soon after, came the news that Mulhouse had had to be evacuated. News from that quarter became both scanty and vague; but there were other topics to keep popular enthusiasm alight: the Russian Steamroller was in action, the Cossacks were within five days' march of Berlin, the British Blockade was already beginning to starve the Germans out. The entry of German troops into Brussels had cast a momentary gloom over the picture; but then French troops also had entered Belgium. In the region of Charleroi . . . .

Fighting had become general in Belgium, in Lorraine, in Alsace. People at home read the communiqués and stuck little flags in their maps. But the line of little flags seldom moved, and long train-loads of wounded soldiers rumbled through the railway stations. This was no triumphant advance (that short-lived hope had faded). A life-and-death struggle had begun. The flames of Louvain served to forge the steely resolution of the people at home. Anyone whispering that an army corps had faltered or fallen back was either a defeatist or a spy. The first flag captured from the enemy was displayed out of the window of the War Ministry, Rue Saint Dominique, "Dangling like a corpse on the gibbet at Montfaucon;* hanging like dead game, doomed to slow decomposition." So wrote Henri Lavedan.

On August 25th the communiqué had announced: "Our offensive has not succeeded in breaking into the enemy lines." A slight withdrawal was necessary, pending more favourable conditions. But there was nothing very alarming in a slight withdrawal in Belgium; nothing to shake one's confidence or make one lose patience. *"Patience"* was a word one began to hear fairly often now. Then came the thunderbolt out of the blue: "From the Somme to the Vosges . . . the speed of the German advance *seems* to have slackened."

The general retreat of the French armies had begun on August 24th, following upon the withdrawal of the 5th Army, threatened with encirclement at Charleroi. On the 27th the Germans had taken Lille and Mêzières; Longwy had surrendered. By the 28th, the 1st German Army, under von Kluck, had forced the passages of the Somme near Péronne. The retreat of the French forces continued.

It was a full-scale retreat, but not a rout, that is to say that the vast operation was being carried out, for the most part, in good order. An immense human tide – of more than a million men in arms – was flowing south; but it was being contained, canalised, divided into rivers that flowed in courses selected by the High Command. The inhabitants of the cities, towns and villages, who had seen, first the cavalry, then the infantry, then the artillery, then the ammunition and supply columns going forward, now saw them come back in the reverse order: the vehicles, the guns, the infantry and finally, the cavalry. A few guns would sometimes bring up the rear, to cover the retreat.

The harvest was over, the weather was still perfect; one of the most magnificent summers for a hundred-and-fifty years. A sleepy, sun-drenched village would hear the sound of distant, random gun-fire. Within a few minutes the first vehicles would appear. Their drivers were on foot, at the

---

*Place of execution, in N.E. quarter of Paris. Erected in the thirteenth century; removed 1761.

horses' heads, bridle in hand. Their uniforms were grey with dust. The gunners followed, marching beside their guns and limbers as if at a soldier's funeral. The famous 75's seemed strangely small; their paint looked scorched. Then came the infantry.

The foot-soldiers had broken step, but they marched in files eight deep, like a broad stream as wide as a road. They filled the main street of the village from wall to wall. Every face amongst them was blotched by a beard of several days' growth and lined with intense fatigue. They looked straight ahead, seeing apparently nothing to right or left, trudging ceaselessly on and on. Without uttering a word. The only sound breaking the silence was the tramp of this mass of soldiers. No one dared question them; they seemed to come from another world. Some had their heads wrapped in a bandage that showed below the képi; others had bandages on their hands.

In some of the towns the stream of soldiers flowed on throughout the day, for a day and a night, sometimes for two days. Women would stand at their doors, watching them pass, for an hour, perhaps two hours, perhaps three; then they would go in and get on with their work, or sit for a while. But they could still hear the ceaseless tramp of marching men; and they would come out again and again to find that human river still flowing by. After a while, overcome by the sound of it, they would break down and weep.

In the torrid heat of August the infantrymen of France were dressed in the most irrational uniform ever known. It was a target and a burden, with its red trousers, long great-coat, broadcloth tunic, flannel shirt and long underpants, winter and summer. Ironically, their boots were known as "Brodequins", which was the name of an ancient instrument of torture. No soldier in any army in the world today would be willing to march ten miles in such boots. The infantryman had to carry his Lebel rifle, a ridiculous kit weighing nearly sixty-six pounds, and, on top of it, the regulation bundle of kindling wood for lighting the bivouac fire at night. Hundreds of thousands of these men had marched a hundred miles or more through vast forests without discarding this precious bundle of firewood; at any rate, during the first week of the greatest military retreat ever recorded in French history.

There were ambulances, too, squeezed into the column until they could reach an entraining point. Through the curtains at the rear a few prone bodies could be seen; a few ashen faces. Now and then a complete convoy of ambulances went by. Some would stop to let the wounded men drink, or relieve themselves. Women would bustle round, eager to help the orderlies, gleaning a little sombre satisfaction from their own compassionate gestures.

Last of all, sometimes escorting the guns covering the retreat, came the cavalry. There were certainly no prancing horses to be seen. Not one of them, indeed, could have been urged, even into a trot. They crawled by at a walk, so slowly that they seemed to be moving in a dream-world. Their riders, clad in the uniforms of another age, were asleep in the saddle, their eyes wide open.

In the slow-moving, solemn procession were helmeted Dragoons, with sabre and lance, in showy, sky-blue tunics, trefoiled epaulettes, red breeches with pale-blue piping. But the dust of defeat lay on all this finery; many of the uniforms were torn. There were Cuirassiers, too, with their straight swords, their carbines in the right-hand bucket, helmets covered with dark brown cloth. Some of the troopers looked like armoured automatons, their torsos bulging with the cuirass worn by their regiments in 1870.

Columns of refugees could be seen streaming through these and other villages, sometimes ahead of the troops, sometimes behind them, sometimes on roads parallel to theirs. This migration differed, however, from the chaotic exodus of June, 1940 in the sense that, during the early days at least, the flood of refugees was not allowed to become involved with the columns of troops. It was directed into specific channels by the local gendarmes, halted when necessary, then set moving again.

The spectacle of a civilian population fleeing from the invader has always left an indelible impression upon those who have witnessed it or even read of it. But the misery of the people crowding along the roads in August and September 1914 had a pathos all its own. Most of these people from Belgium or the north of France had fled from their homes dressed in their Sunday black, soon to be covered with the dust of the sun-bleached roads. There were horse or ox-drawn carts carrying the children and the old people; and all the pitiful makeshifts that appear at such times: handcarts, perambulators and wheelbarrows. No motor-cars in those days. These harassed, dust-covered marchers had no idea where they were bound for; no plan: they simply marched due south. Their plight was so pitiful that other villagers, who had also prepared for flight, abandoned even that hope as they watched this lamentable procession go by.

There were times when the road had to be cleared for a column of troops, and the gendarmes had to deal roughly with this bewildered mass of unhappy creatures, whose staring, vacant eyes showed that they were at the end of their tether. Pathetic old couples, arm in arm, leaning on each other as they had done throughout their lives, would make desperate efforts to quicken their pace, then be thrust aside and pushed into the hedgerows, even into the fields, where they would collapse in utter exhaustion. On each side of the road a fringe of human wreckage had been left behind when the procession had passed on; old men and old women lying dead from sunstroke, lost children, weeping mothers. Such was the price paid to ensure the orderly retreat of the fighting men. Three weeks earlier they had been marching joyfully up to the frontier. Now, in retreat, they had to break through these floods of desolate humanity and march south, day after day, for how long no one could tell.

In 1913 Colonel de Grandmaison, in charge of the Operations Section at G.H.Q., had given two lectures at the Staff College which had greatly impressed his audience:

"The moral factors (he said) are not the most important, but they are the only really decisive factors in war. In practice, everything must be sacrificed to ensure coming to grips at once with the enemy and creating in him a defensive mentality. There must be no undue anxiety over minor errors, incidental risks or possibility of failure. In the offensive, temerity is the safest policy. One's only concern must be to seek out the enemy and attack him. What his intentions may be are of little consequence, since we claim to impose our own will upon him. And our conclusion must be to prepare ourselves – and others – for the offensive by cultivating with passion and fanaticism, even in the minutest details of our teaching, every idea that bears the true mark of the offensive spirit. It is impossible to exaggerate the importance of this teaching, for whatever we achieve in this direction will still fall short of our aim."

The *Rules for the Control of Large Formations* dated October 28th, 1913, had been based directly upon these same principles. "Only by attack," it stated, "can positive results be secured. A resolute commander-in-chief, with confidence in himself, in his subordinates and in his troops, must never, on the pretext of waiting for precise information, let the initiative pass to the enemy. He must, from the outset, conduct all his operations in a spirit of implacable aggressiveness so as to shake the enemy morale, paralyse his movements and force him, in all probability, to remain on the defensive."

To remain on the defensive was considered to be the worst of all evils, an attitude of inferiority inherited from the defeat of 1870, and certain to lead once again to disaster. On August 8, 1914, the French armies, concentrated along an oblique front facing east, from Belfort to Hirson (Aisne), had received General Operation Order Number One, giving each army commander his first objective, and summing up in this superb sentence: "The Commander-in-Chief's intention is to engage the enemy with the combined strength of all forces, the right flank of the operation resting on the Rhine." The final paragraph called upon army commanders to take all the necessary steps to promote the attack and to give it the speed and power of lightning.

But no lightning had struck the German armies. The frontier battle had gone on from August 17th to August 24th. On that day Joffre, the Commander-in-Chief, had written to the Minister for War, informing him that "as our general offensive in Belgium had been definitely checked, we were forced to take defensive action based on our fortified positions and on the strong natural obstacles provided by the terrain, so as to hold on as long as possible, taking, meanwhile, all steps to wear down the enemy's strength and resume the offensive in due course". The Commander-in-Chief had also sent a report to the Prime Minister, René Viviani. That document contained a sentence which still rankles with some of the veterans of 1914: "Fighting in open country, our army corps failed to show the offensive qualities which our partial successes at the outset – achieved in conditions of mountain warfare – had led us to expect."

*   *   *

"I am seventy-three years old, Monsieur. In 1914 I was a regular lieutenant, 103rd Infantry Regiment, IV Corps. It was our regiment that made the attack at Ethe, near Virton, in the Belgian Ardennes. I assure you our men had their tails up all right. In those days, you know, everybody was patriotic. My men were good-natured, but what they said was, let's get on with the job and make Kaiser Bill shut up. Our regiment advanced with no scouts in front and no cover on our flanks, in wooded country and thick fog that lasted for twenty-four hours. General Félineau, commanding the 14th Brigade, was worried about going on blindfold like this, and he told the Divisional Commander, General de Trentinian, how he felt about it. As it happened, I passed quite close to the two generals as they were talking, on the road from Comery to Ethe. I remember it distinctly. I can still hear Trentinian, very haughty, looking down from his horse and saying, 'You are being extremely cautious, General!' So we went on.

"The Germans had been in the district for five days already. They were waiting for us. Under cover of the fog they had got their guns in concealed positions on the wooded hills around Ethe. Their infantry had evacuated the town itself. When we reached the bottom of that' gully they gave us everything they'd got. Our gunners were knocked out almost before they could come into action. A whole regiment of hussars was cut to pieces; 12th Hussars, Colonel de Hautecloque.

"But my men, Monsieur, held their ground. My company went straight in to attack the Ethe railway station, which was held by a regiment of Wurtembergers. Our men would lie down and fire a few rounds, then get up and rush forward, lie down and fire again, rush forward again. The Field Service Regulations assumed that in twenty seconds an assault line could cover fifty yards before the enemy infantry could re-load, raise their rifles, aim, and begin firing again. But the people who wrote those regulations had simply forgotten the existence of such things as machine-guns. We could distinctly hear two of those 'coffee grinders' at work; and every time our men got up to advance the line got thinner. Finally our captain gave the order: 'Fix bayonets and charge!' It was mid-day by now, and the fog had completely lifted; in fact, it was devilish hot. Our men, in full kit, started running heavily up that grassy slope, drums beating, bugles sounding the charge. We didn't even get up to those Wurtembergers. We were all shot down before we reached them. I got hit (like the rest of us) and I lay there until I was picked up later, after a counter-attack. But I don't want to tell you all about my own war experiences. I mentioned that charge because it was typical of what was going on at the time. It was straight out of the drill-book, and (as you might say) inevitable. My memory is good, and I can still repeat by heart some of the sentences in those famous Rules of December 2, 1913: 'Success depends far more upon forcefulness and tenacity than upon tactical skill. Attacks should always be pressed home with the firm intention of engaging the enemy at the point of the bayonet.' As you are interested in that particular period, I suppose you must have heard of the charge of the Second Zouaves at Auvelais, during the Charleroi battle? Drums beating, bugles blowing – like us at Ethe. The German machine-gunners had the time of their lives. And what about the First Tirailleurs,* also at Charleroi! Not only the machine-guns, but even the German 77's opened up on the lines of attacking infantry, over open sights! The Tirailleurs went in with the regimental colours flying. The rare survivors – I've met some of them – were heart-broken because their colours were captured. They had changed hands five times during the assault. The official report of that day's fighting stated that 'the colour-bearer was killed five times'. So now you know, Monsieur, what sort of men these were who (they say) had not shown the necessary 'offensive spirit' in open fighting."

*   *   *

The Germans had a certain liking for the tactical counter-attack; they had been trained in it and they excelled in it. In Alsace – as in the Virton sector – they lay in wait for the

*African Infantry Regiments.

French. From the time fighting began they had put in the field many batteries of 150 mm and 210 mm guns with twice the range of the only heavy mobile French gun, the 155 Rimailho. Their machine-guns were not superior to the French type, but they had more of them and they used them more effectively. Their 77 mm field-gun was inferior to the French 75, but their batteries were always better concealed. And another reason for the German superiority in the early engagements was that, in almost every sector, they outnumbered the French.

In May 1914 the Intelligence Branch of the French General Staff had succeeded in getting possession of the mobilisation plan of the German Army. In it was found this surprising instruction: "Reservist formations will be employed as front-line troops". The Commander-in-Chief's advisers had *refused to believe* this statement because it ran counter to their own assessments and would have forced them to revise the whole scheme for the deployment of the French forces (Plan XVII), which had been drawn up on the assumption that the Germans, even if they entered Belgium, would not extend their operations further north than Namur. On July 13, 1914, the General Staff, after completing its study of the German document, came to the conclusion that the strength of the German forces likely to be concentrated against France was twenty regular army corps, ten reservist army corps, eight cavalry divisions and eight reservist divisions, that is to say, a total of sixty-eight divisions. As a matter of fact, Germany eventually put in the field seventy-eight divisions – plus fourteen "Landwehr" brigades – and ten divisions of cavalry. "It must be admitted" (wrote Joffre in his Memoirs) "that the use made of the German reservist formations in August 1914 took us by surprise, and this fact was at the root of the mistakes that were made, particularly in regard to the extent of the German deployment in the north."

These mistakes had to be redeemed at a high price later, on the field of battle, along with the consequences of the staff's blind faith in the offensive as expressed in the *Rules for the Control of Large Formations, 1913*, and in the Field Service Regulations issued in the same year. A legend has grown up around these "red trouser" battles, giving them an aura of romantic glory, but, to see them in their true light, it is as well to quote at once the following figures of French casualties during August and September 1914: 329,000 killed, missing, taken prisoner, or died in hospital. In other words, the losses during those two months alone were about one-sixth of the total French losses during the war.

* * *

"I, Monsieur, was a sergeant in the light cavalry, 1st Cavalry Corps, under General Sordet – a first-class cavalry officer; very good family. All our officers in fact were very well-bred; several of them belonged to the nobility. We were the first regiment to enter Belgium, and we had a wonderful reception. Our first job was to reconnoitre enemy positions in eastern Belgium. South of Liége we saw some Uhlans moving in the direction of the Meuse. The captain gave the orders: 'Draw swords. Tighten sword-knots, and prepare for action.' We formed line and went off at a trot. I remember feeling a bit tense and excited. But we never got near enough to charge those Uhlans. They cleared off, and we ran straight into their infantry. That's what happened, Monsieur, over and over again – perhaps twenty or thirty times."

* * *

The French High Command had made up its mind that the German army front would be covered by an immense cavalry screen, well ahead of the main body, and that the rôle of the French cavalry would be to break through this screen and reconnoitre the main enemy forces behind it. On the rare occasions when cavalry clashes occurred the French proved to be greatly superior to the Germans. But the Uhlans would usually carry out a reconnaissance and then withdraw behind their infantry support. The result was that the pursuing French cavalry would find themselves under machine-gun, or even field-gun, fire – and be wiped out.

The French cavalry had no infantry support and practically no machine-guns (two only per brigade) because it had been decided that maximum mobility was required. For the same reason it was not burdened with a supply column. Fifteen thousand men and ten thousand horses were expected to "live on the country", by requisitioning their own food and forage.

The Cuirassiers and the Dragoons were armed with the straight sword, called a "latte", and the Hussars and light cavalry with the curved sabre, called a "bancal". The Dragoons and one regiment of light cavalry also carried lances, either of bamboo or hollow steel. The only fire-arm carried by this large body of troops was the magazine-loading carbine of the 1890 model.

General Sordet's First Cavalry Corps had been given the task of clearing the area of all enemy cavalry. But, as the enemy always split up into small groups and dispersed in every direction, the French cavalry had to cover an average of 35 miles a day, without a break. After every sortie they would find orders awaiting them for yet another mission; six of them (all in different directions) between August 15th and 17th. The Higher Command seemed to imagine they were dealing, not with cavalry, but with motorised vehicles; and in any case no motorised unit could have stood up to such an unending wild-goose chase. The French army horses, exhausted, often unshod, short of food and water, were amongst the earliest victims of the war. "Sordet has seen little fighting," wrote Joffre to Messimy, Minister of War; "but he seems half asleep. It's intolerable." The Higher Command had certainly succeeded in tiring out Sordet's cavalry corps without giving it the opportunity or the means of coming to serious grips with the enemy; and it was quite true, during the retreat, that the exhausted French cavalrymen often fell asleep in the saddle.

Every day the news of the great retreat of the French armies penetrated further behind the lines. "The Prussians are coming!" In the country districts they were still called "Prussians", or "Pruscos", as in 1870; rarely "Germans". The name "Boche" came later. Under the threat of invasion, one of the first precautions to be taken was to hide away such valuables as could not easily be moved. In every garden a hole would be dug – preferably at night, unseen by inquisitive neighbours. In the well-built, vaulted cellars of the north and north-east a section would be walled in, but not without the time-honoured device of mixing the mortar with earth, so that the new work would not be detected.

Then came the crucial question: Do we stay? Or do we

leave? Some there were who set out, only to return a few hours later because the roads were blocked, either by troops or by the pitiful stream of refugees. And so one quarter of the population of France would get ready to face – as all too often their forbears had done – the grim prospect of enemy occupation.

2

"NACH PARIS!"

THE OFFICES of the O.H.L. (*Oberste Heeresleitung*, General Headquarters) were in a state of quite unusual activity. All departments were under orders to leave Coblenz and to be in operation the following morning (August 30th) in Luxembourg, capital of the Grand-Duchy. Secretaries and orderlies were hurriedly, packing up files and documents, under the supervision of their impatient officers.

The whole German population had just been thrilled by the communiqué of August 27th: "After a series of successful engagements the German armies on the Western Front have entered French territory. From Cambrai to the southern Vosges the enemy has been everywhere defeated and is now in full retreat. On account of the vast area of the battlefield, part of which is wooded and mountainous, it is not yet possible to assess the losses of the enemy in killed, in prisoners and in war material."

General von Kluck's 1st Army had defeated the British at Mons on August 23rd. On the same day von Bülow's 2nd Army had defeated the French on the Sambre, in the region of Charleroi. The 4th Army, under the Duke of Wurtemberg, had advanced in the Ardennes, and the 5th Army, under the Imperial Crown Prince, in the Woevre district of Lorraine. On the 20th and 21st the 6th Army, under Prince Ruprecht of Bavaria, and the 7th Army, under von Heeringen, had defeated the French in Lorraine, and on August 26th the 1st Army had again defeated the British, at Le Cateau, east of Cambrai. On the 27th, General Helmuth von Moltke, Chief of the General Staff, had submitted to his Supreme Commander, the Emperor, the proposed directive for the continuation of operations. The document ended with these words: "His Majesty orders the German Armies to advance on Paris."

The staff officers at the O.H.L. considered that their head-quarters should have been moved much further forward than Luxembourg. They would have preferred to follow more closely behind the irresistible advance of the armies so that they themselves would be able to hurry forward and join the victorious troops entering Paris.

No one doubted that such a triumphant entry was imminent, and the General Staff officers felt, in common with all other officers of the German armies, that they were entitled to take part in it. The remarkable victory now within their reach was not due to good luck or to the futility of the opposing forces. An army of more than a million Frenchmen was in full retreat after only a few days' fighting; and this for the simple reason that the German High Command had shown crushing superiority in every branch: discipline, training, use of weapons, organisation, tactics, and strategy. The German officer corps had laboured for years to achieve this victory. And von Schlieffen, the brilliant strategist who had planned it, was the arche type of the military caste that was looked upon with pride as the élite of the German nation.

The rôle of the Higher Command in peacetime is (clearly) to prepare for war. Political developments on the Continent of Europe after 1875 had led the German High Command to envisage the possibility of war on two fronts. Marshal Moltke, the aged victor of the 1870 campaign, had declared that, in such conditions, the attack should first be opened against the Russians, a defensive front being maintained, meanwhile, against the French. The German fortified positions along the line, Thionville-Metz-Strasbourg, and thence along the Rhine from Strasbourg to Basle were considered an insuperable barrier against any French attack. Once Russia was de-feated the offensive would be switched to France. Marshal Moltke's successor, Waldersee (1838–1891), had held the same view.

But as soon as von Schlieffen came on the scene he declared the Moltke Plan to be obsolete, useless and quite unsuited to the necessities and potentialities of modern warfare. "The Russian railway system" (he said) "is lamentable. It would take the Russian staff six weeks to transport an army up to our frontier and several months to mount a major offensive. We, however, can crush France in less than two months, and that must be our primary task. In the meantime, we should establish a weak defensive front against Russia.

"It would be foolish to look upon our operations against France as a sort of battering-ram applied to the restricted area of the Franco-German frontier. Our modern army masses require ample space for their effective deployment; what is more, frontal attack is an outmoded, rudimentary conception. Our objective should be, not the enemy's front, but its flanks. The encirclement of the Roman Army by Hannibal at Cannae still remains the classic masterpiece of military strategy and tactics.

"There are geographical reasons preventing us from turning both flanks of the French forces, but we can clamp down their right wing in the fortified areas and turn their left flank by marching through Belgium."

To which certain critics had replied: "Belgian neutrality has been guaranteed since 1839 by Great Britain, France, Russia, Prussia and Austria. That treaty is still in force. Any violation of Belgian territory will mean war with Great Britain."

"No plan is without its risks," was the answer. "It is quite possible that England will declare war; but her intervention will be slow and at first ineffective. Once France has been crushed, England – for economic reasons – will be ready to make peace."

"Our object will be to turn the French left flank by attacking it with our strongest striking force, which, having crossed Belgium, will march on Paris ahead of the French forces, cutting them off from Paris and later falling upon their rear. The French armies will finally be brought to bay in the Jura region."

Such (originally) was the gigantic plan. Von Schlieffen was ready to subordinate everything to this vast turning movement of the German right wing, which was to be made irresistible. The attacking force of thirty-five army corps and eight further divisions of infantry would turn the French left wing somewhere beyond Lille. "The German soldier on the extreme right of the line will be brushing his sleeve against the English Channel." Paris would in fact be outflanked from the lower Seine and be attacked *from the west*.

But another objection had been raised: "We cannot mobilise the number of men required for such an operation."

"We can certainly mobilise them if we get rid of the outdated notion that reservists cannot be used in the front line. They can, if they are well led. By using them as front-line troops we gain twenty divisions."

Such was the second of von Schlieffen's revolutionary ideas; and it was kept even more secret than the famous Plan. Von Schlieffen had retired in 1905 and died in 1913 at the age of eighty. According to members of his family his last words were: "Above all, strengthen the right wing."

But time brings inevitable change. Between 1906 and 1914, a number of factors, including the improvement of the Russian railway system and the raising of military service in France to three years, had led General von Moltke, nephew of the famous Marshal and successor to von Schlieffen, to make slight amendments to the Schlieffen Plan. In order to stiffen the defence against Russia and strengthen the German forces on the Franco-German frontier the colossal right wing had been trimmed a little; even so, it was still very impressive. It would consist of a force of three armies, totalling sixteen army corps, or about 600,000 men; in the centre, eleven army corps, about 400,000 men, and on the left, to cover the Alsace-Lorraine front, 320,000 men.

General von Moltke, Chief of the General Staff, gazed thoughtfully at the large map of the Western Front on the wall. Pencilled arrows showed the marching orders given to the armies by his directives of August 27th. Shaded ovals and circles marked the latest positions of army corps. It was clear that the advancing wing was, if anything, ahead of schedule.

General von Moltke's responsibilities also included the Eastern Front, of which a map was displayed on the other wall of his office. But the German armies shown there gave no impression of an overwhelming mass; on the contrary they seemed rather lost in vast spaces, and a significant line marked the initial Russian penetration into Eastern Prussia. That same morning, however, an A.D.C. had laid on the General's table a long telegram confirming the successful issue of the three-day battle engaged by General von Hindenburg at

Tannenberg: Samsonov's army wiped out, 92,000 prisoners, 350 guns taken. This brilliant victory must be exploited. For the past forty-eight hours two army corps, already withdrawn from the Western Front, had been on their way by rail to the east. There could be surely no danger in such a transfer, given the victorious advance in the west.

In fact, that morning of August 29, 1914, had brought him nothing but good news. And yet his face betrayed no sign of the flush of victory. On the contrary, General von Moltke looked tired and depressed; perhaps even disillusioned . . . .

It was a strange destiny that had made a war-lord of this man. On his desk stood a small daguerrotype portrait of his uncle, Marshal Helmuth von Moltke. This same Christian name for the nephew had been the first sign, his first legacy of the profession of arms. Born a Moltke, he could follow no other career. And yet, as he looked at the portrait with its cold, steely features, he must often have asked himself: "What on earth is there in common between this man and me? I set up a sort of artists' studio; and I began copying landscapes. And I play the violin. Art is the only thing I live for."

How old was Nephew Helmuth when he had said this? (He had even put it in writing!) He was certainly no adolescent, but a man of forty-six, a year after he had become A.D.C. to the Emperor.

His famous name had obviously weighed heavily in the Emperor's decision to appoint him Chief of the General Staff, but William was well aware that the second Moltke was an intellectual, a man of culture, a musician. And William, too, would have himself thought a patron of the arts, an irresistible charmer. His A.D.C. should be a symbol of the Imperial "Kultur". Thus was Helmuth launched on his uncongenial career.

Europe at that time was mistress of the world. The royal courts of the Continent kept up a dazzling display of pomp and splendour, of receptions and diamonds and caviar and champagne, of military parades and State balls. Even their funerals provided spectacles of unforgettable magnificence. Following the coffin of Edward VII, the Emperor William, on a dazzling white charger and wearing the uniform of a *British* field-marshal had raised his baton in salute to the London crowds; and at

The Schlieffen Plan
1905 and 1914

Original Schlieffen Plan, 1905

Schlieffen Plan, modified
and actual, August 1914

XXXX
1 German army initial position

XXXX
6 position of Allied armies
1 September

Windsor Castle that night he had declared: "I am proud to call this place my home and to be a member of this royal family." From 1880 to 1913 this family circle, which included all the crowned heads of Europe, had made and received a continuous series of State visits; and William II's A.D.C. had been kept on the run from one capital to another; from Berlin to St Petersburg, thence to Madrid via Paris, and back to St Petersburg, the peak of imperial grandeur, a city of a thousand-and-one nights. This – and this alone – had been the training ground, the battlefield for the Emperor's A.D.C., the nephew of the great von Moltke. In his sleeping-car, between such junkettings, he had read Nietzsche, Hartmann's *Philosophy of Religion*, Carlyle's *French Revolution*. He was beginning a translation of *Pelléas and Mélisande*. It was said that he was also interested in Christian Science.

Then he was appointed to two years of regimental duty, of training and manoeuvres that had brought a pleasant change, a sort of purification, into the life of the sensitive, artistic von Moltke; but two years are quickly gone. "Here is your promotion to Brigadier-General. Report to Potsdam. You are still A.D.C. to the Emperor." And the festive round had begun all over again, with the same constant attendance on the Emperor. By a great effort of tolerance and understanding, Moltke had kept himself from hating this fantastic monarch, this victim of hysterical adulation, in love with his own "magnetic" personality, which (as he thought) was all-sufficing, a cover for his wildest indiscretions. But, as time went on, Moltke became alarmed: "What new kind of foolishness will he think of next?"

"I appoint you Chief of the General Staff." Von Schlieffen, who had held the post for fifteen years, had retired; and Nephew Moltke suddenly found himself virtually in command of the German Army, with the task before him of putting into operation the famous Schlieffen Plan, of which he knew practically nothing.

"Your Majesty, I am a rather severe judge of my own worth. I wonder if, in case of war, I should prove equal to the demands of such a post? I am not sure."

But William had swept aside his scruples. "You have already established your position in the Army. Everybody likes and respects you, and will have the same confidence in you as I have myself."

To say "No" to the Emperor was out of the question. "The Chief of the General Staff had mastered all the knowledge a soldier can acquire by hard and conscientious study, not only in regard to the fundamental understanding of the conduct of modern warfare but also in regard to the essential difference between theory and practice." In this somewhat ponderous phrase, Foerster, the German military critic, fully recognises the immense effort made by Moltke, lover of the arts, to fulfil the task he had undertaken. He had acquired the knowledge he needed, but he had done more; he had shown foresight and considerable organising ability. He had, in fact, accomplished the tremendous task of perfecting the German war machine.

On August 1, 1914, however, when this gigantic highly-trained force was already mobilising along the western frontier, as laid down by the (modified) Schlieffen Plan, the Emperor had handed to his Chief of the General Staff a telegram from Prince Lichnowsky, German Ambassador in London: "Sir Edward Grey, Secretary of State for Foreign Affairs, has informed me that Great Britain would undertake to keep France out of the war if Germany is willing, in return, to refrain from hostilities against France." William was jubilant: "You see, there is no need to attack France. We can transfer the whole of our armies to the Russian Front."

Moltke felt the ground slipping from under his feet. For the space of a second he had a vision of eleven thousand trains on their way to the Western Front, of lines and stations hopelessly jammed by this crazy counter-order, which, in effect, would mean bringing back a million and a half men, thousands of tons of guns, ammunition and supplies to their point of departure. It would be a devastating tidal wave of men and material.

"But, Your Majesty, that is quite impossible!"

"What do you mean, impossible?"

"If Your Majesty insisted on re-directing the whole army to the East Your Majesty's army would no longer be a fighting machine but a disorganised rabble, deprived of all means of action. General mobilisation cannot be improvised at a moment's notice. It requires a whole year of hard work. Once its plan has been decided upon it is impossible to alter it."

"That is not the kind of answer your uncle would have made."

A moment later an amended telegram arrived from Lichnowsky. Grey had undertaken to secure the neutrality of France if Germany would promise to remain neutral in regard to France *and* Russia. This was quite another matter.

"Very well," William had said, rather vexed, "do what you think best."

A company of the 69th Infantry Regiment had already crossed the Luxembourg frontier. The plan agreed upon was in operation, the nightmarish threat of confusion and disorder had been averted. And the Emperor had not even realised that by this one sentence he had struck a terrible blow at the singleness of purpose so painfully and laboriously achieved by his Chief of the General Staff. "I never recovered from that incident," wrote Moltke afterwards. "Something snapped inside me, and I was never the same again."

The huge German scythe was cutting its way through France; but the man who controlled it stood motionless in front of the great map, and his face was sad, disillusioned. His health (people said) was failing; two seasons at Carlsbad had brought no improvement. The truth was that neither Carlsbad nor doctor could heal the wound within, the gnawing pain of a thwarted career. General Helmuth von Moltke, the mighty warlord, was an unhappy man, unhappy because the profession of arms had been forced upon him, unhappy because the Kaiser had made him Chief of the General Staff. In spite of all his efforts, he had never been able to identify himself with the military caste to which he belonged.

He sometimes found the atmosphere at G.H.Q. utterly intolerable. There was hatred between one department and another; hatred between men in the same department. Most of the officers thus condemned to live and work together seemed to have made up their minds to be thoroughly detestable one to the other by their fanatical cult of Prussian arrogance. But this atmosphere was not distasteful to them all; some officers seemed even to enjoy it.

The German army was sweeping in a curve through France with its axis poised on the east of the line in Alsace and Lorraine. The German front at that point was covered by the 7th Army under General von Heeringen and by the 6th Army under the Crown Prince Ruprecht of Bavaria (who had operational control over both armies). Their original mission had been to pin down the greatest possible number of French formations. (The forceful Ruprecht, with his heavy moustache and keen, piercing eyes bore little resemblance to his soft-hearted royal father, the doting slave of Lola Montez.) On August 20th Ruprecht had telephoned to the O.H.L.:

"The French have had huge losses in fruitless attacks on our defensive positions at Sarrebourg and Morhange; an absolute massacre. We must exploit this success. I agree it's a good thing to pin down the French right wing; but it would be even better to destroy it."

His request was granted, and he had sent his Bavarians into the attack, with strong artillery support. The French line had withdrawn in disorder up to the plateau of the Grand-Couronné, east of Nancy, and to the line of the river Meurthe. But now they were holding their ground. Replying to von Moltke's directive of August 27th, the fire-eating Ruprecht had been forced to say, in effect: I am doing my best. (There was no question for him of a triumphal entry into Paris at the head of his troops.)

The 5th Army, under the Imperial Crown Prince, supported by the 4th Army under the Duke of Wurtemberg, was advancing on Prince Ruprecht's right. On August 23rd the Crown Prince had received a telegram from the Emperor: "Congratulations on your first victory, brilliantly won with the help of Almighty God. I award you the Iron Cross, Second and First Class. Salute your valiant troops and thank them in my name and in the name of the Fatherland."

The valiant troops, very cleverly concealed and then brought into action, had won their success in the region of Virton and were now beginning to cross the Meuse, north of Verdun. But the objective given by the directive of August 27th had been Vitry-le-François. So the Crown Prince (also) had to abandon any hope of entering Paris at the head of his troops – unless (of course) the Emperor summoned him to his side in the hour of triumph. The habitual smile on the Crown Prince's face must have masked some rather complex feelings; in

particular, the complex feelings of the Imperial Heir who
knows that he has a long time to wait. But the Crown Prince
took a genuine interest in the welfare of his troops, and was
undoubtedly popular.

The famous directive "His Majesty orders the German
Armies to march on Paris" was, in fact, addressed to the three
Armies on the right of the line: the 3rd under von Hausen, the
2nd under von Bülow and the 1st under von Kluck. General
Karl von Bülow (not to be confused with Prince Bernhard
von Bülow, the former Imperial Chancellor) had operational
control over the three armies. It was on this part of the front
that the race to Paris had begun, with von Kluck in the extreme
right (outside) position.

On the evening of August 21st von Bülow's advance guards
had come into contact with the 5th French Army in the region
of Charleroi, between the Sambre and the Meuse. The French
had put up a gallant fight and had suffered heavy casualties.
On the 23rd they began their retreat. Von Bülow was bitterly
disappointed at this withdrawal, which had deprived the
advancing German wing of a battle of which the consequences
might be incalculable; possibly a repetition of Sedan. When
von Bülow studied his map on August 22nd he had envisaged
the possibility of the French formations being caught in a
pincer movement between his own army coming from the
north and the 3rd Army coming from the north-east; and
even of the 1st Army coming in to give the coup de grâce
from the north-west. But von Hausen was late, and the pincer
had not closed in time. Or (perhaps) the general commanding
the French army on the extreme left of the line had seen the
danger and had withdrawn before it was too late. Helmuth
von Moltke, Chief of the General Staff (also rather disappointed) asked his Intelligence Branch the name of this French
General; it was Lanrezac.

When von Bülow reproached the Saxon von Hausen for
arriving too late, his reply had been: "I suggest you look at
the map. My troops had to march through the most difficult
country of all."

The wild, tree-clad mass of the Ardennes, with its high
peaks and deep valleys, has always been a formidable obstacle
to an invading army; it was worth fifty battalions to the

defender, and the 3rd (Saxon) Army had had a rough time. Their disciplne was good, but there had been some grumbling as they toiled up the steep slopes, while impatient staff cars drove past them, raising a cloud of dust.

"They're lucky, eh? I bet their feet aren't raw, like mine." By some medieval tradition the Saxon soldier wore no socks. He wrapped his feet in a square of linen; but the linen would shift inside the boot, and their feet became the chief subject in the men's thoughts and conversation; an obsession in fact. The reservists suffered particularly.

"Even when I'm lying down my feet seem to weigh a ton. And we get woken up by the sentries walking on them at night. In the early days of the war we sometimes had a half-day rest for body hygiene and washing our linen. There were even French lessons if you wanted. But afterwards it was just, march, march, march. In Belgium I didn't take my clothes off for four days."

"Wouldn't be so bad if the food was decent. But it's not. Breakfast this morning, just coffee and fat pork. Not a bit of bread. Our bakers don't give a damn."

But the bakers were not to blame. Every large formation of troops on the line of march was followed, not only by the guns, but also by convoys of ammunition, ambulances, sappers' equipment, forage carts and interminable columns of supply wagons. Each army corps had six supply columns, seven reserve supply columns and two convoys of field bakeries. This mass of horse-drawn transport choked the roads of north and north-east France with a vast armada of vehicles.

The field bakeries had, first, to requisition their flour from the local inhabitants. If this source of supply failed or was inadequate they had to indent upon the supply columns; but these were sometimes far behind the troops. The system would have worked perfectly if there had been a twenty-four-hour halt between each day's march. But this never happened. The speed of this victorious advance was depriving these huge armies of bread and sometimes of meat and drink; so the troops resorted to looting in farms and villages on their way. There were times however, when the system of requisitions *was* carried out in a proper manner, payment being duly made in local currency or German marks (which the recipient accepted with suspicious reluctance). In certain deserted towns and villages the uncanny silence of the empty houses, many of which had already been looted by other fugitives, if not by the neighbours, awakened dark, primitive instincts of destruction and depravity.

*   *   *

"That's true. I remember, in particular, a little château at Wibrin where the infantry behaved like a mob of vandals. As an officer I felt ashamed. But there were also moments when one felt a thrill of pride, as for instance, when our army corps converged on Laroche, and the mounted troops and the men on foot flowed in from their respective routes to form one huge river. The various units, Infantry, Hussars and Gunners, fell smoothly into their allotted places in the moving column without a hitch, without a single mistake. On another occasion – also during one of those troop concentrations – at Souet, there was a partial eclipse of the sun, which threw a strange twilight over the scene; then, just as this gigantic flood of men and horses moved on, the sun shone out again...."

"As for us, well, we could hardly think of anything else but our aching feet. As a matter of fact, there were places where we weren't so keen on stopping, anyway. In Luxembourg, at first, it was marvellous; people would hand out chocolate to us; but as soon as we got into Belgium we understood. They had dug trenches, thrown huge trees across the roads. The Belgians loathed us. Their franc-tireurs sniped at us from houses and belfries, from behind hedges. Any straggler who lagged behind vanished for good and all. As a matter of fact, our N.O.C's had warned us what to expect. At Liége the Belgian women had thrown boiling water on us from the windows; some of our wounded had their eyes put out ... At Achene, men of the First Saxon Light Infantry who had taken Dinant told the same story...."

"I saw dead bodies of civilians lying in the street at Leffe-Bouvignes, near Dinant. Many of them had half their heads blown off; been shot point-blank. Franc-tireurs they were; the men were shot and the women and children shut up in a convent. Then they started shooting from the convent. Our infanteers were furious, wanted to burn the whole place down.

In the end the priests paid a fine of fifteen thousand francs and handed over the culprits . . . .

* * *

The treachery of the franc-tireurs became an obsession almost as acute as the torment of aching feet. The incidents reported were always based on hearsay, rarely confirmed by personal experience; but they produced the same effect. There was no doubt as to the existence of a Belgian Resistance movement. Numerous acts of sabotage were committed (especially of telephone lines) and some (at least) of the shots fired at troops on the march came from civilian weapons. But this resistance was sporadic, unorganised, although the German High Command claimed it was an authentic, secret army, encouraged and supplied by the Belgian government and by Paris. What is more, the German troops had been indoctrinated – "conditioned" was the word used – even before they entered Belgium. Throughout the mobilisation centres German propaganda had spread rumours of atrocities committed by civilians (which always took the same form, particularly the putting out of soldiers' eyes). The object of this indoctrination was to demonstrate to the troops that there was ample justification for measures of preventive terrorisation aimed at ensuring the safety and speed of the invasion. Historians and eye-witnesses all agree that these measures were far more severely applied in Belgium than in France. In any case the "franc-tireur" complex acted as a useful stimulant to discipline on the line of march.

* * *

"The first Rothosen (red trousers) we met were at Rostenne, in Belgium. A small French outpost there surrendered without firing a shot. The poor devils had had nothing to eat for forty-eight hours, and we ourselves hadn't much to spare."

"We had our first taste of fighting in France, near Dommery. It was three o'clock in the morning and we had just moved off. Suddenly, as we were going through a wood, we came under heavy, rapid fire; the whole line of the wood seemed to be blazing off at us. There was terrible panic at first. No one thought of taking cover. Luckily it wasn't quite daylight.

Finally, our captain got us together in some sort of defensive position and we started firing back. Then the French cleared off. There must have been some wrong orders given by somebody. You don't send a regiment off on the road at night after three days' forced marches. After that we kept strictly to the drill-book and always had advance guards out in front and patrols on our flanks. But every day we had to march faster and farther, with only about two hours' sleep at night. The villages along the road had been set on fire by our gunners to cover our advance. We sometimes felt as if we were drunk, we were so tired. And yet on the 29th, when a despatch-rider from the divisional staff passed us and shouted, 'Sedan has fallen!' a tremendous cheer went up from the whole column."

*   *   *

The 1st Army, under von Kluck, was advancing on the far right wing, at the extreme point of the immense scythe. It had crossed the Belgian frontier on August 15th (the day of the capture of the last of the Liége forts by the 3rd Army), and since then von Kluck's infantry, except when engaged in actual fighting, had marched twenty or thirty miles a day, carrying a 56 lb. pack and sometimes even *singing* as they marched. For two days and two nights their heavy boots had pounded the pavés of Brussels. The citizens had watched, first with astonishment, then with anger, and finally with consternation, this colossal procession, punctuated at intervals by groups of monocled, mounted officers whose eyes roved contemptuously over the heads of the populace. Behind each regiment were the field kitchens, with fires lit, while the cooks stirred the stew in the kettles as the convoy rumbled on.

The 1st Army had pushed on so quickly and so far westward that the people of the country districts could not believe they were Germans. They sometimes took them for British; sometimes even for French, and offered flowers, sweets or cakes. But they soon discovered their mistake.

Von Kluck would have liked to penetrate even farther westward in order to envelope and capture the Belgian army, one hundred thousand strong, which had dared to stand up to the Germanic onslaught (and even check it for a time at Liége and Hoelen) before retiring on Antwerp. But, once through

Brussels, von Kluck, at von Bülow's request, had taken a more southerly direction, and had been forced to let this humble prize elude him. He was all the more impatient to push on. Von Kluck had the tanned features of a tough old warrior and wore an habitually fierce expression. He had been wounded during the 1870 campaign and was now sixty-eight years old, although he looked much younger. He was raised to the nobility at the age of fifty, but he chafed against the arrogance of the "vons", of the older aristocracy. He chafed, also, against his subordination to von Bülow. All high-ranking German officers chafed against any form of subordination.

The Kaiser had sneered at the "contemptible little British Army", but the first clash at Mons had opened his eyes. The German infantry had found themselves up against well-trained professional soldiers, cool, determined, well-equipped, making good use of the terrain. The British soldiers had found time to dig themselves into positions where their artillery and machine-guns could command a wide field of fire. Losses had been heavy on both sides, for both sides had fought with great courage. British prisoners admitted afterwards: "the Germans fight like devils". The British withdrawal was carried out in good order.

It was carried out in equally good order later, in full day-light, after the fighting at Le Cateau on August 26th. Von Kluck and his Chief of Staff, von Kuhl, had been impressed by the admirable rear-guard action fought by the British gunners and by the controlled withdrawal of the infantry, group by group, under the orders of experienced N.C.O's. Two thousand prisoners and nine batteries of artillery had been captured, and, once again, the losses in killed and wounded had been heavy on both sides.

But the losses in men were less important than the loss of time. The 1st Army had been fighting and marching without a day's respite. After each engagement the pace had to be quickened, for the runner in the outside lane has to run farther than the others. The average day's march had now been raised to thirty miles. General von Kluck always urged his officers to remember the fundamental precept laid down by Field-Marshal Count Haeseler: "On active service the man and the horse are capable of quite extraordinary physical

effort; but only on condition (he added) that discipline,
hygiene and supplies are also maintained at the highest
possible levels."

The 1st Army was truly a thing of steel, a huge mechanism
advancing at maximum speed. On August 28th a radio
message from the Emperor had read: "As a result of its rapid
and decisive operations against the Belgians, the British and
the French, the 1st Army, in its victorious advance, is about to
penetrate into the heart of France. I congratulate the Army
on its splendid achievement and express my Imperial gratitude
and appreciation."

This generous tribute from the Emperor "had put spurs
to the Army". The advance – it was now a race – was resumed
at even greater speed than before.

3

TWO SONS OF THE PEOPLE

LA MARNE was by no means (as yet) a world-famous river.
It meandered through the sun-drenched countryside, while,
on its right bank, the little town of Vitry-le-François and its
seven thousand citizens dozed in the heat of an unusual
summer. But there was a wartime air about the café on the
Place d'Armes, a mere sprinkling of civilians, one elderly
waiter with a somewhat shaky hand. Under the awning of the
"terrasse" officers in uniform wrinkled their eyes as they
watched the comings and goings, in the dazzling sunlight outside, of their fellow-officers from G.H.Q. Now and then a car
would pass with a general or a liaison officer inside. There
was little else to beguile an idle moment.

G.H.Q. was housed in a school in the Place Royer-Collard,
facing the Church of Notre Dame. From the courtyard could
be seen the window of General Joffre's office – the second
window on the left of the first floor. The General and his
two A.D.C's were billeted with M. Chapron, a retired Sapper
officer. The General occupied the "salon", plainly furnished
with a brass bedstead (described in his Memoirs and official
documents as a "camp bed") and a wash-table, concealed
behind a screen.

The Commander-in-Chief rose every morning at five.
Having dressed and breakfasted he left at 6 a.m. for G.H.Q.,
fifty yards away. As soon as he arrived the Morning Meeting
(*Grand Rapport*) began, attended by his Chief of Staff, General
Belin, the deputy Chief of Staff, General Berthelot, Major
Gamelin, the heads of staff departments and the lieutenant-
colonel in charge of railways. Belin and Berthelot would give
their reports of the messages received during the night. The
meeting over the Commander-in-Chief would begin work
at his desk.

At eleven o'clock precisely he would take lunch *chez* Monsieur Chapron. The slightest unpunctuality would bring a reproof. The Commander-in-Chief was joined at table by three of his personal staff, by General Belin and (fairly often) by one or two guests. The cooking was good, and the General, appreciating it, usually took little part in the conversation. He preferred to listen. His customary siesta after lunch had been abandoned at the outbreak of war, but in September this ritual was to be resumed. After lunch he would make a brief return to G.H.Q. to hear the latest situation reports, then take a walk with his A.D.C's or other officers of his personal staff, closely followed by two plain-clothes police officers and – at a distance – two gendarmes. At about three o'clock he would resume work at his desk at G.H.Q. Dinner was at six-thirty. The meal was informal, but it was well understood that "shop" was taboo. At eight o'clock he again returned to G.H.Q. for a short conference – the *Petit Rapport* – and at nine o'clock he retired to bed.

The Commander-in-Chief's entertainment allowance was the equivalent of thirty-seven soldiers' rations, calculated at 1 Fr.50 each, a total of 55.50 (gold) francs. In view of the number of his guests the sum was totally inadequate.

The citizens of Vitry-le-François would bow to the General if they passed him during his daily walk. Not one of them realised, as yet, that this man would one day become a sort of historical monument. They looked at him with curiosity and respect not entirely unmixed with anxiety, for he shouldered the heavy burden of the Allied cause and the responsibility for the lives of millions of men.

I remember seeing Joffre in Paris, after the Marne, during an investiture at Les Invalides. "Look! look! there he is, in front of the other generals." For a few seconds I watched the General (who, to me, seemed very stout) walking with short, irregular steps, his fists clenched, seemingly hurried and pre-occupied; very different from the "Papa Joffre" I had expected. What impressed me most were his beautifully-polished field-boots and the way his cap was pulled down over his eyes.

On ordinary occasions Joffre wore a pair of somewhat non-descript leggings. His careless dressing habits have become a legend – and rightly so, for they contributed to his popularity. From descriptions given me by those who knew him well, and from my reading of foreign biographers it would seem that most photographs of the General convey more successfully his massive physique than his facial expression. General Spears (then a lieutenant) gives this picture of him: "The whiteness of his hair, the lightness of his almost colourless blue eyes, which looked out from under big eyebrows the colour of salt and pepper, white predominating, and the tonelessness of his voice coming through the sieve of his big, whitish moustache all give him the impression of an albino."*

In 1914, Joffre was 62 years old. His life-story had already appeared in all the newspapers. Joseph Jacques Césaire Joffre was the son of a cooper and had ten brothers and sisters. He had won a scholarship to the secondary school at Perpignan and had succeeded by sheer force of character in entering the famous Ecole Polytechnique. Could anything be more romantic? That he was sparing of speech was also considered a point in his favour, a reassuring trait in a soldier's make-up. But the ordinary Frenchman never knew of what surprising taciturnity Joffre could be capable, on occasion.

An officer who had been appointed to the Intelligence Section of the General Headquarters' Staff went to pay his respects to the General, expecting, of course, to receive in reply the usual polite word of welcome from his Chief. There was a silence – prolonged to the point where the officer began to wonder if the General was not deaf – and then:

"So you are working in the British Section?"

"Yes, Sir."

Another long silence. And, finally:

"Well, they've been in the habit of fighting against us. Now we are good friends. *Au revoir*."

On August 3, 1914, Joffre had called a meeting of Army Commanders at the Ministry of War. On such a momentous occasion the generals were expecting the Commander-in-Chief to give his appreciation of the situation, with some remarks upon the probable rôles of the various armies concerned. Not at all. According to accounts confirmed later by everyone present, Joffre simply made a few quite vague remarks.

*Major-General E. L. Spears, *Liaison, 1914*, p. 22, Heinemann, 1930.

General Dubail, commanding the 1st Army, then brought up a point that was giving him some concern. He required reinforcements, he said, for his 7th Corps, which was under orders to open the attack in Alsace.

"That's your plan" (Joffre had replied, with a smile) "not mine."

Thinking that he had not made his point clear, Dubail went on with his exposé. Still smiling, the Commander-in-Chief had made the same reply: "It's your plan, not mine." And the meeting had broken up, leaving the Army Commanders somewhat bewildered.

Joffre broke silence only when he considered he had something useful to say. In the early days of the war, when visiting one or other of the H.Q's he would sit, absolutely silent, listening to reports, explanations and plans, and then leave without having uttered a word other than "Bonjour" and "Au revoir". On another occasion, when a general had been making an impassioned appeal for artillery reinforcements, and had stopped, breathless, Joffre, after a silence, had replied: "You've always been fond of your guns, haven't you? You're quite right."

In spite of his crushing responsibilities and the little time he could spare, he would listen with unlimited patience, and never interrupt. In the end the speaker would come to a halt in mid-air, as it were, beginning to wonder if he had lost the thread of his own argument. And Joffre would reply: "Eh bien, au revoir."

One could almost suggest that this same brooding silence pervaded his office in the G.H.Q. at Vitry. Not a file or sheet of paper on the table. Nothing on the walls. If photographers had to be admitted several maps of the front were hastily produced and displayed. One of his A.D.C's maintains (although it is a controversial point) that somewhere in his office Joffre kept a map to the scale of 1/200,000. This may be so. But the Commander-in-Chief was only concerned with major decisions, and nothing was easier for him than to go and study the appropriate map in some other office. One can make no particular comment on these offices, which all occupied the former classrooms, except the Intelligence Section, which was in the main hall, where rings and trapezes had been coiled and tied high up against the ceiling, as if someone had feared that officers whose duty it was to seek and discover the enemy's nefarious designs would be tempted to try their hand at gymnastics.

General Belin, the Chief of Staff, was not (it seems) a man of outstanding personality. "He was absorbed" (writes Joffre) "in the direction and organisation of the numerous and complex departments for which he was responsible." Berthelot, however, his deputy, comes in for more generous treatment. "A powerful mind; a brilliant brain." Berthelot, stripped, weighed seventeen stone. Suffering from the heat, he had replaced the regulation tunic by a voluminous white overall of the "Père Ubu" type,* and had discarded boots for slippers. Some of the early visitors to G.H.Q. were shocked by this strange apparition, but in course of time, "as General Berthelot's personality made itself felt", this idiosyncrasy was accepted.

The other staff officers at G.H.Q. were far less picturesque, nor had they any desire to be thought so. Their attitude of polite, slightly patronising reserve made it clear that they preferred to consider themselves as belonging to the higher echelons of the Civil Service – the Quai d'Orsay, for example. But this reserve had melted somewhat with the French successes in Alsace at the beginning of the war. The enemy were then described as retreating in disorder, demoralised by the "furia francese" by the inefficiency of German N.C.O's, bad rations and faulty ammunition. In a very short time, however, other news from the front had caused them to resume their traditional circumspection.

In his preface to *Liaison, 1914* (Heinemann, 1930), by Major-General Spears, Winston Churchill wrote with some severity, " . . . It suffices to repeat that hideous and measureless miscalculation of every factor present at the outbreak of the War was made by General Joffre and his officers." The Staff officers at G.H.Q. were no doubt men of more than average intelligence. They had studied hard and long, passed difficult examinations. Having adopted the Army as a vocation they were indifferent to its monetary rewards. And yet, all unconsciously, their outlook was being conditioned by the consequences of their economic and social status.

Ubu Roi was a celebrated farce written by d'A. Jarry in 1896.

Their rates of pay were far lower than those of British officers and they found no social compensations in France comparable, for example, with those of the German officer caste. Many of them had suffered petty persecution, had been frustrated in their career, on account of their religious convictions. For these reasons their own class-consciousness (a perfectly normal and, indeed, inevitable phenomenon), being quite different from that of either British or German officers, had acquired a character of "super-compensation" which led them to over-estimate the value of their own conceptions and to be suspicious or contemptuous of any opinion or even of any information from outside sources. Such a state of mind is not necessarily good in men whose task it is to formulate policies that could have the gravest possible consequences.

In July, 1911, as soon as he was appointed Chief of the General Staff and Vice-President of the War Council (Conseil Supérieur de la Guerre) Joffre had sent one of his junior staff officers, Captain Gamelin, with a message for General Foch, who was then in charge of the Ecole de Guerre.

"Make it clear to him that I should have liked to have him as my Chief of Staff, but that Castelnau had already been nominated and would have been hurt if I had made a change."

"Tell General Joffre he is quite right," Foch had replied. "But, since he values your opinion and because you will one day be concerned with great matters of state, never forget this: The Germans will put thirty-five army corps into the field against us, *with their right wing on the Channel coast.*"

Foch, the strategist, had, in fact, foreseen almost exactly the Schlieffen Plan. But his views had in no way impressed the military experts around Joffre. Their reaction was: "The Germans could not mobilise sufficient forces for such a manoeuvre. As a matter of fact, our Intelligence Branch has just got possession of an interesting *Kriegspiel* carried out by the German General Staff. In it, the German right wing does not extend beyond Namur."

This information must have been more welcome than many other reports which flatly contradicted it; for the mobilisation plan of the French Armies (Plan XVII) was essentially based on the assumption that the enemy would attempt no great turning movement through Belgium.

In all fairness it must be added that the elaboration of the plan had been handicapped by a grave political factor: Britain's military support was conditional upon France's undertaking not to concentrate her forces against a neutral Belgium. But this requirement only lent weight to the already accepted view, which, henceforward, was to become a dogma. When, in 1913, General Lebas, Military Governor of Lille, had protested to Castelnau against a proposal to dismantle the fortifications of the city, the Chief of Staff had shrugged his shoulders: "My dear Lebas, let's be serious. You know as well as I do that the concentration of troops necessary for a determined attack is six men per yard of front. Now, if the Germans pushed their advance as far west as Lille, do you realise what their concentration would be reduced to? To *two* men per yard! We should go through them like a pat of butter. Here's a måp, and here's a ruler. Work it out for yourself."

In March, 1914, General Gallieni, then commanding the 5th Army forming the left wing of the French front, had held a "*Kriegspiel*" at the Cercle des Hautes Etudes Militaires.

"By way of a change," he had said, "I am going to play the part of the German General opposite my own front."

The conclusions arrived at in the report, sent subsequently to the General Staff, were these: (1) The Germans will not hesitate to cross the Meuse and invade Belgium; (2) the 5th Army must be increased from the present five to a strength of nine army corps; the képi and red trousers are too conspicuous, we must put the troops into khaki. The report had had a poor reception.

"In two months' time" (they said) "Gallieni will reach retiring age. He is already Grand-Croix (de la Légion d'Honneur) and a Médaille Militaire.* What more does he want? This is no time to change Army uniform and mess about with Plan XVII."

Admittedly, it was already very late. Twenty weeks later the unchangeable Plan XVII was well and truly buried, along with General Order No. 1, calling for the "lightning" offensive, and close on one hundred thousand dead Frenchmen in red trousers.

*Decoration awarded to N.C.O's and Other Ranks for outstanding gallantry in the field; but also – as a high honour – to certain Commanders-in-Chief.

On August 25th General Order No. 2 was published: "As the offensive manoeuvre previously planned has not materialised, subsequent operations will be prepared with the object of building up, on our left wing, a force capable of resuming the offensive. In the meantime, the rôle of the remaining armies will be to contain the enemy forces." A number of historians and commentators have claimed that the wording of this order reveals the first signs of a "preparation" for the Battle of the Marne; the first order (in fact) showing definite evidence of intuitive genius. From this moment (it was suggested) Joffre had begun preparing his trap – the "bownet" – in which the German armies would be engulfed and destroyed. One wonders how such an idea should have gained credence, since the General in his Memoirs has clearly explained what he had in mind at the time. "What I was envisaging was a battle on a front from Amiens to Rheims, with a newly-formed army, including the British, on the extreme left of our line, capable, when the time came, of turning the German right wing." Nothing could be more explicit than the reference to the Amiens-Rheims line; and the extreme limit of possible withdrawal would, therefore, be sixty miles to the north of the area in which the future battle of the Marne (which could not possibly be foreseen at the time) was to be fought. As to the plan of "turning the German right wing', the tremendous momentum of that right wing would brush it aside before it could even begin to come into action.

Many of the Commander-in-Chief's advisers, instead of throwing light upon his problems, or trying, first, to lighten their own darkness, obstinately maintained their belief in their deadly credo. On August 25th the Intelligence Branch at G.H.Q. circulated a report upon the famous German reservist formations, whose existence they had for years refused to acknowledge and whose weight was now making itself so heavily felt. This report began thus: "If, in fact, these formations exist, they are composed of only partly-integrated units, with inadequate artillery support."

Joffre himself, however, was far less willing to let the accepted credo blind him to the facts. His first display of good sense had consisted in circulating, on August 24th, "A G.H.Q. Instruction (No. 2083) on the tactical employment of troops and the tactical use of artillery". "When attacking a strong point the infantry should always be held back under cover during the preliminary artillery bombardment and sent forward only when the distance is such as to ensure that they will reach their objective. On every occasion when infantry have been sent into the attack too far from the objective and before the artillery bombardment has had its effect, they have come under machine-gun fire and suffered losses that could have been avoided. Infantry units seem to be unaware of the need of organising themselves with a view to survival in battle." One wonders how they could possibly have been aware of it, since for several years of training and manoeuvre they had been taught to consider the idea of organising for survival as the height of stupidity.

This instruction of August 24th was a mere Child's Guide to Tactics that any boy of twelve years old could understand, but it was so contrary to the teaching inherited from Grandmaison that only with the greatest caution was it included by Joffre's colleagues, who drew up the rough copy of his Memoirs. This was their version: "It was obvious that the policy of offensive action we had endeavoured to inculcate into the Army before the war had often been misunderstood and badly followed in practice." In other words, it was always other people who were wrong. In this particular case it was the dead.

Burning the midnight oil, the Commander-in-Chief had spent half the night of August 26–27th in forming (with troops taken from the eastern sector of the line) the new 6th Army under General Maunoury, intended to reinforce the French left with the object of turning the German right wing in the region of Amiens. Forty-eight hours later, when this plan had proved quite impracticable, Joffre came to this decision: "Never mind. We will keep this army up our sleeve, notwithstanding."

Creating an army on paper was an easy task compared with the complicated operation of transferring from east to west (just behind the front line, in the middle of a battle) this large mass of seven or eight divisions, to be moved in three hundred trains cutting across all the normal lines of communication. But here, Joffre was in his element. He had been Director of

Lines of Communication in the War Council, Director of Engineering Services at the Ministry of War, and had built railways in West Africa. Joffre, the Polytechnician, was quite unperturbed by any transport problem, however difficult and complicated it might be.

He had also organised the defences of the Upper Tonkin, and (under General Gallieni) those of Madagascar. He had been an instructor in fortification at the *Ecole d'Application de Fontainebleau.** His only operational exploit as a military commander had been achieved (incidentally with complete success) in 1893, when he had led a column one thousand strong across five hundred miles of the Central African bush and organised thereafter the submission of the tribes of the Timbuctoo region.

The appointment of this expert in transport and fortification as Commander-in-Chief, charged with responsibility for the implementation of a policy based on a fanatical belief in the value of the offensive, had been the result of a compromise, following the dismissal of his predecessor, General Michel, who had opposed the "offensive" fanatics. The group of "Young Turks" who had engineered this minor coup d'état had offered the crown to Gallieni, who, however, had replied: "No, thank you."

"But you voted against Michel?"

"Exactly. It would therefore be improper for me to take his place. What is more, I am too old, and my only experience has been in the Colonies."

Someone had suggested Pau, but he was regarded as too Catholic.

And Gallieni had said: "Joffre is your man."

Joffre, a good Republican, gave no cause for disquiet in any quarter. And even his corpulence was a point in his favour. Under cover of Joffre's protection the "Young Turks" – fervent believers in the Grandmaison doctrine – had been able to carry out their radical change of official policy: "The French Army" (so it ran) "reverting to its traditional principles, declares its unshakeable belief in the offensive." Now, at the end of August 1914, the more thoughtful amongst them felt a twinge of anxiety as they watched the reactions of this

*Officers' Training College.

strangely silent man, about whom (after all) they knew relatively little. "What is he going to *do*?"

The enemy was still a long way from Vitry-le-François. But officers at their windows in search of the cooler night air from the river would listen thoughtfully to the ceaseless rumble of trains. The route of Maunoury's army on its way from Alsace passed through Vitry. Rumours of the move had some-how leaked out but, by a strange presentment, the whispered talk was of an army from Paris that was on its way north to repulse the invader and deny him once for all the route to the capital.

One of the officers in that army was (like Joffre) a former scholarship-boy, and a son of the people. His father had been a joiner, his mother a mender of rush-bottom chairs. He himself, through sheer grit and hard work, became a graduate of the famous Ecole Normale. There were but a few days of life left to him now, but his name was to endure and reach heights of fame seldom attained by any general. It was Charles Péguy.

Even today our knowledge of Péguy as a lieutenant of infantry is incomplete and obscure; all we really know is his pathetic grave in the middle of a field. And yet his brief army career is almost the story of a new vocation.

"My intention is to cover the same ground from a Christian standpoint as Goethe covered from a pagan one." So wrote the author of the *Cahiers de la Quinzaine* to his wife in September 1913, and he went on: "You cannot imagine how much I still have to write. I really must keep alive somehow." And on August 18, 1914, one of his friends, Madame G. Faure, received this: "If I should never come back, remember me, but do not grieve. What we shall have accomplished in a few weeks' time will be worth more than thirty years of living."

This indefatigable little lieutenant from the Reserve of Officers with his pince-nez, his fair beard and moustache, his somewhat dowdy uniform, would march up and down the column from front to rear, oblivious to the scorching sun (you just tie a handkerchief over the back of your neck) or to drenching rain; the perfect type of the efficient, humane, regimental officer. When war came, this ex-Socialist turned poet had made the discovery that the most wonderful thing in life was to be the captain and foster-father of the 19th

Company of the 276th Reserve Battalion, two hundred and fifty of them, "a good third of them are from Paris, the other lads are from Seine-et-Marne, the rest from your beloved Crécy and Voulangis, in other words, just the people you like so much". It seems that these men had a real affection for their little lieutenant who was so obstinately concerned about their welfare and training. They good-naturedly nicknamed him "le Pion".*

After the flower-decked delirium of the mobilisation period had come the fighting in Alsace. There had been days of long, exhausting marches through villages lined with anxious faces. "The Uhlans have just been through here." But Péguy's men had never met any Uhlans. In billets, training continued as in peace-time. Péguy would deploy his Company in extended order and shout: "Prepare to charge, – fix——bayonets!" And he would lead them off at the double, waving his sword and shouting at the top of his voice: "En avant, chargez!" When it was over he would sheathe his sword, "with a sigh of satisfaction that made us all smile".

On August 20th Lieutenant Péguy had been ordered to occupy the farm at Sainte-Marie, two and a half miles from Viéville, close to the frontier, and to establish a complete system of forward posts there. He was convinced that the whole of his division (the 55th) was to move forward and lay siege to Metz. But, on the twenty-third, heavy gun-fire had been heard from the north-west.

"It must be near Etain they're fighting," said the local peasants.

As so often happened, they were mistaken. That same evening the battalion had been taken out of the line and sent to protect Pont-à-Mousson, which was being shelled by German heavy artillery. They marched through the cool, star-lit night and went on next day through blistering heat. But Pont-à-Mousson, apparently, had not been badly damaged. There was another alarm on August 25th at two o'clock in the morning, and they set off for Thiaucourt. From there – without a halt – they had marched on to Saint-Benoît-en-Woëvre, Haumont, La Chaussée, Hadonville and (finally) Joinville. Between two o'clock in the morning and five on the following afternoon

*School-boy slang for "pupil-teacher".

they had covered thirty-two miles in full marching order. Péguy shared his men's sufferings as keenly as if he had carried a pack himself; and yet the pace had to be kept up, there must be no stragglers; the Germans were on their heels. Le Pion urged his men on, rallied and cheered these companions of his – these brothers in arms. If only (he thought) he could lead them into battle!

But after that exhausting march had come the withdrawal (in rain and mud this time) to the high ground above the Meuse valley. Péguy was then forty-one years' old, but many younger men envied his stamina. At Saint-Mihiel, for the first time for several days, they had been able to read the newspapers. The news was bad. But the company commander with the pince-nez looked up from his reading to reassure those around him:

"There has been, no doubt, an unfortunate set-back, the causes of which are not apparent, but there seems to have been no decline in morale, which is the main thing. And, in any case, I have complete confidence in our General Staff. We shall certainly get over this slight reverse. Ultimate victory is absolutely beyond question."

Just then the news came that the 55th Division had been allotted to the Army of Paris. Péguy and his men had entrained on the morning of August 28th at the junction station of Lérouville. There was no singing this time, and their train moved along more quickly than during mobilisation. There were brief halts at Bar-le-Duc, Vitry-le-François, Châlons, Rheims, Soissons, Villers-Cotterêts. On the twenty-ninth, in daylight, they stopped at Crépy-en-Valois.

Lieutenant Péguy had a painful shock as he looked at his map. Crépy-en-Valois was less than seventy-five miles north of Paris. "We thought the Germans were somewhere near Lille."

But what Péguy told his men was: "We shall no doubt be moving up to the Nord (Department) on foot. By stages, of course."

The first stage ordered was Roye, eighteen miles away. They had hardly covered six miles when they met the first groups of refugees. The grey, weary faces turned towards the troops: "The Boches are coming!" they said.

4

GENERAL CASSANDRA

EARLY ON the morning of August 29th three staff cars from
G.H.Q. were travelling north-west at high speed on the N.44
road. In the pilot car was an officer of the Commander-in-
Chief's personal staff, with two detectives from the Sureté
and two gendarmes. In the closed car flying the Commander-
in-Chief's pennant were Majors de Galbert and Gamelin and
the Commander-in-Chief himself, in the right-hand corner at
the back. His face was dark and set, and he was even more
silent than usual. General Joffre was on his way to H.Q. of
5th Army at Laon for the purpose of performing the most
distressing – and most unusual – duty ever falling to the lot of a
Commander-in-Chief. He was about to relieve of his command
an officer whom he looked upon as the most able of all his
subordinates: General Lanrezac.

As a matter of fact, Lanrezac was not dismissed on that
day, but a few days later; in any case, before the battle of
the Marne. Strictly speaking he plays no part in the drama
itself, but it is impossible not to mention him, because the
operation he successfully directed on August 29th was to have
an important bearing upon the situation as it existed immediately before the great battle began. But, quite apart from this
factor, the psychological aspect of the Lanrezac affair has a
magnetic attraction that is irresistible.

Poincaré, in his "Journal", makes this comment: "Lanrezac
was a member of the Conseil Supérieur de la Guerre (War
Council) and one of the most eminent soldiers of his time.
He came to lunch with me soon after his appointment and was
described to me by the Commander-in-Chief as a master of
the art of war. 'He has a very quick brain, and seems full
of fire, but is also very cool-headed', General Joffre told me:
'He is a future Commander-in-Chief'."

His reputation was all the more remarkable because Lanrezac's views were in direct opposition to the accepted dogma that the offensive should take precedence over every other consideration. But, in spite of this "unfortunate defect", his colleagues always listened to his ideas with considerable pleasure, and indeed (as they all have admitted) with intense interest; but they always went back afterwards to their credo.

On July 31, 1914, Lanrezac had written to Joffre, anticipating (amongst other possibilities) a German attack through Namur, Dinant and Givet. "In such a case" (he wrote) "the 5th Army, which is under orders to attack in the Ardennes, could do nothing to prevent a possible encircling movement against our left wing." Lanrezac's own proposal was to remain on the defensive until the British troops were ready for effective action and then to mount a counter-offensive "in the light of the situation of the enemy forces at that time". Joffre had received this letter on August 1st, while he was engaged in the formidable task of committing to memory the movement of the thousands of trains mobilising the French army. How could he find time for a discussion with Lanrezac, or even to reply to his letter?

On August 7th, when he heard of the German attack on Liége, Lanrezac had sent his Chief of Staff to G.H.Q. with a letter in which he wrote: "This time there can be no doubt about it. They are planning a wide encircling movement through Belgium. I ask permission to change the direction of the 5th Army towards the north." No reply. At last, on the thirteenth, he had been allowed to divert one of his army corps towards Givet. On the fourteenth he went himself to G.H.Q.

"I am under orders" (he told Joffre) "to advance through the Ardennes. But I am now quite certain that the Germans intend to attack in force on the left bank of the Meuse. In the course of my advance I shall be attacked from the flank."

"Our view is that the Germans have got nothing ready up there as yet," Joffre had replied.

And Berthelot (smiling above the folds of his enormous white smock) had echoed his chief's remark.

"Up there" meant west of the Meuse. Now Lanrezac had only just returned to his own H.Q. when an officer placed on his table Information Bulletin No. 38, which read: "Threat of a German encircling movement to the west of the Meuse by eight army corps and from four to six artillery divisions." Lanrezac had sent immediately for his secretary.

Take this down: "Commander 5th Army to Commander-in-Chief. Beg to call your attention to B.R. No. 38 issued by your own H.Q. In order to meet the threat reported I ask permission to divert 5th Army towards the sector Givet-Maubeuge."

Joffre's reply was: "I see no objection (on the contrary) to your considering the movement you propose. But the threat is as yet only a long-term possibility and we are not absolutely certain that it actually exists."

At that time the Commander-in-Chief had seemed neither annoyed nor surprised. But how long is it possible (without growing irritation) to go on listening to a subordinate whose ideas are always proved to be right? Although, by sheer persistence, Lanrezac had finally won Joffre's permission to move his army seventy-five miles further north, it had, nevertheless, been outflanked by the German right wing and only narrowly escaped the pincer closing in upon it at Charleroi. Lanrezac had then refused to cross the Sambre and, on the evening of the twenty-third, had deliberately given the order to retreat. Subsequent events had proved that this order had been the salvation of the French left wing.

But it was not merely because he was always right that Lanrezac had become so objectionable to the Commander-in-Chief. A brief glance at any map of the front on August 28th will suffice to explain the clash – now reaching a climax – between the two men. A study of that map will, in fact, be useful in view of later developments.

On the extreme east, in the right-hand lower corner of the map, the thick line represents the 1st Army under General Dubail, extending from Munster to Baccarat. Above it is the 2nd Army, under General de Castelnau, with its flank secured on the Grand Couronné plateau, just beyond Nancy. Above that, again, is the 3rd Army under General Ruffey, protected by Verdun. This part of the front was relatively stable, or so, at least, it was reported two days previously. It was beyond this point that the front was becoming fluid, that is, in the sector of the 4th Army, under General Langle de Cary, who

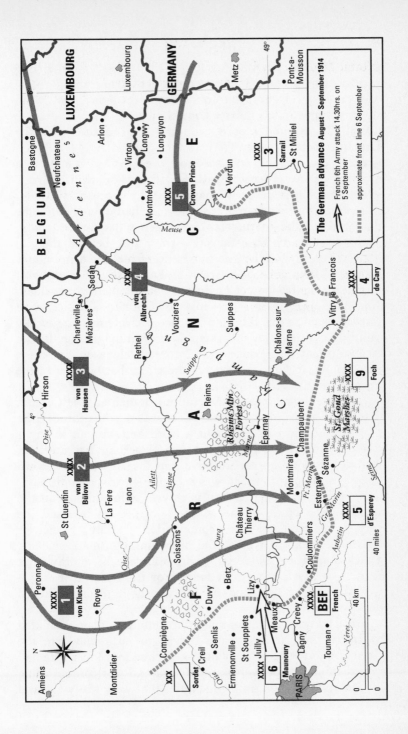

The German advance August – September 1914

French 6th Army attack 14.30hrs. on 5 September

approximate front line 6 September

was falling back and disengaging his left wing. A disquieting gap had been opened between the 4th Army and General Lanrezac's 5th Army, but Joffre had already planned to fill it by sending in an "Army Detachment", (later to become the 9th Army) under Foch, who had been recalled from the Lorraine sector.

Since the fighting at Charleroi, the 5th Army had been carrying out an orderly retreat. On its left, the British Army, which had been severely mauled at Le Cateau, was also retreating, but much more quickly. It had thereby become detached, to the extent of some fifteen miles further south, from the main body of the 5th Army, and, beyond the gap between them, was the line representing the 6th Army under General Maunoury – the Army of Paris – still in process of formation, its troops not having as yet completely detrained. And the black arrows showing the German advance were already penetrating this empty space, threatening the highly vulnerable 6th Army, threatening to annihilate the British Army, threatening, once again, to encircle the 5th Army, threatening, in fact, to dislocate the entire battle order of the French front.

Joffre had gone into the Operations Branch at G.H.Q. and, seated saddle-wise on a chair (a characteristic attitude), he had studied the map. Without a word and without asking a single question he had remained thus for perhaps half-an-hour, waiting for the map itself to give him the answer. In its own language the map, in fact, was speaking clearly enough.

From this point onwards it is easy to follow almost all the stages of the battle of the Marne if one keeps in mind the very simple fact that every commander of a large French or German formation lived in the perpetual nightmare of being attacked *from a flank*. A large formation is like a drawer, it is built to move from front to rear or from rear to front; a blow from either side could be very damaging; it might indeed destroy it completely.

Joffre by now had abandoned the ambitious plan circulated in Instruction No. 2, which sought to out-manoeuvre the German right wing by a counter-encircling movement. He had ceased thinking about this pipe-dream and was concentrating his attention only on simple measures that were ready to hand to cover the retreat and avoid the disastrous possibility of envelopment of the French left wing. Now what the map was telling him, in no uncertain terms, was that one of the possible moves available was to use the 5th Army for a counter-attack from the *inside* against the flank of the German right wing.

Joffre had already conceived this plan on August 27th, and had sent a liaison officer with it to Lanrezac. This officer, Colonel Alexandre, had presented the order in an off-hand manner, suggesting that it was incredibly easy of execution, child's play in fact; a mere flick of the hand over the map, and the thing's done. When his attention was called to certain difficulties in the way he had made this unfortunate remark: "Of course, if you'd rather do nothing at all . . . . "

Furious, Lanrezac had retorted: "Before presuming to teach me my job, Sir, go and tell your half-baked little strategists to learn theirs!"

Thus ran the official version (somewhat milder than the more picturesque original) for Lanrezac, choleric and impatient by nature, never minced his words. Joffre himself had arrived next day, white with anger: "I repeat my orders to you to march on Saint-Quentin and press home your attack with the utmost vigour."

"But, General, I am already changing front with that intention."

Slightly nonplussed, Joffre, after a short silence, said: "Ah! bon." And then Lanrezac, with a somewhat theatrical gesture, had pointed to the map. Lanrezac was taller than Joffre; he had a deep voice, expressed himself with fluency and ease: "I should like, nevertheless, to point out to you, General, that the German forces that attacked me at Charleroi are still hot on my heels. Consequently, as soon as I begin my advance on Saint-Quentin my right flank will be exposed to attack. To do this they are likely to deploy their troops in the region of Guise."

Yet another lesson in tactics! Another of his pessimistic intuitions that would probably prove correct! Really, this was beyond endurance! Joffre had exploded like an overcharged boiler and launched himself into one of his rare, short, but violent fits of temper. With fists clenched, and quick, almost convulsive gestures of the arms, he had poured out his pent-up feelings in a splutter of jerky, half-finished phrases. Lanrezac had offended the British, and they were now throwing up the sponge; he was a wet-blanket, he raised objections to every order he was given, his attitude was obstructive, insubordinate. "Do you want me to relieve you of your command? If not, do as you're told, and don't argue. If you refuse to carry out my orders I'll have you shot!"

Lanrezac later denied that Joffre had used these last words, although Poincaré affirms it. True or not, they expressed Joffre's feelings. He only calmed down when Lanrezac repeated his assurance that he would carry out the Commander-in-Chief's orders.

"Good. I shall come back tomorrow."

Night brings counsel. In this instance it had counselled Joffre to sack Lanrezac, deprive him of his command and send him to the devil along with twenty other generals already *"limogés"** since the war began. That would be the last of this maddening General Cassandra, whose every word was a thorn in the flesh, this creator of disasters by the sheer fact of always foreseeing them. It was no good shelving the issue; it must be faced "in spite of the grave objections" (wrote Joffre later) "to such a move in the middle of a battle. What was wanted at this juncture was a man of action and resolution. I was thinking of General Franchet d'Esperey . . . ."

A little before nine Laon came into view, perched on its high ridge three hundred feet above the surrounding plain. There, centuries before, the Gauls had halted the Belgae; later the Romans, holding Laon, had thrown back the Francs, the Vandals and the Huns. Would the new wave of German invasion reach this brave old bastion? The three cars from G.H.Q. were now climbing up the winding road to the town above.

The H.Q. of 5th Army – also housed in a school – was mean and shabby. Its officers were squeezed uncomfortably into children's desks and working in an atmosphere redolent of dust and ink. As soon as the usual polite greetings were over, Hély d'Oissel, Lanrezac's chief of staff, handed the Commander

---

*Sent to Limoges – a command far removed from the fighting line; out of harm's way.

in-Chief an order signed during the morning by his army commander: "The 1st German Army has attacked Péronne from the right. It is of the utmost importance that the attack now being launched by us upon his left flank should be pressed home with the utmost rapidity and vigour. The opening phase will be directed upon Saint-Quentin." The operation had in fact begun, and two reserve divisions, together with the 18th Corps, had already crossed the Oise in a westerly direction on their way to the objective ordered.

Without a word Joffre handed back the paper and went out with Majors Gamelin and de Galbert into the playground, where they paced up and down for a few moments. They then returned to the classroom. It was less than ten minutes after their arrival at the H.Q. that an orderly brought a telegram from General Defforges: "The 10th Corps, in process of establishing a protective flank behind the Oise above Guise, is being attacked by superior forces deploying from Guise-Englancourt. My left is holding, my right has had to give ground." Exactly what Lanrezac had forecast on the previous day.

The scene that follows is probably unique in French military annals. Seated at the table in the classroom was General Hély d'Oissel, tall, slim, perfectly groomed, well-trimmed moustache, a model of the dashing cavalry officer of pre-war days, a "gentleman" in the English sense. Lanrezac, also tall, but somewhat flabby and corpulent, was pacing to and fro in front of the table. Sixty-two, the same age as Joffre. His hair and moustache were turning grey, his complexion sallow, strangely exotic (he had been born in Guadeloupe). His eyes were vivid and clear, sparkling with intelligence (with fever, too, it was said) in contrast with the cynical curl of the lower lip. He was tidily but – like Joffre – indifferently dressed. A curious mannerism was to carry his pince-nez perched over his right ear, putting them on only to read.

Seated, facing the two men a few feet away, were Joffre (in a black tunic bulging at the waist-line and ill-fitting red breeches) and Major Gamelin in the dark "Chasseurs" uniform, rosy-cheeked, looking very young, but self-assured, unruffled, very much the G.H.Q. type.

Lanrezac begins dictating orders, then stops and looks up: "I take it you are in agreement, General?"

He repeats the question once or twice, but, as Joffre makes absolutely no reply – none whatever – he goes on dictating his orders as if he were alone with his Chief of Staff. The attack towards Saint-Quentin is to be continued north-westward, but, at the same time, counter-measures must be taken to meet the German attack developing from Guise in the north. But further reports show that this attack from the north is becoming more and more dangerous; all forces available must be concentrated to contain it. Lanrezac continues to make his decisions without any consultation with Joffre, and Joffre still says nothing, not a word.

Clear and precise, Lanrezac's orders go out to his units, the appropriate moves are initiated, and the 1st Corps, under Franchet d'Esperey, moved in the nick of time to support and rally the sorely-tried 3rd and 10th Corps on the right. "When it became evident that the original plan had miscarried and that the 5th Army must fight facing north to save its very existence he rose to the occasion ... displaying the greatest quickness and comprehension of events."*

This comment by Spears, one of Lanrezac's most determined detractors, summarises what others have written. Historians are unanimous that Lanrezac's handling of the battle of Guise was an exceptionally brilliant performance, a model of its kind. Joffre himself admits this: "My impression was that he was directing the battle with precision and method." For the moment there could be no question of "sending him to Limoges". Nevertheless nothing had been decided when, at noon, the Commander-in-Chief left Laon to pay a visit to Field-Marshal French at Compiègne.

Lieutenant-General Sir Archibald Murray, the Chief of Staff to the British Expeditionary Force, walked across the forecourt of the château to meet his Commander-in-Chief.

"General Joffre will be arriving, Sir, in half-an-hour's time."

Sir John French dismounted, a short, sturdy figure. A groom appeared and put his hand to the horse's bridle.

"That gives me time to change," he said, and went quickly up the steps beside his Chief of Staff. It was certainly very hot;

*Major-General E. L. Spears, *Liaison, 1914,* p. 276.

and a damp patch was visible on the back of his tunic. His
white moustache contrasted sharply with his high colour,
but his congested appearance was not merely due to the heat;
he seldom looked otherwise. The sentries to right and left of the
entrance presented arms with the automatic precision born
of long training in a professional army.

"What do you think he wants?" asked Sir John.

"I don't know, Sir; but I am sure he will not persuade
you to change your mind."

Mercifully, the G.H.Q. staff had not been obliged to make
their abode in some shabby, dusty school. This château was a
most suitable place. The light streamed in through the tall
windows. The offices were installed in the gallery, which was
magnified into gigantic dimensions by its huge mirrors. Many
of the pictures lining the walls were famous master-pieces; but
alas, a squad of workmen were now busy taking them down and
packing them into wooden cases.

"This hammering is dreadful," said the Field-Marshal.
"We shan't be able to hear ourselves speak."

"We'll get them to keep quiet for a few minutes, Sir."

A few minutes, yes, that was all that was necessary. No
need to go on discussing for hours; people always talk too
much. Especially Frenchmen. Since he arrived on the Continent
the Commander-in-Chief had decided (and in this he was
following the directives he had been given) to adopt a policy
of "wait and see". On the rare occasions he had departed
from it he had lived to regret it.

"General Joffre has left General Lanrezac's H.Q. and is
on his way here," said the Chief of Staff.

The mention of Lanrezac's name could hardly fail to bring
a shadow of annoyance across the rubicund, mobile features of
the Commander-in-Chief. French, hero of the Boer War, the
dashing cavalryman who had cut his way through the Boer
defences to relieve Kimberley had, in fact, an impulsive,
sensitive nature. And, in any case, no gentleman could help
feeling annoyed at any reference to this officer commanding
the 5th Army. Who would wish to have any further dealings
with a man who had been so abominably rude to the Commander-in-Chief of the British Expeditionary Force, when,
on August 17th, he had gone out of his way to make a polite –

and, indeed, what was intended as a gracious – gesture by paying a call on the 5th Army Commander? Rather with the object of keeping a difficult conversation going (for Lanrezac's attitude had been icy) French, at one point, had put his finger on the map at a spot where German troops had been reported: "Do you think they intend to cross the Meuse there?"

He said this, of course, in English. Every time French had spoken Lanrezac had impatiently asked, "What did he say? What did he say?" This time, when French's question had been translated, Lanrezac, with an almost imperceptible shrug of the shoulders, had replied: "Tell him the Germans have come there for a bit of fishing!"

Sir Henry Wilson, the Deputy Chief of Staff, had given his Chief a diplomatically-amended English version, but Sir John had sensed the tone of the reply, and, very soon after, he had learnt the truth. So far as French was concerned, Lanrezac's remark betrayed, once and for all, the man's breeding. Incidentally – and this was yet another incredible faux pas – Lanrezac never returned the Commander-in-Chief's visit; which perhaps, was just as well.

By the time General Joffre was announced Sir John had had time to take a bath and change. General Joffre, however, was neither ill-mannered nor unpleasant. His appearance, admittedly, was not very impressive. It was a pity he had let himself put on so much weight. And dressed so badly. So many of these French officers, with their badly-cut uniforms, their long hair and untidy moustaches gave the impression that the French Army was becoming alarmingly democratic. Sir John had written as much – and plainly enough – in a letter to Lord Kitchener, Minister of War: "One must always bear in mind the class of society from which most of these French generals have come."* But this was no time to bring all that up again. We must go and listen very politely to what General Joffre has to say.

"A somewhat difficult situation has arisen on the left wing of our 5th Army," said Joffre. "It is important that the British Army should make every effort to maintain contact with it and also with the reserve divisions of General Valabrègue, which

*Barbara Tuchman, *August 1914*, Constable, 1962.

are the only troops available at present to cover the 6th Army, now in process of formation."

Ah, so the British Expeditionary Force was expected to make yet another effort. But whose fault was it if the French left wing was in danger? The Field-Marshal, on August 16th, had made contact, by a personal visit, with the French G.H.Q. at Vitry-le-François. (He had been cordially received; there had even been whisky, although he had never guessed the amount of trouble taken to unearth that half-empty bottle in a café in the town.) But at that time the French were expecting to make mincemeat of the German Army. Two weeks later, the French strategical plan had proved itself a complete failure. The interpreter went on: "The Russian offensive now in progress will certainly force the Germans to withdraw troops from our front. General Broussilov is making good progress in Galicia."

Sir John was tempted to reply: "Galicia is a long way off!" but, instead, he said, "Yes, yes, exactly," in a very conciliatory tone. (One must always seem very conciliatory when one has no intention whatever of giving way.)

"The pressure on this front will therefore be relieved," went on General Joffre. "If, therefore, you could keep your army up in line with our own front until our 6th Army is fully operational we could resume the offensive shortly afterwards. I would suggest, for instance, that your troops would be lying in an excellent defensive position if they were behind the Crozat canal . . . ."

The French Commander-in-Chief obviously did not realise that his advice on tactical questions now lacked weight; what is more, he was going beyond the existing conventions in claiming to give orders to the commander of the British Expeditionary Force.

The truth was that, from the beginning, a misunderstanding had existed as between the French and British commanders, due to what may be called the sentimental reactions to the alliance of the French people themselves. Sir John still remembered the wild enthusiasm of his reception in Paris (Vive French! Vive l'Angleterre, Vivent les Engliches!). From the time they disembarked at Rouen, Le Havre or Boulogne until they reached their allotted sector in the Le Cateau-Maubeuge area the khaki-clad British soldiers had been cheered, fêted, covered with flowers and kisses (although their officers had been warned, in a confidential memorandum, to beware of French women). Every Frenchman was clearly convinced that an eternal friendship – a sort of blood-bond – had been established between the two peoples. The British Army had certainly done its duty – and even more – during the opening attack, which had been expected to sweep everything before it. But now the time had come for a cool-headed assessment of the situation.

Another difficulty in dealing with the French was that they were quite incapable of accepting – even for a brief moment – any point of view other than their own. The worthy Joffre would certainly have been surprised therefore (and perhaps profoundly shocked) if he had suddenly been informed of the secret directives given to Field-Marshal French for the conduct of the campaign:

" . . . . The greatest care must be exercised towards a minimum of losses and wastage. Therefore, while every effort must be made to coincide most sympathetically with the plans and wishes of our Allies, the greatest consideration will devolve upon you as to participation in forward movements where large bodies of French troops are not engaged and where your Force may be unduly exposed to attack . . . . I wish you distinctly to understand that your command is an entirely independent one, and that you will in no case come in any sense under the command of an Allied General."*

Field-Marshal Lord Kitchener, Minister of War, who had dictated these orders, was certainly no enemy of France. He had fought as a volunteer in the French Army in 1870. But Lord Kitchener was taking the long view. In London in early August, 1914, at a meeting of the Cabinet, he had clearly stated the policy he proposed to follow: "We must be prepared to put armies of millions in the field and maintain them for several years."†

Hence the directives given to Sir John. Meanwhile, at Compiègne, in the tall-windowed room of the château, the burly French general went on with his pleading. Sir John kept

*Field-Marshal Sir John French, 1914, p. 14, Constable, 1919.

†Sir W. S. Churchill, *The World Crisis, 1911–1918*, p. 140, abridged and revised edition, Butterworth, 1931.

silent, and Sir Archibald Murray made discreet gestures now and then, to forestall any weakening on the part of his chief. But Sir Archibald's fears were groundless, for Sir John had not the slightest intention of acting against the secret orders he had received. When, finally, Joffre asked if he might count on the British troops moving north next morning, Sir John, composed and polite, had replied: "I am very sorry. But my troops need at least forty-eight hours' complete rest. After that I shall be willing to take part in the operation you propose; but not before."

No great risk was involved in such a promise. How much further would the French have retreated in two days' time? Joffre seemed somewhat annoyed, but from Sir John's tone he had realised, no doubt, that it was useless to insist. He had made no attempt, as he took his leave, to conceal his disappointment.

Passing through Rheims on his way back to his headquarters, Joffre saw General Wilson, standing beside his car on the square in front of the cathedral. "I stopped my car at once and went across to him. He told me he was on his way back from Vitry-le-François. We began talking, and, without any attempt to hide the impression I had gained from my meeting with his chief, I explained my own point of view. Wilson was fully aware of the gravity of the situation, and he promised to do his best to persuade the Field-Marshal, as diplomatically as possible, to modify the views to which, at the moment, he seemed so obstinately attached." As diplomatically as possible, no doubt. General Wilson was so fully aware of the gravity of the situation that he had given orders the previous day to Lieutenant-Colonel Marr Johnson, a staff officer in the Railways Branch, to reconnoitre the bridges that would need to be destroyed between Compiègne and La Rochelle in order to cover the possible withdrawal of the British Expeditionary Force to that port of embarkation. And, next day, Field-Marshal French was to telegraph General Joffre, informing him that "in no circumstances" could the British Army resume its position in the front line in less than ten days' time.

There was at least one item of good news for the somewhat care-laden Joffre when he returned to Vitry-le-François on the evening of August 29th. The 5th Army had won the battle of Guise. Thanks to Lanrezac's brilliant tactics, his left wing, and the 1st Corps in particular, under Franchet d'Esperey, had thrown back the German attack north of the Oise. The attacking forces had included the 2nd Guards Division, the pride of the German Army.

But, in spite of this success, orders had to be given to the 5th Army to continue its retreat, because its left flank was still uncovered owing to French's refusal to move up in support. Orders had also to be given to the 6th Army to continue its retreat, because (for the same reason) its right flank was in the air, and this notwithstanding a brilliant counter-attack by the 7th Corps at Proyart-en-Santerre. The 4th Army, under General Langle de Cary (who repeatedly assured Joffre he was ready to counter-attack, and asked permission to do so) was also ordered to retreat because, on his right, Foch's Army Group was taking heavy punishment. The Germans were bringing the enormous pressure of their attack to bear on each of the French armies in turn, and each had to be pulled out, like a drawer, as and when its flanks were endangered.

On September 1st, General Instruction No. 4 was issued, and was completed on September 2nd by Secret and Personal Note No. 3463 to Army Commanders, fixing as follows the extreme limit of withdrawal of the French Armies: (from west to east) Pont-sur-Yonne, Nogent-sur-Seine, Arcis-sur-Aube, Brienne-le-Château (Haute-Marne). Pont-sur-Yonne is fifty-three miles south-east of Paris. The Instruction made it clear that "the withdrawal need not necessarily extend as far as this line". (Nor, one might be tempted to add, necessarily stop there). The truth was that for several days from now onwards the movements of the retreating armies were to elude all possible anticipation, all possible orders or counter-orders.

5

"*À OUTRANCE!*"

August 30th was a Sunday. A few French regiments were still marching north on that day. The 276th Infantry Battalion, which had detrained at Tricot (Oise) was making its way towards Roye (Somme) when, at nine o'clock in the morning the artillery received orders to come into action.

"Don't see many Boches about," said one soldier of the 19th Company.

"Don't worry; you'll see plenty of them," replied Lieutenant Péguy.

Very soon after, the guns opened fire and the whole battalion went forward to attack. In columns of fours through a field of beetroot. The men cursed as they slithered on the dew-drenched leaves.

"Steady there! Don't wander about!" said Lieutenant Péguy. "Close ranks, and keep your ears open for orders!"

He himself was marching, as if on parade, beside the column, his képi pulled down over his eyes against the low, morning sun. But beneath the peak his eyes were gleaming with happy excitement. Away towards the north-west the Germans, like a swarm of ants, were debouching from the wood at l'Echelle-Saint-Léger. Fighting had already begun beyond the village of Armancourt, but the 5th Battalion was ordered to occupy a crest, in support of the artillery, to prevent any turning manoeuvre by the enemy.

From this vantage point the 246th, 289th, 231st and part of the 276th Companies could be seen marching abreast under fire, like regiments in the battle pictures of the Napoleonic wars. The sharp crack of the 75's was answering the deep boom of the German guns. At two o'clock the battalion commander galloped up.

"The General is asking for a company of volunteers to defend the village."

"The 19th is ready, Sir!" replied Captain Guérin.

And off they went again – into the beetroot. The dew was off them now, but the sun was terribly hot. A few men dropped to the ground even before the company came under shell-fire, and the N.C.O's shouted at them: "Get up, there!" But the men lay prone. Their faces were bright scarlet; sunstroke.

Although there was no enemy in the village, the place was a raging inferno. Shells went screaming over their heads and burst a few yards away.

The company had been holding the village for about ten minutes. Dead bodies lay here and there in the streets. An aeroplane, marked with the German black cross, circled overhead; and the shelling increased.

"Withdraw to Marquevilliers!" Its steeple could be seen above a line of trees a little under a mile distant. "In column of fours," ordered Péguy.

The shells came over on a very flat trajectory, ploughing into the ground and leaving a repulsive furrow of green smoke. Hearing their warning screech, the men would throw themselves flat on the ground and cover their heads with their packs; then they would get up and move on. The officers remained standing, Péguy smiling to himself, La Cornillière carelessly tapping his boots with a cane cut from a hedge. Captain Guérin, with monocle and a walking-stick, was leading his Company on foot. He had a pronounced limp – a legacy from a serious wound received during the Moroccan campaign. Next day, Péguy was to read out to his men (or to those who were still with him) a despatch from Divisional Headquarters congratulating the 19th Company of the 276th Battalion on its gallant conduct and its retreat in perfect order under fire during the fighting on August 30th.

In perfect order then, but not later. For the 19th Company, the whole of the 276th Battalion – and, indeed, the whole division – became engulfed in the flood of the main retreat. In some of the villages on their way all the inhabitants had fled, leaving nothing but empty homes behind them. "Looting is strictly forbidden! Leave everything alone!"

They went on, and there seemed no end to it. "What the hell" they muttered "what about our hourly halt?" But there was no hourly halt. Gendarmes behind the column chivvied them along. "It's all right for them, the bastards, they're as fresh as paint! And they've got no pack!" Captain Guérin, covered in dust, but still wearing his monocle, walked on in silence, hanging on to his horse's tail. Péguy alone seemed utterly tireless. ("How the hell does the Pion do it?"). He would run – actually run – from one end of the company column to the other: "You're not falling out, are you? All right then, have a breather; and then get a move on and catch us up."

It was getting dark, but they marched on, hunger gnawing their vitals, through Remangis, Rollot, Courcelles, Montgeran and Vaumont (names one would have forgotten long since, but for the vivid memory of what was endured there; a curious thing, surely?)

At one o'clock in the morning an order was given: "Company, right wheel. Forward. Across country."

"Bloody hell! What next! We can't go on like this! We're finished!"

They stumbled in the darkness over ground as hard as iron. Groaning and almost weeping with exhaustion, they suddenly heard, quite close, a friendly, ghostly voice: "Now look here, lads, I'm just as tired as you are and just as hungry; but – for goodness' sake – do as I do. I promise you, this time we're nearly there."

It was the Pion, of course. In the space of twenty-four hours, with no food, the men of the 19th Company had been through very heavy shelling and had then marched thirty-seven miles. That night, sleeping on straw in a barn was Heaven. They were up next morning at seven, and moving forward again (or more exactly backward) in the direction of Paris. Still no rations. Their only food was a few green apples picked along the roadside; with inevitable results. Captain Guérin's old wound re-opened and he was forced to give up. The Pion was now in command of the company, a company reduced to sixty men. Along the interminable road of retreat, rumours spread like the plague between one unit and another:

"The Government has left Paris and taken refuge at Tours."

"No, not Tours, Bordeaux."

"That is untrue!" shouted Lieutenant Péguy. It's just a rumour!"

But, when some of the men began throwing away their packs, the Pion could stand no more. He protested: "Don't do that, lad!"

"Sorry, Sir, but I'm all in."

"Very well, give it to me."

And Péguy would carry this man's pack a while and then another's; carrying the cross for his exhausted men, whose numbers grew hourly less. Leaving Saint-Aubin on August 31st there were but thirty left, shuffling wearily along, leaning one on the other. Péguy blew a blast on his whistle: "Fifteen minutes' rest!"

Péguy, the pilgrim of the Chartres road, looked with infinite compassion on these wretched pilgrims of defeat, lying like corpses along the hedgerow. But not of defeat; surely not of defeat? He refused to believe it. In spite of everything one must have faith in France, in her leaders. Péguy was too sensitive even to speak of those other secret sources that nourished his courage and his hopes: Notre-Dame, Saint Joan, Saint Geneviève, the Holy Innocents . . . .

But the fifteen minutes break had passed like a flash for these exhausted foot-sloggers. Péguy got to his feet, and blew his whistle once again. No one moved. There seemed no life left in these prostrate figures. And yet Péguy knew they were not dead. They must get up. They must. For France. "Come on, now! 19th Company! Up you get!"

No one moved. The only answer, when it came, was in the unmistakable accent of the Paris streets: "There isn't a 19th now! It's done for!"

"Ah, that's what you think, is it?"

The voice of the tireless Pion roused them, ordered, begged, cajoled. And one by one the prostrate figures stumbled to their feet.

The 19th Company of the 276th Infantry had become a tiny pebble rolled along in a huge flood, and the Retreat was now a vast world of its own, weird and remote, with its own colour, its own mass; a law unto itself. A grey world. Under the blazing sun and the fantastic mid-day heat, the same dust covered the incongruous clothing of civilians in flight and soldiers in uniform. Red trousers, battered képis, blue, dead-weighted great-coats were merged into an indistinguishable uniformity of grey. "I could hardly believe that men could bear so much and still survive," wrote a British liaison officer. These infantrymen, with their cracked, half-open lips, their unkempt beards and haggard faces, were covering an average of thirty-five miles every twenty-four hours, marching day and night, with rarely more than four hours' sleep. They were without food, because they were cut off from their supply wagons, which had got lost or been abandoned on some hill or other when their half-dead horses could go no further. Hundreds of men died of sunstroke and hundreds of others collapsed from exhaustion, even though they had discarded their arms and their packs. Others would fall asleep on the march and drop in their tracks; their képis would fall off and they would then die of sunstroke, or be run over by a passing vehicle.

The Retreat was a world of its own, and in it the best rubbed shoulders with the worst. In some villages the troops passed through as they had done a week before, tired and anxious, but in good order, keeping their formation in files eight abreast with their packs and arms; halting and moving off under the orders of their officers. But in others, where the roads and streets were already littered with soldiers' packs, rifles and odd scraps of uniform, unorganised groups of limping stragglers could shuffle through, leaning on their sticks or on each other. Here and there on the roadside, guns had been abandoned, undamaged, in perfect working order.

In other villages, officers in search of billets or supplies would find themselves talking to half-dazed individuals utterly ignorant, even of the name of the village itself. These people were not, in fact, the inhabitants at all, but refugees from elsewhere, who had stopped for an hour or for half a day in houses evacuated a day or a few hours before. Some villages were filled with these temporary occupants, lying asleep on beds, tables or on the floor, too tired to go in search of food, gloomily accustomed to the incessant and plaintive protests of the famished animals left unattended in the cattle-sheds.

Reluctance to part with their livestock had been, in many instances, the determining factor in persuading a whole village population to stay in their homes. A number of villages and hamlets had shown great courage and tenacity in so doing, and an example of stony determination that contrasted strangely with the panic-stricken confusion around them. They had even dug huge trenches to bury dead horses, for their elders had warned them that when the Prussians arrived they would give orders for this to be done – if it were not done already.

One of the nightmare memories of veterans of 1914 was the sight of thousands of horribly distended bodies of dead horses, lying along the roadsides during the retreat.

They died, most of them, from thirst and exhaustion; and death often came all too slowly. Twisting their necks in any effort to raise their heads they would watch pathetically as the men moved on. Their mouths and nostrils were thick with dust. Sometimes an officer, passing, would draw his revolver and put them out of their misery.

In some cases where the inhabitants would have stayed in their homes, villages would be suddenly evacuated as a result of terrifying stories of German atrocities – true or false – put around by small groups of unrepentant deserters fleeing from the troops behind them. No sooner had civilians abandoned their homes than these uniformed bandits would go in to loot. Some were captured, however, by the gendarmes, and there were soldiers, during the retreat, who would come across a group of these men, lined up against the wall after a summary trial. All available evidence confirms that their numbers were small, but these bandits undoubtedly existed, and their audacity, combined with the frightening rumours they spread, created the impression that they were more numerous than, in fact, they were.

A number of soldiers – lost or forgotten in the course of the colossal retreat – found themselves eventually behind the German lines. Many of them were simply made prisoners; but others who refused to give themselves up had formed themselves into a sort of maquis. If caught, they were considered as franc-tireurs having contravened the laws of war; and they were immediately shot.

The most famous of these maquis was led by Captain de Colbert, who, having been left behind in the Ardennes, collected some three hundred men, mostly of the 205th Infantry Battalion, and, until November 1914, carried on a successful guerilla campaign against isolated German soldiers and the

German lines of communication. Although hunted throughout the Ardennes by two divisions of *Landwehr*, de Colbert's maquis successfully avoided capture. In November the French High Command, having heard of Colbert's men, was able to establish contact with them. A French airman landed behind the German lines with special orders from G.H.Q. for de Colbert to attempt a raid on an important German command post installed at Mézières. But de Colbert was forced to abandon the project, the objective being too strongly guarded. By the end of December the maquis' existence had become extremely precarious, for the Germans were systematically destroying any village suspected of supplying them.

"I am disbanding the unit," said de Colbert. "You must all disperse and each man do his best to find his way alone to the Dutch frontier."

Some were successful, others failed. De Colbert himself was captured. It has never been established what happened to him.

It is difficult to resist the temptation to recall these scenes from a drama that created such totally unexpected situations and revealed so many diverse passions, virtues and personalities. One thinks of Lanrezac, on August 31st, reciting the Odes of Horace – in Latin – on the terrace of the Château at Craonne in the cool of a perfect summer night; or Lanrezac's officers, after the tough fight at Guise, white with anger and humiliation on the bridge at Orbais, where the girls shook their fists in their faces and screamed: "You are leaving us to the Germans!" or the sub-mistress of the post-office at Châtillon-sur-Marne, the only woman left in the town, sitting alone behind her counter and being urged to leave: "The Boche will be here in two hours time," they told her.

"No; I stay here. I've received no orders."

The Germans were here, they were there; no, they were not there yet, it was not certain, anyway. And even the Germans themselves were sometimes trapped by the prevailing confusion. A Uhlan's officer, impeccably dressed, immaculately groomed and polished, in silk shirt, gets out of a car at La Fère, thinking it to be in German hands. His driver stares somewhat anxiously at the French soldiers – unarmed, incidentally – around him; but the officer, quite convinced that these are prisoners, goes to the post-office and sends off a number of enthusiastic postcards: "Marvellous success! The French and British are scuttling away like rabbits!" He was quite surprised, on returning to his car, to find it surrounded, his driver a prisoner and he himself firmly grabbed by the scruff of the neck.

The British, in retreat, behaved no more like scuttling rabbits than the French. In obedience to the Field-Marshal's orders they had withdrawn more quickly, but their retreat was as bitter a *via dolorosa* for them as for their French comrades. It was also a demonstration of the sound discipline of a professional army. Only a short time before, the people of France had given a vociferous welcome to these men, admired their brand-new equipment, their polished leathers and well-kept uniforms; had looked on, with amused astonishment, as these strange soldiers shaved and cleaned their teeth every morning at the village pump. But now, as they watched, their faces were set: "Les Engliches foutent le camp,"* they muttered.

But they could not repress a new upsurge of curiosity – and even of admiration – when they saw how some regiments, the Irish Guards and the Highlanders among them, would suddenly march at attention as if on parade when they went through the village. The British cavalrymen for the most part were on foot, leading their horses. For this reason the British Army lost far fewer horses than the French.

The sweltering, dusty hours dragged by and the marching men longed for the night and the cooler air. It came at last, bringing welcome relief to a million weary soldiers in retreat and to the no-less weary Germans in relentless pursuit at their heels. But the dust still hung in the air increasing the darkness and hindering their progress by repeated stops and starts, wrong turnings, altercations and curses.

"Halt! Four hours' rest. No sleeping in the open."

In spite of the heat of the day, the exhausted men instinctively sought shelter under cover at night. But inside the barns the air was suffocating, intolerable. When at four a.m. the N.C.O's roused them, they thought they had been asleep for no more than a few minutes.

"Joffre is incompetent. He should be removed."
"He should be court-martialled! Shot!"

*Polite equivalent: "The English are clearing out!"

"When you think he has sacked more than twenty generals already! He has just sacked Ruffey and replaced him by Sarrail."

"Messimy was all for having them shot."

"Perhaps he was right!"

"No; you mean *they* were right. Anyhow, they were not so stupid as Joffre."

"They've sacked Messimy – who appointed Joffre – but they keep Joffre! It's idiotic!"

"Well, Millerand's no better than Messimy. He's scared stiff of Joffre."

Comments such as these are not to be found in the official war histories, but there seems ample evidence to confirm their truth. The Higher Command came in for very little praise in the lobbies of the Palais-Bourbon* at the end of August or during the early days of September; nor, indeed, in political clubs or drawing-rooms not as yet departed south of the Loire.

"Gallieni should be made Commander-in-Chief. He is already Joffre's designated successor."

"Joffre can't stand him. He has refused to work with him. Messimy sent Gallieni to see Joffre a fortnight ago, and Joffre talked to him for no more than five minutes. In the passage. And yet Joffre will always listen to anyone!"

"Gallieni was at the Elysée yesterday. Poincaré is very pessimistic. He told Gallieni: I am sorry you were not made Military Governor of Paris earlier. But I know the defences are not ready yet."

"All the same, the 6th Army has been put under Gallieni. He and Maunoury get on very well."

"The 6th Army? Can you tell me what it consists of? Nothing but the remains of disbanded units."

"The Paris fortifications would be useless against heavy artillery. And have you seen the ridiculous defences at the gates of Paris?"

I remember, as a child, the barbed wire, the pavé chicanes, the railway-sleeper barricades guarded by "Territoriaux"† who looked terribly old to me. And even to my childish eyes (which usually magnified everything) those defences seemed minute. I could not imagine that they could stop this enormous

*French Chamber of Deputies. †Elderly Reservists.

army of Germans that people around me talked about (lowering their voices if I was within hearing). I had a new – and strange – feeling that the grown-ups were frightened.

There were women at prayer in all the churches. Many were seen to be weeping in the dim candle-light. Paris (the preachers dared to proclaim) was being punished for its wickedness and immorality. But the good must pay for the bad. No news from the front; or what news came was so much out of date that it meant nothing. The newspapers said so little, and what they said was so stupidly reassuring, that it only increased our fears.

A squadron of Dragoons gallops down the street. No one raises a cheer. Not a word. A few days before the crowd had shouted: Vivent les Fusiliers Marins!* But now they are silent and anxious. Even the clatter of these galloping horses in the empty street has a touch of drama. Paris has become a silent city, filled with rumour. The Germans are much nearer than they say. Uhlans have been seen at Luzarches and Ecouen, "and they can see the Eiffel Tower from there".

Five thousand unhappy-looking Belgian refugees have arrived in Paris. But many more are on the way. Huge convoys of them, that we never see because they were diverted from Paris and sent elsewhere. There are some grumblers (it seems) amongst them. "Of course those people have nothing in their own country. And what's more, there are spies amongst these Belgian refugees. Bound to be."

The smart quarters of Paris are emptying fast. The wealthy are off to Bordeaux, to which town the Government has (now officially) decided to withdraw. The move produces a spate of caustic witticisms, including a parody of La Marseillaise: "Aux gares, citoyens! Montez dans les wagons!" But the main railway-lines, Paris-Lyon-Mediterranée, Paris-Orléans and even the Ouest-Etat, are hopelesly overcrowded, almost chaotic. Passenger trains take three days to cover sixty miles, for priority must be given to troop-trains, ammunition and the wounded. (The caption to a photograph in *l'Illustration* reads: "Our wounded keep smiling.") All who can use any other available means of transport. Up to fifteen hundred francs (sixty pounds sterling in those days) is demanded

*Marines.

by taxi-drivers and others for the trip to Bordeaux – and
eagerly paid. The main-line terminals (Gare de Lyon, d'Orsay,
d'Austerlitz, Montparnasse and Saint-Lazare) are thronged
with a seething mass of humanity, and people queue for
thirty-six hours for tickets available six days later. But, in
the meantime, the Germans will have arrived.

The first German plane flies over the city and drops two
bombs. Its name – *Taube* – at once becomes a household word.
Two days later, two more planes come over, and a bomb falls
in the rue La Fayette, killing a few people, wounding others.
But no report of it appears in the newspapers until a month
later, when the people of Paris are assured that these raids have
excited nothing more than idle curiosity – and more witticisms.
The people of Paris certainly took them calmly, but I well
remember the impression they created of a strange new threat
to óur daily existence. The word *Taube* took on a sinister
meaning.

A black-out was ordered, and, although far less strict than
that of the Second War, it was, nevertheless, an impressive
novelty. From the open window at night I would watch the
long, cone-like beams of the searchlights, wheeling and
halting in an endless rhythm until, finally, I would drop off to
sleep. The nights were strangely still, broken only by the
strident whistle of trains. So now, even in Paris, their long
shrill note could be heard at night . . .

The Government had finally decided to leave. On September
2nd, at seven in the evening, the Minister for War sent for
Gallieni.

"The Ministry looked gloomy, dark and deserted. The
courtyard was full of enormous furniture vans being loaded
with files and documents to be sent by rail to Bordeaux. In the
circumstances, the whole scene was decidedly depressing.
There was no light on the staircase."

Millerand was seated at a table in his completely empty
office. With his gruff features, his eyes staring fixedly through
pince-nez, he looked somewhat like a prisoner awaiting the
verdict. But the verdict, in fact, must be found and given by
him. Gallieni was brought in, and he asked at once for clari-
fication of a point arising from the directives he had been
given. The Government, now engaged in packing bag and

baggage, had decided that Paris was to be defended to the last ("*à outrance*"): "You realise, no doubt, Monsieur le Ministre, what is meant by these words, '*à outrance*'? They envisage the possibility of exceedingly grave measures, demolition, destruction, even ruins. I might, therefore, be obliged to blow up certain monuments, bridges; the Pont de la Concorde, for instance."

Millerand nodded his shaggy head: "*À outrance!*" he said.

6

TROUBLE ON OLYMPUS

SINCE THE early hours of August 30th General von Moltke's headquarters had been installed in Luxembourg, the trim, prosperous capital of the Grand Duchy; but in the most unpretentious and uncomfortable accommodation it could be possible to find there: a small school for girls, built in local red brick. The benches and desks in the class-rooms had simply been pushed against the walls and replaced by tables. And not even by tables. The monocled officers (whose servants spent three-quarters of an hour each morning shining their masters' field-boots) arrived at G.H.Q. to find themselves forced to sit in front of a few planks laid across trestles. No carpet on the bare boards under their feet. The Operations Branch was housed in a passage formerly used as the children's cloakroom, and so narrow that it was now barely possible to walk along it. For lighting there was neither electricity nor gas; oil lamps had to suffice, and even, in places – incredible as it may seem – candles.

"Avoid any action likely to inconvenience the local population; reduce requisitioning to a minimum." These had been General von Moltke's own orders. "This school will do us very well. And we shall be on our own here."

"On our own," that is to say, away from the restless hubbub of Imperial Headquarters; away from the chattering, gilded Officers-in-Waiting, the indiscretions of Imperial A.D.C's, the time-wasting military attachés; and, above all, away from those princelings of reigning houses, all that arrogant camarilla, secretly at daggers drawn, endlessly engaged in intrigue; in defending their privileges and honours; more active than ever now that victory held out alluring promise of even greater splendours, more lavish entertainment.

"Joffre is a lucky man," von Moltke would murmur, with a sigh. "In France a prince means nothing."

The officers of the O.H.L. often heard a sigh escape this Mecklenburger giant with the tired, sad face. And now, in spite of all these victories, he sighed again. Joffre, it's true, was carrying the heavy burden of retreat; but victory, too, had its problems. And here was a telegram from von Hausen, the 3rd Army Commander, dated August 30th, 14.00 hours: "Should I continue moving south tomorrow in pursuit of the forces engaged today, or resume my advance towards Château-Thierry?" By following the Directive of August 27th and marching south-west on Château-Thierry, von Hausen would let French troops escape that he might otherwise have captured or destroyed. Which was better, to conform strictly to the Plan, or exploit a local success?

Lieutenant-Colonel Tappen, Chief of the Operations Branch, was resolutely optimistic: "Your Excellency, practically speaking, we have successes to exploit in every sector. Here is a message we have intercepted from General von Kluck to General von Bülow: '16.00 hours. Enemy thrown back over the river Avre, south of Amiens. The 1st Army will move tomorrow towards the Oise in the Compiègne-Chauny area.' Here is another intercepted message from von Bülow to von Kluck at 16.00 hours: 'The enemy has suffered a decisive defeat. In order to take full advantage of our success it is of the utmost importance that the 1st Army converge around Chauny in the direction La Fère-Laon'." Without knowing it, von Kluck's intention and von Bülow's wishes seemed to be in complete accord.

Von Moltke listened carefully and thought hard. The engagement von Bülow had referred to had taken place around Guise. If the 2nd Army Commander had won such a complete and decisive victory why was it so highly important that von Kluck should come to his aid? Was it possible that the crafty and conceited von Bülow had suffered a rather nasty knock from the French before they withdrew? The army commanders reported as little as possible to the O.H.L.; and their independent habits often came near to sheer insubordination. The position was aggravated by the almost exclusive use of wireless telegraphy, a brilliant invention no doubt, but far from perfect, as yet, in practice. The powerful French station on the Eiffel Tower could swamp or jam the feeble, portable German transmitters, and every message had to be repeated several times, and subsequently decoded.

At six o'clock that evening Tappen brought in two more telegrams. The Duke of Wurtemberg reported: "The 4th Army began its advance southward at 13.00 hours"; from the Imperial Crown Prince: "It is highly desirable that the 4th Army should advance in order to facilitate the crossing of the Meuse by the 5th Army." In the centre of the German front therefore, as on the right wing, the army commanders' intentions seemed to harmonize completely one with the other, as Tappen had suggested. As for Prince Ruprecht of Bavaria, after having impatiently tugged at the leash for several days, he seemed now to be in no great hurry to push forward the two armies on the extreme left wing. But that part of the front was only looked upon, in any case, as a kind of strategic pivot.

"Do you not think, your Excellency, that the situation, as reported here, gives you the answer to the only important question raised, that is to say, von Hausen's? By pursuing the enemy southwards the 3rd Army will help the advance of the 4th Army, as proposed by the Imperial Crown Prince. As for the two armies on the right, it seems difficult not to allow them to exploit their success."

One, at least, of the arguments put forward by Tappen appealed to the Chief of the General Staff. At this very moment the Emperor was arriving at the Crown Prince's headquarters. Any reluctance on von Moltke's part to support the 5th Army would certainly offend both father and son.

"Very good, I agree," said von Moltke.

At 20.00 hours two telegrams went out over the wireless; the first to von Hausen, 3rd Army: "Yes, continue your advance southward"; the second to the Duke of Wurtemberg, 4th Army: "Advance, coordinating your movements with those of the 3rd Army." An hour later, as a sort of unimportant post-scriptum, a third wireless message was sent to both von Kluck and von Bülow: "The movements initiated by the 1st and 2nd Armies are in accordance with the intentions of the Supreme Command."

No historian has recorded whether von Moltke slept well or badly after signing that last message. No one on the German side seems to have realised that this approval of von Kluck's

and von Bülow's initiative was the first stage in the abandonment of the plan followed since the opening of the campaign.
In one short sentence von Moltke was giving his approval to the
abandonment, not only of von Kluck's march on Paris, but
also of his envelopment of the French left wing. He thought –
or tried to persuade himself – that this concession would be
only temporary.

* * *

"My men go on marching until they drop" (wrote a Saxon
officer) "and then the regimental ambulance picks them up.
A rumour has gone round in certain units that officers have
shot men who said they could not go on. I find this hard to
believe. We are told to maintain very strict discipline, but
circumstances often make this impossible. I mean, it is not
always easy, for instance, to forbid looting entirely when we
come to some place that has been left intact, after seeing so
many villages in ruins.

"The 178th had its first taste of fighting at Launois, against
troops of some African regiments dressed in baggy, grey canvas
trousers, and dirty shirts. These men knew how to make good
use of the terrain, but, like most French soldiers, they always
aimed too high. Another time we had a scrap at Faissault, in
dreadful country, wooded and full of hazards; attractive
scenery, no doubt, but hopeless from a military point of view.
The French artillery did some excellent work spraying our
reserve troops in the rear of our guns. They say the 102nd had
heavy losses. After fighting this rear-guard action the French
withdrew.

"On August 31st, just before we reached the village of Faux,
a mile or so from Auboncourt, we passed close to some French
gun positions that had been wiped out by our howitzers. It
was a terrible sight. The dead were scattered about amongst
the enormous shell-holes, the gunners in blue, the infantry
in their red trousers. A little further on the wounded were
limping away towards the village. Auboncourt itself had not
been completely evacuated, and there was no looting. We
requisitioned eggs, sides of beef and a few casks of wine. After
this unexpected stroke of luck we all set off again in better
spirits on the road *nach Paris*.

"Our conquest of France will no doubt be recorded and

commented upon later, and its strategical sequences analysed by the experts. I, as an officer, am putting this down in writing so that it can never be forgotten: nothing will have counted so much for us as the physical hardships we endured, and particularly what we suffered with our feet. Only one thought can make us forget them, and that is Paris. Paris is the Promised Land for us. Without that name in our minds night and day we should have given up. I sometimes wonder how the French have not collapsed from exhaustion long ago, when they have nothing to look forward to but defeat."

The man who wrote this was a *leutnant*, equivalent to a second-lieutenant in the British Army. He belonged to the 178th Infantry Regiment (or 13th Saxons) which had been on garrison duty at Kamens, in Saxony. The 178th, together with the 177th (or 12th Saxons, from Dresden), made up the 64th Brigade of the 32nd Division of the 12th corps in General von Hausen's 3rd Army. This officer was killed later during an attack by the French on the Aisne, on September 25th. His diary was found on him. Many similar records were recovered from the bodies of French and German soldiers, and these brief, pencilled notes are nearly always more vivid, sometimes almost more revealing, than many official Histories of the War. For the sake of brevity and simplicity I propose to make frequent use of these eye-witnesses' accounts, condensing them here and there, but adding, when necessary, some explanatory comment. I hope, in this way, to avoid any distortion of the truth and also to preserve the authentic idiom of these records. Here is a cavalryman's story:

"Fourth Cavalry Division. Our rôle was to cover the right flank of the 4th Reserve Corps. Early in the morning of September 1st we came into action at Néry, south of the Forest of Compiègne against the 1st British Cavalry Brigade. We first saw the British, through the mist, just before sunrise. They had seen us, too. This brigade was covering the British retreat. First, a battery of horse-artillery opened fire on us; then the British troopers charged. After that others dismounted and opened on us with rifle fire. The British cavalry fight just as well on foot as on horseback. Their equipment was wonderful, their horses in first-class condition. Our infantry came up in support and the British withdrew. All the officers in their horse-artillery battery were killed. Our own losses were heavy, too. Our next orders were to follow the course of the river Oise to a point just beyond Senlis, and then march straight on Paris. We were counting on being the first to enter the French capital."

"When we infantrymen arrived at Senlis we saw on a sign-post: Paris 28 miles. We all said, 'At last!' We entered the town by the Compiègne gate at about three in the afternoon. My patrol was ordered to follow the boulevards and ramparts round the town, while the others marched straight through. I remember we said, 'They're lucky; they have a chance of finding something to drink'; we were absolutely parched. The streets were empty in the baking sun. The town had just been shelled. We had just reached the southern limits of the town when some shots rang out. A French rear-guard detach-ment was firing on some of our men who had gone into a café for a drink; Débit Simon was the name; I saw it on the sign outside. The café-proprietor was taken out and shot on the spot. Then we came to the Faubourg-Saint-Martin, and there, again, we were fired on. South of the town the French had dug trenches on each side of the road. To make a detour round these defences we got into the gardens of a hospital, and there again we were fired on. So then our N.C.O's arrested a number of civilians and made them march down the centre of the road, while we crept along close to the walls. Two or three civilians were killed by bullets fired by their own com-patriots, and the others began to shout and scream in a dreadful manner. When the French heard this they stopped firing. Soon afterwards they withdrew. I heard that evening that the mayor and several other civilians had been shot. The General Staff installed themselves in the Hotel du Grand-Cerf and there was a dinner at night for thirty people, with ices and cham-pagne. For us it was red wine."

*   *   *

Champagne . . . No picture of invasion on French soil can be complete without some passing reference to its fantastic prestige in the eyes of victorious foreign soldiery. When the Germans swarmed into the vineyard country between Rheims and Château-Thierry the war in that sector took on – for a brief spell – a character all its own. Kindly inhabitants have revived for my benefit distant memories of those days. They told me, first, of the coming of the Uhlan officers, immaculate, miraculously preserved, even from the dust of the roads; then of the weary, travel-stained infantry, bivouacked in the fields at night, within walking distance of cellars famous the world over. What could be expected? The lower orders of soldiery – Prussian, Pomeranian and Bavarian alike – were seen drinking from the bottle, choking over its bubbling contents; one bottle, another and another, until the inevitable happened and they would drop in their tracks, only to be kicked on to their feet again by their sergeants. If one has never witnessed tragi-burlesque incidents such as these the expression: "The victor vanquished by his own conquest" has no meaning. But even floods of champagne cannot repel invaders; and by dawn next day they had all gone; leaving a few thousand empty bottles behind.

Meanwhile, the troopers who had fought against the 1st British Cavalry Brigade at Néry were trotting along through the valley of the Oise river, and thence on to the route nationale No. 16 though Creil, Chantilly and Luzarches. On their way the Uhlans and Dragoons passed through silent villages, overwhelmed by the sweltering heat. Women at their doors seemed transfixed, in a sort of stupor. The German troopers felt that Paris now was only just beyond the horizon, almost defenceless, practically at their mercy. And yet this fabulous city could still intimidate the unwelcome stranger at the gate. His pulse would surely quicken when the order came to march in.

"Change direction! The 4th Cavalry Division will move east towards Meaux, covering the flank of the 4th Corps." The order cracked out like a whip, rousing the astonished troopers from an idle dream.

September 2nd, at dawn. General von Moltke, with his two A.D.C's, comes out of the Hotel de Cologne in Luxembourg. A quiet, cool morning. Just the day for a long walk in the gardens along the old ramparts, or a ride down the Pulvermühl valley. Let's get along to the little red-brick school. Tappen will be waiting there, with a sheaf of papers:

"A wireless message from the 3rd Army, your Excellency.

Everything going well. Von Hausen expects to reach Mour-
melon-le-Grand and Suippes in the course of the day; which
shows he is meeting no opposition on his front."

"Still no news from von Kluck?"

"Yes, your Excellency, also by wireless. But it gives no news
of yesterday's doing. His report is dated August 31st, at 21.00
hours."

"And it has only just arrived? It's intolerable!"

A radio message sent over the air at a speed of two hundred
thousand miles a second has taken thirty hours to reach its
destination, only one hundred and twenty miles away. And the
explanation is that, owing to the weakness of the 1st Army
transmitter, this message had to be repeated several times
before it reached the main signals office in Metz (in the afternoon of September 1st) and then be retransmitted to G.H.Q.
But the Signals H.Q. in Metz, where all messages had to be
decoded before being sent on by telephone or telegram, now
resembled a hive where the over-worked bees had gone mad.
The tables in the telegraph and cipher offices were piled high,
not only with operational orders and reports, but also with long
messages from the service departments to Government offices,
to district and sub-district commanders; a mass of correspond-
ence, unimportant in the main, but rendered necessary by
the now well-established traditions of Imperial red-tape,
which, in certain respects, could almost challenge the unique
ineptitude of the Russian administrative system. And this
immense pile of messages – some of them quite unimportant –
was swollen by private telegrams from Very Important
Persons and other officials at Imperial H.Q., quite apart
from Royal and other Highnesses serving in the field. In
spite of the scale of operations in progress, and while the
Chief of the General Staff was impatiently awaiting news of
von Kluck, the Grand Duke of Mecklenbourg-Schwerin, who
was on the staff of 9th Corps, 1st Army, had that day sent
telegrams to the Crown Princess Cecile to congratulate her
upon her husband's success, and to several other titled friends
to give them news about himself. Moltke is exasperated by all
these delays, and by the increasing chaos apparent in a system
of communications vitally important to him at this moment.
And his exasperation is even more excusable than, perhaps, he

realises, because this faulty system is to prove a terrible handi-cap during the coming battle.

The day goes on, and the shadows of the trees in the play-ground outside move slowly over the red-brick walls. General von Moltke is now alone in his office, alone with the large maps in front of him. From the papers lying on his desk he must now draw up tomorrow's orders; and in the middle of those papers stands the daguerrotype portrait of the uncle, Helmuth von Moltke, the victor of 1870. The cold, hard face in the small oval frame seems colder and harder than ever. Inscrutable. Nephew Helmuth alone must find the answer – with no help from his uncle – to the terrible problem tormenting him all day, in spite of its cheerful background of good news. And it is this: should he now return to his Directive of August 27th (that is, to the amended Schlieffen Plan) and divert his advancing right wing towards the south-east; or allow it to continue its advance south? Once again he looks at the map.

"What is the position? The Imperial Crown Prince, still fighting north-west of Verdun, is advancing more slowly than the Duke of Wurtemberg on his right. If I deflect the Duke towards the south-west I open a gap between him and the Crown Prince, which will allow the enemy to get away."

The meditations of Nephew Moltke are well worth following step by step, for a minute or two. No effort of imagination is required; we can know them with certainty, because he will soon reveal them to Tappen, chief of the Operations Branch.

"It is therefore absolutely imperative that Wurtemberg and Hausen continue to march south. But this also means that von Bülow, on their right, must also march south; if not, a gap will open between him and Hausen, and my whole front will collapse. Very well. So the three armies in the centre must continue marching south.

"And what about von Kluck? What about this Sledge Hammer out on the right wing, this Arrow launched from the start on its far flight to the west? After the Guise affair, von Kluck's momentum had shifted slightly eastward, to exploit von Bülow's success (so it was said). If it is allowed to follow its present course, the right wing of von Kluck's army will reach Paris. "But that is out of the question, because the gap would then open between von Kluck and von Bülow.

Von Kluck's right wing must be directed on Meaux, that is, it must pass to the east of Paris."

East of Paris? We (who know the sequel) can almost hear the astonished reaction of the Press: Schlieffen Plan abandoned! Official! New Strategical Conception. An Historic Decision, etc. But decisions, even when historic, are not necessarily spectacular. Just a shabby classroom, used as an office, and a tall, heavily-built, tired-looking man bent over some papers.

"Can there be any objection to passing east of Paris, so far as the continued pursuit of the enemy is concerned? None whatever. We are, in fact, merely following the direction of the French retreat. To capture or destroy the enemy is our first and principal objective.

"All we have now to consider is the strength of the forces within Paris itself. According to our information, it is hardly impressive. But we have no figures. Taking a pessimistic view, let us assume that it includes the six French reserve divisions so far unaccounted for; assume also that these have been reinforced; let us even assume that a considerable force – an army perhaps – is available in the Paris area, ready to march east. Would it constitute a real danger to my central armies advancing towards the Marne?"

Moltke's methodical and logical processes have brought him to the hub of the problem; and he resolves it thus:

"No danger whatever, on condition that von Kluck moves to cover the central armies by placing his formation in echelon on their right rear."

That is the answer. Von Kluck, passing to the east of Paris, but slightly in rear of the other armies, will form a shield between them and Paris while they are engaged in liquidating the retreating French forces. Neither Moltke nor anyone else will ever know what his plan was worth, since History took a different course; but anyone who has ever found the solution to a difficult problem may be excused for thinking it particularly attractive, endowed, in fact, with every virtue.

"We halt the march on Paris, but only momentarily. Once the main enemy forces have been captured or destroyed, the defences of Paris will not be a very serious matter. Our entry into Paris will be all the more spectacular, after final victory."

Moltke's sighs are over. Now be breathes freely again. All

the more so as Tappen, in complete agreement with his Chief's idea, begins to draft the necessary orders. At 21.20 hours on September 2nd, von Moltke signs a wireless message, jointly addressed to von Bülow and von Kluck: "The Supreme Command's intention is to drive the French in a south-easterly direction, cutting them off from Paris. The 1st Army will follow in echelon behind the 2nd Army, covering, in so doing, the flank of the main body." The second message is addressed to von Kluck alone: "It is desirable that your cavalry should continue to make a reconnaissance in force at the approaches to Paris, and destroy the railways leading into it."

Morning on September 3rd. The telegrams read out by Tappen have the same cheerful ring as the cathedral bells of Notre Dame, close by. Without a shot fired, von Bülow has occupied Laon and La Fère, and captured twenty-six guns. Von Hausen and the Duke of Wurtemberg are making short work of the French rear-guards, and taking prisoners. A little later it is learnt that the Crown Prince has sent the following order to the 3rd Cavalry Division: "Engage and destroy the enemy, direction Sainte-Menehould." Engage and destroy! This is quite a different language from his reports of a few days earlier. At 16.30 hours von Bülow sends in another report: "The 2nd Army, hot on the enemy's heels, has pursued them throughout the day and driven them across the Marne. South of the river, the enemy retreat continues in complete disorder. The greater part of the bridges over the Marne have been destroyed. I await further orders."

Dear Bülow! Would not any Commander-in-Chief's bosom swell with pride when one of his generals, having driven the enemy even further than anyone could have hoped, says: "I await further orders"?

"Reply at once: 'Your action approved. Occupy the south bank of the Marne'."

Champagne was served that night at dinner, while von Stein, the Quartermaster-General, read out the press communiqué: "Our troops are covering the north-east approaches to Paris. The enemy, including the British, are withdrawing at a speed suggesting headlong flight. General von Kluck's cavalry units are patrolling the whole area up to the gates of

Paris." From the Russian front the news was no less exhilarating :"Further results of the battle of Tannenberg. General von Hindenburg's troops are continuing to reap the fruits of their recent victory. The number of prisoners increases daily. The Commander-in-Chief of the Russian Army is reported killed. It is not possible, as yet, to estimate the number of guns and the quantity of booty left behind in the Prussian forests and marshes."

Splendid. Not a false note anywhere in the heroic symphony. In order to conceal his inner feelings of intense relief, von Moltke, Chief of the General Staff, and responsible for both Eastern and Western fronts, does his best not to appear overjoyed. All that was wanted, after all, was a touch of audacity, self-confidence. And it came off.

Yes, it had come off, but not quite as von Moltke and his friends at table imagined. There was, in fact, a false – a terribly jarring – note in the general rejoicing; and it took the form of a telegram, signed by von Kluck, addressed to the Supreme Command, to von Bülow and to von Hausen. It did not reach Supreme Command until the following day, for the simple reason that it was at that moment buried under the pile of footling and useless telegrams cluttering the tables of over-worked cipher-clerks in the Signals Headquarters at Metz. And this was von Kluck's message: "The 1st Army crossed the Marne at Château-Thierry and west of the town."

With complete disregard of orders, von Kluck, instead of moving forward in echelon *behind* the 2nd Army, was in fact advancing *in front* of it.

Moltke's order, von Kluck considered, was senseless. The 1st Army was a day's march ahead of von Bülow's and in a far better position to exert pressure on the French left wing. To force it to follow in echelon behind von Bülow would bring it to a complete halt for the forty-eight hours required for the 2nd Army to catch it up and move past it. The delay would give breathing-space to the British and French troops, and remove all chances of the quick, crushing victory planned by von Moltke himself.

Von Kluck's flagrant disobedience of orders could be amply justified from a strategic point of view; and he and others claimed to do so later. But a moment's study of the photograph

of the tough old veteran of 1870 (whose sixty-eight years sit
so lightly on his shoulders) explains clearly enough the furious
reaction of a man of his temperament.

He was in command of the largest, most powerful, best
equipped, best led, and the fastest-moving army in the field.
No other army had fought so gallantly. They had just completed, in record time, a fantastic march on the outer rim of
an immense arc from Aix-la-Chapelle to Paris, further than
all the rest. He had swept aside all opposition from the British
and French. And now he was being ordered to bring his
victorious troops to a halt, to twiddle his thumbs for two
whole days in a defensive rôle, as if his were second-line
troops! He was being denied the hard-won (and well-deserved)
honour of being the first to lead an army into Paris, as well
as the credit of sharing in the final *coup de grâce* for which his own
irresistible advance was largely responsible. Really, this was
beyond endurance! This thinly-disguised attempt to make him
do the donkey-work for the others was tantamount to an
insult, not only to him as Commander but also to his officers,
N.C.O's and men. He could not accept it. The Royal Highnesses and blue-blooded "vons" who had plotted this swindle
were quite mistaken if they imagined that he would meekly
comply, with a bow and a scrape like some lackey at Court.
Efficiency was the only law he acknowledged; and the 1st
Army had certainly proved itself the most efficient of them all,
and would go on doing so. And who would dare tell him then,
"This was not in the programme"? Since these lordlings now
judged that victory was imminent he would get ahead of them;
and be in at the kill. He sent for his Chief of Staff, von Kuhl,
as rugged and obstinate a type as von Kluck himself, if not
more so. Von Kuhl had won a mention in despatches, which
read: "Keen, penetrating judgment; highly developed mental
faculties. Utterly imperturbable. Brave to a point where his
recklessness under fire has more than once been reproved by
his commanding officer."

"My dear Kuhl, I propose tomorrow to cross the Marne on a
front from La Ferté-sous-Jouarre to Château-Thierry. Please
prepare the necessary orders for the Corps Commanders."

No trace can be found, in the list of wireless messages
received or intercepted by the German G.H.Q. Signals on

September 3rd, of any acknowledgment by von Kluck of
Moltke's order to him to take up position in echelon behind the
2nd Army. The only message recorded from von Kluck is
timed 16.50 hours, and states (as we already know) that the
1st Army was crossing the Marne. It was not until next day,
September 4th, that the grim-faced, insubordinate old warrior
drafted his reply:

"First Army requests information on situation of other
armies whose reports of decisive victories are frequently
followed by requests for support. As a result of continuous
fighting and exhausting marches, 1st Army has now reached
limit of resources. Only thus could it have succeeded in opening
up front to allow progress of other armies. We now hope to
exploit our success. Instruction No. 2220 from G.H.Q. ordering
1st Army to take up position in echelon behind 2nd Army
cannot in these circumstances be complied with. The plan to
drive the enemy south-east cannot succeed unless the 1st Army
moves forward."

It would be difficult to find, amongst the records of the
French military staff, any message in terms as impertinent as
these from an army commander to his commander-in-chief;
nevertheless, von Kluck was not sacked. Although official
propaganda was assuring the French people that the German
Army, from top to bottom, was subjected to a ruthless discipline
and that the German soldier was little more than a slave under
the Kaiser's heel, a fault was becoming apparent (although,
as yet, only to a small number of discerning observers) that
was to rob it of the quick success that, by virtue of superior
numbers, equipment and training, it might have achieved.
Signs of trouble, in fact; at the Top.

7

GALLIENI'S FINEST HOUR

NIGHTS WERE becoming cold now, but the sun still blazed all day. The morning of September 3rd brought nothing to lift the fear of impending calamity that brooded everywhere. No one could foresee the dramatic change that would soon turn the threatening tide away from the city.

General Gallieni, appointed Governor of Paris less than a week before, was making the customary round of courtesy calls upon the members of the diplomatic corps who had not yet left the city.

"I love France, and I shall do my utmost to prevent historic monuments from being destroyed." The face, under a crown of thick, curly hair, was curiously un-American; but the speaker was Myron T. Herrick, the American Ambassador. He was, no doubt, genuinely fond of France, and was speaking with obvious emotion; but no international agreement could now prevent Paris being shelled or destroyed by fire; for Paris was no longer an open city, but a fortified place, an entrenched camp that the refugee government (in Bordeaux) was prepared to defend to the last. Nevertheless, Gallieni politely expressed his thanks. He was in great pain; for the past few days there had been a recurrence of prostate trouble.

"May I have your permission, Monsieur le Gouverneur, to display these posters?"

"Certainly," replied Gallieni. The posters, in German and French, were intended to protect the homes of American citizens resident in Paris. Displayed above the text was the American flag. Myron T. Herrick took up the telephone immediately, and gave the necessary orders. He evidently felt that there was no time to lose.

To the Spanish Embassy: The Ambassador's reception was icy. The military attaché (who took some part in the conversation) had studied at the German *Kriegsakademie* and was convinced of an early German victory. His Ambassador looked sharply at him at times, thinking no doubt, that all the same, he was talking over-much.

To the Norwegian Legation: A change in atmosphere here. Norway had the friendliest sentiments in regard to France, but her sentiments were no less friendly in regard to Germany. "This war is, indeed, a dreadful business. And it might so easily have been avoided!" The Norwegian Minister was only too willing to give what help he could, "when the time comes". He expressed the hope that international agreements would be respected; that negotiations might be opened.

To headquarters: In the car, the A.D.C., on the General's left, looked somewhat anxiously at his chief. "Are you in pain, Sir?"

"No, thank you. I'm all right."

Could anyone have the slightest doubt now, that the Germans would enter Paris? The Government had fled. As for Joffre, his General Instruction No. 4 envisaged the possible withdrawal of the French armies as far as Nogent-sur-Seine, fifty-five miles south-east of Paris. Joffre was intelligent enough to realise that the Paris garrison and Maunoury's exhausted little army were quite incapable of withstanding the onslaught of von Kluck's victorious troops in full cry. Therefore, the main preoccupation of the military experts at G.H.Q. was to save the mass of the French armies from annihilation. Paris was just one town like any other. It could be recaptured later.

After four days at Les Invalides (the Military Governor's traditional headquarters) Gallieni had tired of the interminable corridors, the hundreds of doors where all and sundry came and went as they pleased, the red-tape and the all-pervading dust. He had moved to the Lycée Victor-Duruy, a girls' school near by. He had posted sentries everywhere, forbidden unauthorised entry, installed an efficient telephone service. A fleet of cars was standing by night and day. His staff officers took their meals in the mess and slept on the premises.

Immediately after lunch on that day, September 3rd, Gallieni drove to the headquarters of the 6th Army at Tremblay-les-Gonesse. Sapper officers along the road were supervising *Territoriaux* erecting road-blocks and barbed wire. Refugees were still streaming in. There was something re-assuring (to them) in the idea that Paris was to be a "defended city"; they were anxious at least to reach the suburbs. Their hand-carts and wheel-barrows were squeezed into a weird collection of vehicles of every kind; brightly-painted lorries, including some with British names in large letters. A British dépôt and loading quay had been installed at the station of Villeneuve-Saint-Georges; in readiness for possible evacuation.

General Maunoury, however, was in process of assembling his 6th Army – more or less intact – along the line Pontoise-Louvres-Dammartin, and was now engaged in the task of reorganising it. No need to mince matters with Maunoury. He had served as a lieutenant in 1870 and was at one time a member of the Ecole Supérieure de la Guerre. (Joffre once described him as "le type du soldat complet".) Maunoury was always ready to face hard facts. He also had received a copy of Joffre's Instruction No. 4, envisaging withdrawal as far as the Seine, and the resumption of offensive operations at some (unspecified) later date.

"I can let you have the 45th Algerian Division," said Gallieni. "I am expecting the 4th Corps, to reinforce my Paris garrison. Joffre has given me Sordet's cavalry corps, but you know what state their horses are in. Ebener's reservist troops are covering the marshalling yards at Pontoise. And there is also the Brigade of Marines from Ronarc'h."*

The total strength of the forces available for the defence of Paris against von Kluck's army of 250,000 men was less than 150,000, of whom only a few could be described as fighting fit. The problem was to know from what direction the assault would come. From cavalry reconnaissances on August 31st, Maunoury formed the impression that a part of von Kluck's army was moving south-east; he had in fact reported this to G.H.Q. But, since then, the pressure on the retreating 6th Army had come from the north, and was directed on Paris.

"My aeroplanes (nine in all) are out on reconnaissance every day," said Gallieni. "Perhaps we shall know the answer before it is too late."

Too late for what? To defend – with any hope of success – such a crowded, exposed city as Paris would seem well-nigh

*In Brittany.

impossible. Nevertheless, in all the north and north-west suburbs, trenches were being dug, barbed wire and strong-points erected. If concreting could not be completed, railway lines were piled up to replace it. The orders were that not a minute must be lost. The Military Governor gave neither himself nor others any respite. "He expects everything to be done in no time," said Clergerie, his Chief of Staff, with an indulgent smile.

In five days' work the whole defensive system came to life. Batteries of siege-guns were put in proper working order and provided with fifty rounds of ammunition per gun. A few days before they had been lying about in disorder, not even mounted on their emplacements. Even now they were grossly inadequate for the task that (it was feared) would be theirs, but they would be of even less use if nothing was done at all. As a second-lieutenant, Gallieni had been made prisoner at Sedan, in 1870. During his captivity he had learnt German; he also spoke English and Italian; later he had conquered Madagascar and organised its civil administration. Gallieni knew better than anyone that action need not wait upon hope.

He drove back to his headquarters. In the working-class suburbs of St Denis, Le Bourget, and Pantin the streets were filled with people. To leave their homes and flee south was out of the question for them. On the whole they looked calm and resigned. From police reports it would appear that most of the inhabitants of Paris and the suburbs who stayed in their homes did so because they imagined that the city would be besieged and defended, as in 1870. Their thoughts went no further than that.

That morning two white broadsheets were posted in the streets. People gathered to read them. The first was a lengthy proclamation by the Government: "People of France, for several weeks our heroic troops have been engaged in stubborn fighting against the enemy's forces. Our valiant soldiers have won notable successes at several points on the front. But in the north the weight of the German attack has forced us to retire. As a measure of national security the Government's duty is to leave Paris for the time being. Let us all show ourselves willing to face this tragic situation. In the end victory will be ours, etc." A few rude comments had already been scribbled over the sheet. The second, a proclamation by the Governor of Paris, scored heavily, not only by its brevity and courage, but also by the veiled taunt, which Millerand (who had approved it the day before) had not even noticed. For the benefit of readers to whom the First World War may seem mere ancient history, this was Gallieni's text (Tacitus himself could hardly have been more concise): "Army of Paris, People of Paris: The members of the Government have left Paris in order to give a new impetus to the defence of the nation. I have been given the mandate to defend Paris against the invader. I shall fulfil this mandate, come what may. Gallieni."

G.H.Q. had left Vitry-le-François on September 1st and was now busy unpacking two hundred cases and parcels of documents in the boys' school at Bar-sur-Aube. The Commander-in-Chief was lodged at "Le Jard", an attractive eighteenth-century house belonging to a Paris barrister, on the outskirts of the town.

At 13.00 hours on September 3rd the Commander-in-Chief's convoy of three cars left Bar-sur-Aube for Sézanne, Headquarters of the 5th Army. Coming out of Troyes, from the high bridge over the railway an endless line of stationary troop-trains came into view below. An officer from the leading car reported: "Mon général, these are the 4th Corps troops."

Without a word, Joffre sank back into his corner. The 4th Corps had been allotted to the 6th Army. When on earth would it arrive? Within a radius of nearly one hundred miles from Paris all railway transport was disorganised, sometimes completely blocked as a result of the movement of civilian refugees, the diversion of all trains going east, the evacuation of material by the retreating armies and the despatch of material and supplies for the defence of Paris. Up to now, chaos had been narrowly averted.

There could certainly be no question of resuming the offensive for several days to come. On September 2nd Joffre had written to the Minister of War: "The slightest set-back would run a grave risk of developing into an irretrievable disaster. Our chances of success would be further diminished by the fact that our troops are all extremely tired." The Commander-in-Chief had made no mention either of the semi-paralysis of the transport services or of the quasi-impossibility of coming to any definite conclusion as to the present position or movements of the German forces. On August 31st Maunoury and the British G.H.Q. had both reported quite independently: "The German right wing is turning south-east." On the following day a map had been found on a wounded German officer in a car captured near Coucy-le-Château. The map was bloodstained, but the arrows showing the direction of the 1st Army's advance were faintly visible. South-east. Very good. But on September 2nd the Information Service put out a quite different story: "The Germans are marching straight on Paris." Which was right? – and what should one do now?

"Wait a few days before resuming the offensive and, in the meanwhile, put sufficient space between ourselves and the enemy to avoid sporadic fighting. The further the enemy advances over territory in which communications in the main will have been destroyed, the weaker he will become, and the greater will be our chances of ultimate victory." Millerand and his colleagues, reading this letter from Joffre, might very well have thought that this strategic concept was not unlike the Russian retreat during the Napoleonic campaign. The French countryside – admittedly – was hardly comparable with the Russian steppes; but had anyone a better idea to put forward?

The Commander-in-Chief was going today to the 5th Army headquarters with the intention of relieving General Lanrezac of his command. This was the third time he had done so. On the first occasion, at Marle on August 28th, Lanrezac's docile attitude ("I will attack, in accordance with your instructions; the preliminary orders have already gone out") had decided Joffre to postpone his decision until the next day. But, next day, Lanrezac had won the Battle of Guise, where the 5th Army Commander had fought the only successful engagement recorded on that part of the front since the beginning of the war. Then, acting strictly in accordance with orders, he had brought his army – more or less intact, although (like the others) in an exhausted state – into position on the south bank of the Marne. In spite of all this, the Commander-in-Chief was leaving his G.H.Q. once again with the firm intention of "sending him to Limoges".

Joffre was convinced, in fact, that Lanrezac's removal was absolutely necessary. From what has been already written regarding Lanrezac's relations with Joffre and with the other staff officers at G.H.Q., it is clear that Joffre's decision had not been taken in cold blood; personal animosity certainly had some part in it. Joffre, nevertheless, was not merely giving way to his feelings. In his view, Lanrezac's dismissal was a necessary step in the preparation of plans for the resumption of the offensive.

The Commander-in-Chief had no idea, on September 3rd, how soon this resumption could be expected; but his own common sense warned him that the conditions for it would, in any case, be far from ideal; on the contrary, after such a retreat they would be extremely difficult, probably not entirely free of actual muddle and confusion. One could be reasonably certain also that, when the order was given to turn about and face the enemy, Lanrezac's domineering voice would be heard mouthing a series of objections, each one as valid as the other; and this Joffre would not tolerate at any price. He must have army commanders who were ready to press forward under the worst conditions, and willing (without discussion) to carry out – or attempt to carry out – what might seem to them to be quite senseless orders.

This, at least, was the first reason for Joffre's decision. No trace is to be found, in any official document, of a second reason, namely, an approach by French, who had certainly not forgotten Lanrezac's unpleasant manners, nor his brusque comments upon the extreme caution being shown by the British command. Nothing, however, would justify any assertion that such an approach was ever made, although a rumour to that effect persisted for many years and still persists today. Be that as it may, any such intervention by French accorded only too well with Joffre's own feelings; there was no need to force his hand.

Lanrezac's dismissal was carried out in a class-room of the boys' school at Sézanne, on September 3rd. Before taking this step, however, Joffre (to guard against any further weakening on his own part) had asked Franchet d'Esperey, commanding the 1st Corps, to meet him at a cross-roads just outside Sézanne: "I shall have to replace Lanrezac. I thought of appointing you. Do you feel capable of taking over command of an army?"

Franchet d'Esperey wished for nothing better. So it was impossible, now, for Joffre to go back on his decision.

Joffre and Lanrezac walked into the class-room alone. Later, each gave his own version of the interview. Lanrezac said: "He took me aside and said: '*My dear Lanrezac, you know how fond I am of you, but I really must relieve you of your command of the 5th Army. You are hesitant, and you lack decision*'. He accompanied these remarks by a play of features suggesting that I had exhausted his patience, keeping his eyes carefully averted from mine. I vehemently protested, and asked the General to quote facts to support his opinion. But he merely repeated that I was hesitant and indecisive; that I raised objections to every order I was given."

Joffre's version: " '*My friend*' " (I told him) " '*you know that I have always given you my support and help in your career. But now you are tired and hesitant, and you must relinquish command of the 5th Army. It is painful for me to tell you this, but I cannot do otherwise*'. Lanrezac hesitated a moment, and then he answered: '*You are quite right, mon Général*', and, to my great surprise, he seemed as if he had been relieved of a crushing burden, and his face literally glowed."

One can take one's choice between the two accounts. For my own part, I merely suggest that the men who drafted Joffre's Memoirs (and then submitted later for his approval their own version of what he had told them) were somewhat over-zealous in their assumption that the dismissed general's face "literally glowed". According to other accounts, the interview took place partly in the playground, with several witnesses at a respectful distance, out of earshot. Spears' version was: "General Lanrezac was obviously dispirited and depressed. He talked a good deal and interrupted his walk now and then, to make a point."[*] No mention of any glowing reaction.

My impression is that Joffre himself was not feeling very happy, either. Immediately afterwards, Joffre sent for Franchet d'Esperey and confirmed his appointment from then onwards as Commander of the 5th Army. Joffre then drove back to Bar-sur-Aube.

September 3rd 18.30 hours. On returning to his H.Q. in the Lycée Victor-Duruy, Gallieni sends for General Clergerie, his

[*] Major-General E. L. Spears, *op cit.*, p. 377.

Chief of Staff, Major Bourdeau, Chief of the Intelligence Branch, and Colonel Girodon. (Girodon, crippled by a serious wound during the Moroccan campaign, had made a special request to serve under Gallieni.) The three men speak in order of seniority.

Clergerie: "Mon Général, the situation has changed since midday. Up to that time the main body of von Kluck's army seemed to be marching on Paris. But since then, according to reports both from our aeroplanes and from the cavalry, it has turned south-east, with the exception of one army corps moving south towards Luzarches."

Girodon: "It seems certain that we are witnessing a major change in the movement of the whole of the German right wing. This morning our interpreter, Fréchet, showed me the report on the interrogation of a refugee from the Somme department, who, for a short time, had been made prisoner by the Germans in the region of Saint-Just-en-Chaussée. This man maintains that at St Just he saw columns of German infantry and artillery, all marching due east. Fréchet himself made a reconnaissance by car this afternoon in the area, Chambry-Lizy-sur-Ourcq and Meaux. Towards the north and north-east he saw columns of smoke from villages being set on fire by the Germans as they marched through. Refugees told him they had seen Germans this morning at Plessis-Bellevue."

Bourdeau: "The latest aeroplane report is timed five o'clock this afternoon. No German troops or transport seen between Pointoise and Creil, or between Creil and Luzarches. Senlis is in flames. Several columns were seen marching south-east. One of them, seven or eight miles long, was passing through Etrepilly."

Gallieni rises from his chair: "Let us mark all that on the map."

Information from a refugee is all very well, but nine times out of ten a refugee will be forty-five degrees out in his compass-bearing. It is only possible to arrive at an interesting probability by co-ordinating all information received with the greatest caution. By 20.00 hours that evening Gallieni's three staff officers had plotted on the map the conclusions they had reached. The numerous names involved may seem tedious to the reader; they meant much more to the four men studying a large map, dotted with coloured pins. For them, everything was at stake.

One German army corps is marching south-east on a front from Luzarches to Mortefontaine, followed by detached units moving towards Creil and Beauvais; another army corps in marching order between Nanteuil-le-Haudouin and Lizy-sur-Ourcq; another column between Ormoy and Mareuil-sur-Ourcq, preceded by yet another, of which the head had already reached Château-Thierry. Finally, further east, the tail of another column is leaving Soissons, while its head has already crossed the railway from Rheims to Paris in the region of Oulchy-le-Château.

"We have accounted for every army corps in von Kluck's army; not one is missing," says Major Bourdeau.

Gallieni makes no answer. The tall, spare figure, with the thin face, exceptionally keen eyes behind those pince-nez, has an air of authority which is slightly intimidating. Unless he asks a question little talk goes on around him. But this time, the picture on the map is really too exciting. Clergerie and Girodon (leaning on his crutches) exclaim together: "Their flank is wide open! It's a gift!"

Gallieni turns to his Chief of Staff: "The Army of Paris will take the offensive against the enemy right wing."

The scene described above and the actual words used by the actors concerned are based, either on details given in their Memoirs or on statements made later by their colleagues, which differ only on points of detail. No one since then has been able to dispute the claim that it was Gallieni and his two staff officers, in the late afternoon of September 3rd, who discovered from the evidence before them that von Kluck's right flank was open to attack; and that Gallieni immediately decided to take advantage of this situation. ("From that moment, therefore, my idea was to take the offensive against the enemy's right wing, in spite of the risks involved.")

It is easy enough to write (after the event) that one had thought this and that at such-and-such a time, but Gallieni did more. After having made a full report to G.H.Q. he dictated to Major Bourdeau the orders for the reconnaissances to be made the following morning: "It is vitally important to find out if the area north-north-east of Paris has been evacuated and if the German army that was marching on Paris is now moving towards the Ourcq river and beyond. At dawn tomorrow, September 4th, aerial reconnaissances will be carried out as follows . . . ." Following the road from Paris to Creil, the Oise valley and the Paris-Compiègne road, the airmen were to comb the whole north-eastern portion of this vital part of France, now pockmarked with the charred ruins of what were once villages, and dotted with columns of smoke and flame from fires still burning fiercely. And their objective must be to determine, with absolute certainty, whether or not this enemy, so formidable from the front, was now presenting a vulnerable flank. "These reconnaissances are of vital importance, because important decisions may depend upon their result. The Army Commander is particularly anxious that they should be carried out with all speed and that the information obtained be made available by 10 a.m."

Ten o'clock on the night of September 3rd. General Gallieni is bent over his desk, his bushy eyebrows almost hiding the pince-nez. He must push on with the static defence of Paris itself (it would be folly to neglect any aspect of it) but he must also plan his attack, if the enemy movement east is confirmed. And then there is the question of food ("I insist that the people of Paris should not go short of bread; and even that white bread should still be made available"); and of transport (there is a shortage of motor transport, horse-drawn vehicles and even handcarts). Public administration must also be attended to; he must reply to this "député" who (before leaving for Bordeaux) has added a recommendation to a letter from the owner of a café in the military area asking permission to remain open. If this "député" does not receive a more-than-polite reply there will be a complaint from the Minister.

Midnight. Must he really wait until ten o'clock tomorrow morning – another ten hours – before knowing with certainty (or reasonable certainty) the answer to this insistent, obsessive, terribly fascinating problem of von Kluck's movements? Aeroplanes (it's true) cannot fly at night. But cavalry could start off before dawn. "Clergerie, let's send out some cavalry patrols, too."

"I sat up almost the whole night, impatiently waiting for information." He had acute stabs of pain at times, but pain,

that night, was dulled by his excited impatience. After his wife's
death only a few weeks' before, he had thought that life had lost all
meaning, but tonight he was living more intensely than at any
time in his career; for the papers and maps on his desk represented
perhaps one of the most sensational military events in history.

Bar-sur-Aube, September 3rd, 20.15 hours. Less than a
quarter of an hour had passed since the Commander-in-Chief
arrived back from Sézanne.

"The letter, Sir, from General Foch." His aide handed
it to him.

Foch, like Joffre, has little use for the telephone. The two
men exchange letters almost every day. Joffre knows that this
letter will bring an answer to the question he asked Foch the
previous day: "Do you feel capable of resuming the offensive in
the very near future?" Foch's answer was: "The 9th Army is
still in process of reorganisation and General Foch considers
it would be premature, in these conditions, to undertake any
offensive operations for a few days to come."

Joffre puts the letter down again on his desk and makes no
comment. He is already two hours late for dinner. Was anything else urgent?

"Yes, Sir. Lieutenant-colonel Bernard, on the staff of the
4th Army, came to ask if he could have railway transport for the
12th Corps infantry, at least for a stage or two. These men,
under General Roques, have done extremely good work ever
since the beginning."

"Yes. I know."

"General Roques says that his infantry are now at the end of
their tether."

And it was with such material as this that, sooner or later,
one would have to turn round and face the enemy? One
could go on withdrawing as far as the Morvan,* even as far
as the Auvergne;* but not as far as the sea. This question of
physical exhaustion was the most serious of them all.

"Agreed for the 12th Corps. Tell Ragueneau to fix it up with
the Railways."

It is not going to be easy to squeeze a force of 30,000 men into
an already half-choked railway schedule; but is anything easy

*Provinces of south-eastern France.

at present? How long is it since we had anything but bad news? No hope of getting to bed at nine tonight; here are some more letters to attend to. Gallieni says that the German right wing is turning south-east; but he also says that some of the troops in the Paris garrison are in poor shape and is asking what rôle I "propose to allot to it and to the Army of Paris in the general scheme of operations".

It is late in the evening when Joffre dictates his reply, which is an important document, because it raised considerable controversy later.

First point: *Territoriaux* stationed in the entrenched camp of Paris will not take part with the regular formations in any field operations in the vicinity of Paris. Second point: "On the other hand, I must reserve the right to call upon the front line and reserve units of the Paris garrison to take part in operations directed on Meaux during the offensive envisaged by Instruction No. 4 and Memorandum No. 3463, of which I send you copies herewith." (Memorandum No. 3463, amending and amplifying Instruction No. 4, envisaged the withdrawal of the French armies up to a line Pont-sur-Yonne, Nogent-sur-Seine, Arcis-sur-Aube, Brienne-le-Château, and Joinville.) "I must reserve the right" clearly suggests that Joffre will himself give the orders for the movement of these troops when he thinks the time ripe to do so.

Joffre then writes – in his own hand – a personal and unofficial letter (not mentioned in Gallieni's Memoirs, but described later as "secret") of which the following are the essential passages: "My dear friend, I am sending you, in an official letter, my instructions regarding the employment of the troops under your command . . . . As from now, a part of General Maunoury's front-line troops may be pushed forward in an easterly direction as a threat to the German right, so as to give a feeling of support on that side to the British left."

"Joffrist" supporters have since used these two documents in an attempt to demonstrate that the idea of the Marne offensive had originated from the Commander-in-Chief himself, and that Gallieni had merely adopted and carried it out.

But Joffre expressly states: "As from now a *part* of General Maunoury's front-line troops *may* be pushed forward in an easterly direction, as a *threat*." This hardly amounts to a formal and precise order to attack, especially as Gallieni receives at the same time an official memorandum containing the words: "I must reserve the right to call upon you," once again envisaging the withdrawal to the Seine.

Was Joffre's ambiguity intentional? Was he covering himself against either eventuality? What would have been his reply if Gallieni had asked: Yes or no, must I act, or wait? At what time did the two messages – the official and the unofficial one – reach Gallieni the next day, September 4th? None of these questions has ever been answered.

In order to avoid returning to this subject later, I should like, at this point, to express briefly my own feelings in regard to the quarrel between "Joffrists" and "Gallienists", which is apparent not only in all accounts in public circulation, but also in the official records.

Gallieni died on May 27, 1916. His Memoirs, written entirely unaided, and covering the period from the end of 1914 to June 1915, betray here and there a lack of calm, unbiased judgment in regard to his own rôle in launching the opening stage of the battle. The tension noticeable in certain passages is, nevertheless, excusable. Gallieni was then suffering from the malady from which, after an operation, he died. He was constantly in pain, and constantly forcing himself to bear it stoically. In such conditions he could hardly fail to resent the efforts being made in certain quarters to minimise his part in the battle. He had, in the first place, to accept – with soldierly discipline – the deliberately restrictive wording used in his mention in army despatches: "Showed the greatest skill, through the information he had obtained, in helping to determine the direction of movement of the German right wing, in the judicious orientation of the mobile forces at his disposal with a view to their rôle in the battle and in facilitating by every means in his power the successful accomplishment of the task *assigned by the Commander-in-Chief* to these mobile forces." The italics are mine.

This text was, unquestionably, the starting point of a wordy quarrel in which the Commander-in-Chief (largely through the fault of the editors of his Memoirs) became personally involved. Their judgment in the matter was, in several instances, definitely at fault, for Joffre (over his own signature) is made to appear vindictive and irresolute, constantly changing his mind.

It is to be regretted that Joffre himself did not end the quarrel once and for all by attending Gallieni's funeral. But even a Commander-in-Chief has his weaker side. Looked at in historical perspective, the conduct of each of the two men, Joffre and Gallieni, would seem, after all, perfectly logical, bearing in mind their respective positions and temperaments. It was quite natural for Gallieni, in command of forces greatly inferior to the huge armies for which Joffre was responsible, to think and act more quickly; and it is difficult to imagine the Military Governor of Paris in the rôle of the man who could preserve such unshaken composure amid reports of fresh disasters pouring in on every side.

In certain official – or semi-official – accounts the senior staff officers at French G.H.Q. are depicted, during the retreat, as sitting in Olympian isolation in their offices, elaborating plans for counter-offensive operations, their plans becoming the more ingenious as the situation deteriorated. Such accounts belong only to legend. The truth – as many of them have confirmed since – was that they spent a great deal of their time listening (with growing concern) to the highly dramatic reports brought in by liaison officers returning from the front; they naturally wondered to what point their own headquarters would be forced to withdraw; and some began to worry about the fate of their own families. In the midst of it all Joffre was like a rock in the tempest. To anyone whom he overheard expressing any kind of alarm or despondency he would say, in a tone of gruff astonishment: "So you have lost confidence in France?"

Even the worst of Joffre's detractors (and there are many) recognise that anyone holding a position of authority, great or small, in France at that time, felt more or less dependent upon and protected by this irreplaceable, rock-like personality. But, once the danger had passed, there were certain clever men at G.H.Q. who could not bear the thought that the brilliant idea that had averted disaster had come from other brains than their own.

My view is that it is neither useful nor interesting, nor does it enhance the reputation of anyone – whoever he may be – to probe into the details of this private war, with its stories of over-written or re-written documents, or documents withdrawn from official archives, or documents preserved that were ordered to be destroyed. These are no more than part of the scrap-heap of history.

In this chapter on the opening stage of the battle – and, indeed, throughout the book – I have quoted, as reliable evidence, only simple, obvious and undisputed facts, elaborated and coloured, when necessary, by the openly avowed feelings and opinions of the persons concerned.

Impatient readers waiting for the curtain to rise upon the battle itself should, nevertheless, give a moment's attention to the more prosaic happenings of this memorable day of September 4th 1914; to the goings and comings, the telephone calls and even the silences of the principal actors; for (as in all dramatic situations) their gestures, words and silences give a sort of fatal significance to their actions.

At seven-thirty in the morning of September 4th, Gallieni comes back to his office in the Lycée Victor-Duruy. Half-an-hour later, the first reconnaissance reports arrive from the cavalry. They confirm in every respect the air reports of the previous day. Senlis and Creil are in flames, but *the road from Senlis to Paris is completely clear of the enemy*. Nanteuil-le-Haudouin and Crépy-en-Valois have also been evacuated. A few cavalry patrols only are reported on the right bank of the Oise and in the Beauvais area.

Gallieni's pulse must have quickened as he read. The morning reports from the aeroplanes should arrive in about an hour. Must he wait until then?

There is no time to lose. People make a terrible mistake who think otherwise. Joffre's latest orders make it clear that, once the French forces have withdrawn south of the Seine, the Yonne and the Aube, they will be "brought up to strength by drafts from the dépôts". How long will that take? "Simultaneously the Paris garrison will begin operations in the direction of Meaux." But when? In two days' time – even, perhaps, by tomorrow – it will be too late for these troops to begin their move. If the Germans are not attacked at once, with all forces available, they will wipe out the retreating 5th French and the British armies, and fall upon the rear of the main mass of the

French forces. The Paris garrison, which Joffre imagines operating in the direction of Meaux will, in fact, be marching towards the area where the French armies are being rounded up and liquidated. Now is the time for the Paris garrison to move out. Now.

"Clergerie, we will get an order out to Maunoury."

Although not perhaps the best known, this was one of the most important orders issued during the battle of the Marne: "Paris, September 4, 1914, 9.01 hours. Special Order No. 1. Divisional General Gallieni, commanding the Armies of Paris, to General Maunoury, commanding the 6th Army, le Raincy. In view of the fact that the German armies seem to be moving across our front in a south-easterly direction, I propose to order your army forward against their flank, that is to say, in an easterly direction, in liaison with the British troops. But please make all preparations at once for your troops to be ready to move this afternoon and to initiate a general movement forward tomorrow to the east of the entrenched camp of Paris. Order your cavalry to make deep reconnaissances in the whole area between the Paris-Chantilly road and the Marne. I am placing the 45th Division under your command as from now. Come and discuss situations personally with me as soon as possible. Gallieni."

The order is typed, registered, and despatched. At 9.45 Gallieni asks his Chief of Staff to call the Commander-in-Chief to the telephone.

This (of course) is merely a manner of speaking. Gallieni wants to talk to Joffre himself, but he knows that Joffre never replies personally to telephone calls. He always refuses even to pick up the receiver. Newspapers facetiously quote him as saying: "I don't understand the first thing about these machines." The truth is that the Commander-in-Chief of the French forces lives and operates at a level where it is difficult for him not to be conscious at all times of the significance that may be attached later to any one of his actions. Joffre knows exactly his strength and his weakness. He likes always to check and revise at leisure every paper he is asked to sign. He hates being called upon to reply Yes or No on the spot, and this is what – to a certain extent – the telephone forces him to do. What actually happens, therefore, in the present

instance, is that Clergerie picks up the telephone and gets
Colonel Pont, head of the Operations Branch, on the line.
The substance of their conversation is that General Gallieni
proposes to launch the Army of Paris against von Kluck's
exposed flank. Preparatory orders have already been sent out.
According to what the Commander-in-Chief decides, the
Army of Paris can go into action, either north of the Marne
(in which case their attack could begin on the 6th) or south
of the Marne, twenty-four hours later. Gallieni would prefer
the action to begin north of the Marne on the 6th. Pont's
reply was: "I will ring you back as soon as possible."

Ten o'clock; and no news from the aeroplanes. Gallieni says
nothing, but is obviously impatiently awaiting their reports.
Perhaps the Commander-in-Chief may think him rather
presumptuous to have sent orders to Maunoury before the
final reports had come in? It is now fifteen minutes past ten.
Here is the first report: "Two groups of German artillery at
Bouleurs." (Bouleurs is five miles south of Meaux.) A minute
later: "Two regiments of German infantry at Sancy, north-
east of Crécy." A third report states: "A division of infantry,
with artillery, at Pierre-Levée, seven miles south of Meaux."
Everyone of Gallieni's nine aircraft – the wood-and-canvas
contraptions of those days – has spotted von Kluck's columns
of troops on the march; and there can be no further doubt
whatever that his whole army has left Paris well on its right,
is now hurrying across the Marne and beginning to envelop
the French left wing. There is not a moment to lose.

Meanwhile, at G.H.Q., a long discussion goes on.

"I have taken part" (wrote General Gamelin later) "in
enough discussions of national importance to know that each
person present will subsequently give a different version of
what actually took place." What follows gives ample proof
of the truth of this remark.

At some unspecified time during the earlier part of the
morning a group of staff officers in the Operations Branch
were talking in front of a map on which the positions of
French and German Armies had been plotted, partly from the
information supplied by Gallieni, whose liaison officer was
actually present at the time.

According to General Alexandre, Gamelin suddenly exclaimed: "But we've got them! For the first time in four weeks they are *in our hands*. We must exploit this situation at once; give up our plan of reorganisation behind the Seine; and attack tomorrow." Several officers agree, others raise objections. Colonel Pont goes to General Berthelot, Deputy Chief of Staff (the heavy-weight in overall and slippers), and points out the possibilities of this new situation. Berthelot says no. He has other ideas. He will not hear of this hurriedly-planned counter-offensive. Pont, greatly disappointed, goes back to his colleagues; and the discussion goes on.

"Just then" (writes Gamelin) "General Joffre came into the office, as he had often done during the early months of the war." But another officer, Major de Partouneaux, of the Operations Branch, declares: "Our discussion was getting so heated that Joffre could hear us from the adjoining office, where he was working with General Berthelot. Suddenly the door opened and the Commander-in-Chief himself appeared in the operations room; which had *never* happened before." (The italics are de Partouneaux's.) Whether it was his habit or not (and one hopes it was) to visit the Operations Branch, the Commander-in-Chief sits astride a chair and looks at the map. At this point all our informants are agreed on one thing; each of them claims the credit for having been the first to put the plan to Joffre. And they go on:

Alexandre: "The General did not reply immediately; then, as he got out of his seat, he said, 'Very good: we will fight on the Marne, and not on the Seine'."

Gamelin: "The General did not say exactly: 'We will fight on the Marne' (which was impossible anyway, because the Germans had already crossed it). What he said was: 'It would suit our purpose better to fight the battle in the Marne valley rather than on the Seine'."

Partouneaux: "General Joffre, in his usual laconic style, made no reply except to ask one or two questions as to the exact positions of certain army corps; but he studied the map for some time and then left the office without telling us what he had decided to do. Generals Belin and Berthelot, who were with him, were equally reticent . . . ."

Neither Joffre himself nor anyone else present at the time

seems to have remembered that Belin and Berthelot were with him, for (in his Memoirs) he writes: "As I wished to discuss the question with General Berthelot, I went to his office, which adjoined that of the Operations Branch." Let us follow him there.

Berthelot (still draped in his voluminous overalls) maintains his objections to the idea of resuming the offensive. His own plan is an eventual counter-attack on the centre of the front, directed not against the outside but against the inside of the German right wing and in a north-westerly direction. But for the moment he is in favour of continuing the retreat, "in order to draw the Germans further into the net". Joffre, impressed by the arguments put forward only a few minutes earlier, points out that here is a chance that must not be missed, that the Germans may suddenly realise the danger and manoeuvre accordingly; but Berthelot will not agree. The discussion is still going on when, at about ten o'clock, Clergerie's call comes through. Berthelot, quite unshaken, criticises Gallieni's plan and obstinately refuses to give way. Joffre listens, weighs up the arguments on both sides, and is still undecided. His hesitation is understandable. To attack von Kluck's right flank is all very well, but it means that the vast, combined counter-offensive must also take place at the same time. Joffre is still unconvinced that this can be done, and is therefore impressed by Berthelot's stubborn opposition. And the discussion goes on.

At eleven o'clock Maunoury arrives at 6th Army H.Q., in the Lycée Victor-Duruy. Gallieni takes him over to the map.

"Von Kluck is pushing on fast. Either he is completely ignorant of our existence or else he thinks we are a negligible quantity. See here, all he has left on the Ourcq is a flank-guard, probably the 4th (reserve) Corps. We ought to make an all-out attack on it, get it rattled, drive it in and then attack, not only von Kluck's flank, but also his rear. Our attack should be on a broad front, north of the Marne, in the direction of Villers-Cotterêts."

"What does the Commander-in-Chief say?" asks Maunoury.

"Clergerie, still no news from G.H.Q.?" Gallieni says.

"Still nothing, Sir."

"How is your Army coming along, Maunoury?"

Gallieni knows well enough that the 6th Army could not have been transformed overnight into a formidable array of fit, well-trained troops. One of its most serious handicaps was that, since they arrived in the western sector of the front, these men had seen nothing around them but refugees in flight, villages in ruins, and troops in retreat. Maunoury would have liked to rest them for two or three days, but Gallieni's plan made this impossible. The attack must be made at once. It is part of a military commander's duty to know that, when conditions are favourable, the weaker force can sometimes defeat the stronger one.

It is now fifteen minutes past twelve. "Clergerie, is there still no news from G.H.Q.? Give them another ring."

The telephone, this time, is answered by Colonel Pellé, who says: "The General gives his approval, in principle, to the proposal that Maunoury's army shall move east. As regards the question of operating north or south of the Marne, and the date of the operation, the reply will be given a little later."

"They are probably at lunch," says Gallieni. "Let us go and lunch, too. Immediately afterwards we will go and see French at Melun." Gallieni wants to know if he can count on the British.

"They", in fact, are not at lunch; or not yet. Hours of meals are becoming more and more irregular – a clear indication that the Commander-in-Chief realises the gravity of the situation. And the Commander-in-Chief, before coming to his final decision, is still seeking information.

He sends a telegram to Franchet d'Esperey: "A situation has arisen in which it might be to our advantage to go into the attack, tomorrow or the following day, together with the British Army and the mobile forces of Paris, against the 1st and 2nd German armies. Please inform me if you consider your army is in a position to do this with reasonable chance of success." Gallieni's plan is obviously making headway. At the same time Joffre sends an officer to see Foch, whom he had questioned the day before. And Joffre repeats his question: "Can you attack?"

13.00 hours. Joffre sends a coded telegram to Gallieni: "Of the two proposals you make regarding employment of General Maunoury's troops, I consider the more advantageous to be that consisting of sending 6th Army along left bank of Marne north of Lagny." So Joffre has chosen the 7th for the date of the attack. His telegram will arrive at the Lycée Victor-Duruy at 14.50 hours. But, at that moment, Gallieni, accompanied by Clergerie, Maunoury and a group of staff officers is about to arrive at the British Army Headquarters.

Yes, Gallieni wanted to know if he could "count on the British" ("*compter sur les Anglais*"). For the rift was still unhealed. The high-ranking officers of the British Expeditionary Force, who, for their part, had counted on the French and on the confident strategy of the French military experts, now felt that they must count only on themselves to ensure a minimum of cohesion between the units of their retreating army.

The British headquarters was now installed in the Secondary School at Melun, in an ordinary school building, just like any French headquarters staff. And there was something rather pathetic in the sight of these exhausted British soldiers asleep on the lawns around the school (if one could give the name of lawn to a dried-up patch of bare ground). A bitter experience, indeed, for the United Kingdom of Great Britain and Ireland! But an army of gentlemen could never entirely lose its self-respect, and, a few yards away from these weary, sleeping men, the two kilted sentries of the Scots Guards came smartly to attention and presented arms with the same slapping, mechanical precision as ever.

And this ceremonial now greeted the group of French officers as they got out of their two cars in front of the school, at three o'clock in the afternoon of September 4. Amongst them – surprisingly enough – was an officer who spoke English; and he was the Military Governor of Paris, now asking to speak to the British Commander-in-Chief. But Sir John was out on a tour round the front line; it was not known at what time he would be back.

"Could I then speak to General Murray? Or is he also out?"

No. Sir Archibald, the Chief of Staff, should be somewhere in the building. He would be here in a few minutes. In the meantime Colonel Huguet, head of the French Mission, appeared. Huguet was a Gunner, small, brisk, a rather sallow complexion, but (thank God!) reasonably successful in adapting himself to British ways. General Murray kept them waiting for some time, and the French officers began to show signs of annoyance, as if they had expected Sir John and Sir Archibald to welcome them with open arms. However, here comes Sir Archibald at last, who says: "Very glad to see you."

The Chief of Staff's manner was polite, but his expression became increasingly non-committal as General Gallieni unfolded his plan and concluded with these words: "It is therefore absolutely necessary that the British Army should bring its retreat to a halt and be prepared to resume the offensive as from tomorrow."

"I am very sorry," said General Murray, "but I can decide nothing in the absence of Sir John."

These Frenchmen obviously did not realise how inconsistent – and, indeed, inconsiderate – their conduct had been towards the British High Command. On August 31st Field-Marshal French had informed Lord Kitchener that, as the French seemed unable or unwilling to resume the offensive, he was withdrawing his troops from the front line and retiring as quickly as possible across the Seine. This decision caused a considerable stir, first in London, and then in Paris. At Joffre's urgent request, the French President had intervened, and Sir John had found himself in the unpleasant situation of being more or less ordered to keep his troops in the front line.

Sir John, however, had quickly and generously overlooked what amounted to a personal snub, and had written to the French Minister of War, saying that the present situation demanded that a plan of action be drawn up, easily understood by all concerned, so that concerted action could carry it out and a new line of defence established along the river Marne. Joffre had replied: "Impossible." His actual words were: "The present situation of the 5th Army would not permit it to give adequate support to the right wing of the British Army if the need arose . . . . The British Army could hold out on the Marne for a certain time and then withdraw to the left bank of the Seine." This letter was dated September 2nd. And now this new Governor of Paris wanted to launch the British Expeditionary Force on an attack in an *easterly* direction! What was one to think? The whole scheme was preposterous.

But they were very insistent. The staff officers accompanying General Gallieni went over the plan again and again, rather as if they were dealing with somewhat backward pupils; an attitude which was bound to be resented. The atmosphere became strained.

The group of French officers took their leave at last, and Sir Archibald accompanied Gallieni to his car. This French general certainly seemed very intelligent – and spoke remarkably good English – but he apparently did not realise that a high command that was always changing its mind could not expect to inspire confidence; nor did he seem to realise – alas! – that a general who wishes to inspire confidence should not wear yellow puttees with black boots.

The weeping ash in the middle of the playground of the boys' school at Bar-sur-Aube was now a pathetic sight. Its leaves were burnt and shrivelled; it seemed to be dying from the heat. The hands on the yellow dial of the clock above marked half-past two. The sun was blazing as fiercely as during the hottest days of August. Under the tree's shade was a school-master's rush-bottomed chair, and sitting astride, with his arms resting on the back of it, was the Commander-in-Chief.

His black tunic and cloth trousers were hardly suited to such heat; and lunch had finished at two. Yet the Commander-in-Chief (who so much enjoyed an afternoon nap) was wide awake. The back of his neck was rigid and motionless; under the bushy eyebrows the pale blue eyes were lost in contemplation of some distant, imagined scene.

The latest reports had brought nothing significant or dramatic; nothing to help him towards his decision. Huguet, the head of the French Mission at British G.H.Q., had telephoned to the effect that French, on the advice of his Chief of Staff, had decided to withdraw his troops behind the Seine. Would Gallieni succeed in making French change his mind? Most unlikely. A report had also come in from Conneau's cavalry corps, which was covering – ineffectively – the left wing of the 5th Army. "Under pressure of German columns of all arms am crossing over to south bank of the Petit-Morin." Von Kluck's army was pressing on faster than ever. And still no reply from Franchet d'Esperey. Nor from Foch. As motionless as a statue, Joffre waited; and waiting can be the hardest test of all.

The Deputy Chief of Staff, General Berthelot, coming out of the bathroom (he took a shower every two hours) looked cool and refreshed under that ridiculous, bulging overall of his. Shuffling in his slippers along the passages, he carefully stepped on to the gravelled courtyard and walked over to the rush-bottomed chair. Joffre, lifting his head and shoulders, looked round at him: "Well?"

No, Berthelot had no news to bring. What he wanted to discuss – once again – was his pet idea of an attack in the centre. He was interested in nothing else. Impassive and resigned, Joffre listened patiently as the tireless, bulging feather-bed went on talking.

"Mon Général, whatever your final decision may be, we can at least take steps to modify the existing order of battle."

The "feather-bed" had drawn up an Instruction affecting, in particular, the 3rd and 4th Armies. It envisaged an attack in the centre; but it would not interfere with whatever other decision might be taken. His Instruction, in fact, was an omnibus affair. It was getting hotter than ever. "We were thinking of the hardships the troops were suffering, and wondered if they would be in a fit state to carry out the manoeuvres we were planning."

"Will you sign it, please, Sir?"

Joffre signed. This Instruction, after all, was harmless enough. He then signed an administrative order clearly indicating that no one was pre-judging the results of the coming offensive: as from September 5th, G.H.Q. would be moved (further south) to Châtillon-sur-Seine.

The hardships the troops were suffering were certainly as great as any Commander-in-Chief could imagine; and considerably more varied.

And yet, the immense retreat went on. Some regiments had withdrawn without even firing a shot, and the men kept repeating: "It's 1870 all over again."

The 55th Division formed part of the 6th Army – the Army of Paris – and the 276th was one of the regiments of the 55th Division. So far as the 276th was concerned, the retreat had been resumed on September 2nd at Liancourt, after a few hours' halt. Lieutenant Charles Péguy of the 19th Company had requisitioned bread from every bakery in Liancourt, and (although it amounted to no more than a large slice for each man) no dainty brioche could have tasted so good. An absolute feast, in fact, for these half-starved soldiers. ("The officers had the same ration as the men.")

The 276th formed part of the rearguard. When they arrived at Villiers-Saint-Paul they found – to their utter astonishment – the whole town decorated with Allied flags.

What does it mean? They must be mad!

All the inhabitants had left, with the exception of two very old people, who were just able to explain that this gay bunting had been put up on mobilisation in the early days of the war. Incredible as it may sound, it had never been taken down, even during the exodus of refugees. The blue had faded from the French flags, leaving but a pathetic remnant of shattered hopes . . . .

The sappers had built a bridge over the Oise on twelve brand-new (requisitioned) barges. While the infantry marched over, in a noisy thunder of hob-nailed boots, the sappers, with grim faces, were emptying cans of petrol over the sleepers; others were fixing demolition charges. The last to cross were Brigadier-General de Manbrey and Major-General Leguay, the divisional commander. A few moments later the bridge was blown. The brand-new barges went hurtling up in a whirl of smoke and flame and plunged into the water below. And the men grumbled: "God! what a bloody waste!"

The retreat was gathering speed now. There were anxious faces amongst the officers in command. At every halt, field-guns and machine-guns were prepared for action. On the road to Verneuil, along the edge of the forest of Halatte, a column of buses from Paris was halted; but no one was to be seen around them.

"I say! Perhaps they're for us!"

"Don't be a fool; they're for bringing up reinforcements."

"No they're not. It must be for the rations."

But they were carrying neither reinforcements nor rations. They were simply empty buses, left abandoned along the edge of the forest after fulfilling their mysterious mission. Large areas of the French countryside were littered with abandoned material of every kind.

Approaching Senlis they saw some Uhlans galloping away

across the fields. From a forage dump, set alight by the French, great wreaths of smoke and flame were curling into the sky. Senlis was burning, too. Lieutenant Péguy muttered, under his breath, "Savage brutes!"

Night came on once again. Marching on sand is torture for aching, blistered feet, and the men of the 276th Infantry sank up to their ankles in the sandy tracks of the Chantilly forest. But they must hurry on, and keep their ears open for the slightest sound. The regimental supply train had been captured by the Uhlans. The man in charge of the convoy had got away with a few bullet-riddled vehicles, in one of which was a dead soldier. There was no time to bury him; so the regiment followed behind this improvised hearse. There had been nothing – literally nothing – to eat since the small slice of bread at Liancourt; and now it was midnight. They went through another forest: Coye. The sweltering heat of the day had been followed by damp, chilling mist.

"Halt. You can lie down and sleep."

There was no comfort but the bare ground and no cover from the cold mist; but these men were near the limit of endurance and they were already asleep.

"As you were! Get up, everybody! Forward!"

In certain states of abnormal fatigue, men – and horses – can march in their sleep. The 276th had become a regiment of automatons. Every now and then the mechanism would snap; and a man would drop to the ground.

Other units joined them as they marched farther and farther south. Beyond Luzarches hundreds of camp fires had been lit in the fields, and thousands of soldiers were warming themselves around them. Groups of wagons, parked in dozens, line upon line, stood out in the fiery glow, giving the scene the appearance of some gigantic migration. In the village itself, men were sleeping on the pavements; thousands of men, packed close together along the street. Whole regiments were alseep in the fitful light of the fires burning in the fields.

The 276th had arrived at Puiseux-lès-Louvres in the morning of September 3rd, and had turned east towards Villebon. There it was that the men had seen, on a signpost at the cross-roads: "Paris, twenty-two kilometres."

Some said, "The Germans are at Saint-Witz." In fact they

were not – or they were there no longer. Lieutenant Péguy
gave permission for a party of men to go there in search of food
and water. Of the whole population, the only person left was
one frightened woman who timidly half-opened a shuttered
window. The soldiers found some chickens and rabbits in a
deserted farm and hurriedly roasted them on the end of their
bayonets. Burnt or under-cooked, nothing mattered to the
hungry men devouring them.

At five o'clock that evening the colonel sent the company
forward to advanced positions near Montmélian, in the woods
around Saint-Witz. Lieutenant Péguy carefully selected the
positions for his scouts:

"Well, Sir" (they said) "we've covered ninety-five miles in
three days; but we're going the wrong way!"

"Don't you worry, my friends. We'll soon be putting that
right!"

The men took turns to sleep on the damp ground under a
starlit sky. When they awoke they could see the long, sweeping
beams of the Paris searchlights.

Next morning the sun seemed as hot as ever. The 19th
Company stayed in their positions as advance-guards, three
hundred yards from a wood occupied by the Germans, whose
own sentries had been seen amongst the trees. The sweltering day
wore on, and not a shot was fired; everything was quiet. The
men were glad enough of the rest, but the atmosphere was
tense and puzzling. Why had they halted here, so close to the
enemy? And why did not the Germans attack? What the
soldiers of the 276th did not know was that the Germans in
front of them were the flank-guards covering their 4th Corps
on the Paris side while the remainder of von Kluck's army was
hurrying with all speed south-east. Nor did they know that
many of their company were looking their last on the rolling
fields of stubble, the lines of slender poplars, the pointing
steeples and the blue sky of the land that bred them.

Bar-sur-Aube, September 4th, 16.00 hours. Joffre is still
seated, motionless, astride his chair. Footsteps rasp on the
gravel as an A.D.C. walks across to him.

"Mon Général, a telegram from Colonel Huguet."

Joffre takes the paper, reads it once, and then again, as he always does. His lips open slightly, but they close again; he gives the paper back without a word. Nevertheless, his attitude seems to have changed, and he straightens himself on his chair. Huguet's telegram was unhoped for. It brings at least a little relief to the burden of doubt that makes Joffre's decision so intolerably difficult. Huguet explains that Gallieni has just met French at the British H.Q. at Melun, and that French has agreed to halt the retreat of the British forces. French had told Gallieni that he would remain as long as possible in his present position south of the Marne, and that he was willing to cooperate either with the 5th or the 6th Army (or with both) "in accordance with the needs of the situation". So French is ready to do exactly what we want! Splendid!

It would seem, therefore, that Colonel Huguet, who was at the British G.H.Q. during the Gallieni-Murray meeting, had seen Gallieni and French in conversation and had actually heard French give his consent? But French was, in fact, not there at all! Huguet's incredible blunder – amounting almost to hallucination – is without historical precedent; and yet no commentator appears to have been particularly impressed by it. All Joffre noted in his Memoirs was: "This telegram had a very considerable influence upon my decisions." How then could he have imagined that the reported conversation between Gallieni and French was a complete fiction?

At the same time, Huguet informs Joffre that Franchet d'Esperey also is arranging to see French; and, shortly afterwards, a reply arrives from Foch: "I am ready to attack." Joffre asks himself: Is this all I need; or must I still go on waiting until Franchet d'Esperey gives his answer?

From their windows some of his staff watch their Commander-in-Chief sitting astride his chair. He has been there now for nearly three hours. The shade of the weeping ash moves round, and Joffre from time to time shifts his chair out of the sun; and then resumes his seat, as motionless as before. Even the toughest, most insensitive spirits amongst his officers cannot repress a strange feeling of respectful sympathy as they watch him. This man has to decide – once and for all – whether or not to order more than a million men to turn and face the enemy. To miss the opportunity would be catastrophic; but if the operation miscarried the catastrophe might be even greater.

It is now five to six, and still no answer from Franchet d'Esperey. Von Kluck's advanced guard must at this moment be outflanking Conneau's cavalry corps; and the flank of the 5th Army will be in the air.

The clock in the playground strikes six. Officers at the windows, still discreetly watching their chief, see him shake his head, pass his hand over his face and get to his feet. They hurry out towards him.

"Ask Belin and Berthelot to come to my office."

Three of his personal staff are already there. "I asked the Chief of Staff and his deputy to give me their views once more." Berthelot has already done this often enough, but Joffre insists on hearing him again. Joffre (as usual) turns every idea over and over in his mind, in order to integrate himself, as it were, with the problem.

Berthelot, understandably, maintains his point of view. Belin is undecided. Then, at about 18.30 hours, Joffre, as Commander-in-Chief, makes his decision, and it is this: the left group of the French armies will attack von Kluck's right wing *from the outside*, while the remaining armies will turn and counter-attack the enemy on their respective fronts.

"In view, however, of the objections to this manoeuvre, repeatedly raised by Berthelot since that same morning, I decided to fix the opening date of the offensive at September 7th." Gamelin immediately begins drafting the necessary orders.

Joffre's guests at dinner that night were two Japanese officers (an unexpected intrusion into the atmosphere of French G.H.Q. at such a time). The Allies were engaged in negotiations for military aid from far Japan; but, as usual, no mention of military operations was permitted at table. The talk was of the Japanese Navy, of Fujiyama, of the famous Admiral Togo, whom Joffre had met in Formosa in 1884.

Towards the middle of the meal an officer of the Operations Branch brought a note to the Commander-in-Chief. Joffre read it, put it into his pocket, and the conversation was resumed. But a little later, as soon as dessert had been served, he said: "I must ask you, gentlemen, to excuse me."

The message was that Franchet d'Esperey was ready to attack. At G.H.Q., a few minutes later, Joffre read the full text of the telegram: "The battle cannot begin until the day

after tomorrow, that is, September 6th." Franchet d'Esperey
went on to give full and precise details of the conditions under
which the three armies – the 6th, 5th and British Armies –
would open this epoch-making battle.

Joffre immediately told Gamelin to revise the draft of the
orders in accordance with Franchet d'Esperey's reply; but he
maintained his decision that the operation should begin on
September 7th.

Important visitors come and go; orders are given, and
sometimes misunderstood, but are acted on, notwithstanding.
And time ticks on, making history every hour.

Gallieni is back from Melun. As soon as he arrives at the
Lycée Victor-Duruy an A.D.C. shows him the coded telegram from Joffre, timed 13.00 hours, received at 14.50. "I
think it preferable to attack on the left bank of the Marne."
In other words, the attack is postponed until the 7th.

Almost immediately another telegram arrives, timed 18.30
hours, this time from General Wilson, French's Deputy Chief
of Staff. "The Field-Marshal is not yet returned. But orders
have already been given for the British Army to occupy the line
Ozoir-la-Ferrière, Tournan-Ormeau." So the British line is
moving in towards the south-west. It is perfectly clear that
French is continuing his retreat, after all.

Gallieni sees an obvious and important co-relation between
the two messages. Joffre is no doubt well-advised to refuse to
attack before the 7th. He wants, perhaps, to give time for the
British to make up their minds, and a breathing-space to the
6th Army before launching it against undoubtedly tough
opposition. Time is necessary, too, to prepare the gigantic
counter-march of the other armies. Obviously, one cannot
risk creating chaotic confusion. Yes, Joffre, no doubt, is quite
right . . . .

No, Joffre is wrong. In the present situation speed is the only
important factor. Admittedly, the troops are tired, they
should be given more time, the British retreat has opened a
gap; but all that is as nothing compared with the vital importance of a surprise attack on that vulnerable German flank.
Even if the enemy are not staggered by it they will have
to halt and change front; and now they will be given time to
meet and avert the immediate threat. No, Joffre is wrong.

"Get me the Commander-in-Chief," asks Gallieni.

"G.H.Q. on the line, Sir. General Belin."

"I don't want General Belin. I want to speak to the Commander-in-Chief."

Gallieni's insistence – at this precise moment of time – is a deliberate challenge. At one end of the line is a Commander-in-Chief who hates the telephone ("He wishes to speak to you, personally, Sir"); at the other is the ex-Governor of Madagascar who had had Joffre serving under him and who feels sure today, that, if he can adopt the right tone, Joffre will give way.

"Mon Général, the Commander-in-Chief is on the line."

The actual words are of minor importance; the substance of their conversation is well-known and was confirmed later by both parties:

Gallieni: The 6th Army, with the addition of the 45th Division, has already begun to deploy for attack on the 6th. I insist on nothing being changed.

Joffre: Agreed. (*D'accord*)

Joffre, in fact, did not reply so quickly, nor so briefly. This is the version given in his Memoirs: "I re-assured him by stating that, since sending him my telegram at 13.00 hours, I had resolved to open a general offensive, in which the 6th Army would participate; what is more" (I added) "orders were already in preparation, and they envisaged action by Maunoury's army to the north of the Marne."

Nevertheless, the orders in preparation gave September 7th as the opening date of the attack. Having given his consent to Gallieni, Joffre went back to his office and ordered the date to be changed. The attack would open along the whole front on the 6th.

"I must admit" (he writes in his Memoirs) "that it was with great reluctance that I amended these instructions by altering the date of the offensive. I was then, and I am still convinced, that if it had been possible to postpone the battle until the 7th its result would have been far more satisfactory." *With great reluctance*. Joffre admits, therefore, that Gallieni forced his hand. As to his opinion upon the result, many others – even Gamelin – later disagreed. Churchill, for his part, bluntly asserts: "The battle of the Marne was won when Joffre had finished his conversation with Gallieni on the night of Septem-

1. The Kaiser, Wilhelm II (centre), with his Chief of Staff, Helmut von Moltke, during the initial German assault on France, 1914.

2. General Joffre, the French Commander-in-Chief.

3. (*Above*) General von Kluck, Commander of the German First Army, crossing the Marne, August 1914. Fresh artillery is being unloaded from railway carriages.
4. (*Below*) German forces marching through Belgium, August 1914.

5. (*Above*) German infantry taking a short rest on the way to the Marne front.
6. (*Below*) Dead horses and destroyed materiel on the road of retreating British forces near Clery
(Peronne).

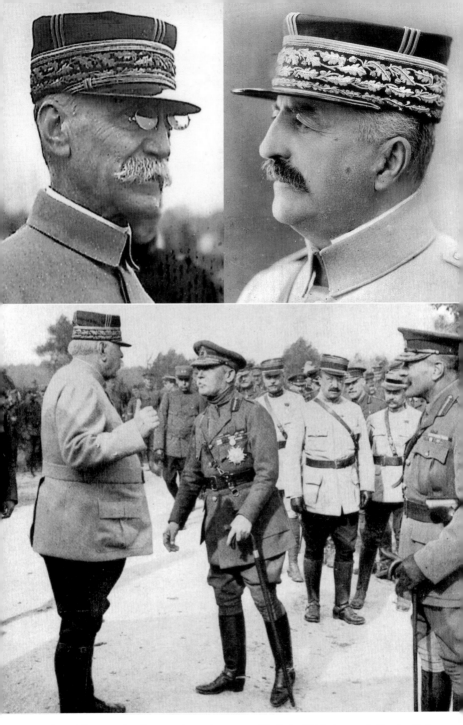

7. (*Above, left*) General Galliéni, Military Governor of Paris, in 1915, the year before he died.
8. (*Above, right*) General Franchet-d'Esperey, Commander of the French Fifth Army.
9. (*Below*) General Joffre talking to Field Marshal Sir John French, Commander of the British Expeditionary Force. General Wilson is on the right.

10. French troops from the Paris garrison arrive at the Marne front by taxi, September 1914. Some 1200 taxis were used to rush forces to the front line; some are visible in the background.

11. (*Above*) German soldiers in position, awaiting a counter attack.
12. (*Below*) French bayonet charge in the streets of Rembercourt (Meuse).

ber 4th."* That conversation undoubtedly had an enormous influence upon the subsequent course of events. But one must not lose sight of the fact that no battle could be won without the intervention of a third person, one of a host of exhausted, hungry and thirsty fighting soldiers with blistered feet, who, a few hours hence, when the order comes to turn to the right-about and face the enemy, will reply, in Joffre's words: "D'accord."

At 20.30 hours Gallieni sends out his General Order No. 5, which had been drafted during the morning. It says, in effect: "The 6th Army will move tomorrow in an easterly direction along the right (north) bank of the Marne with the object of establishing a front based on Meaux, from which it must be ready to open an attack on the morning of the 6th."

At 21.30 hours a telephoned message from G.H.Q. informs Gallieni of the dispositions of the respective armies in readiness for the attack on the 6th. Joffre's General Order No. 6 dated September 4th at 22.00 hours, begins with these words: "Advantage should be taken of the highly vulnerable situation of the 1st German Army by concentrating against it the combined strength of the extreme left wing of the Allied forces." The movements ordered apply to the 6th, 5th and 9th (now under Foch on the right of the 5th) and the British Armies. On the morning of September 5th an addendum is issued defining the rôles of the remaining armies.

Thus it came about that a decision was reached to fight one of the greatest battles of all time. And that decision was based on incorrect information. Gallieni had not seen French; he had seen Murray only; and Murray had promised nothing.

Nor had Franchet d'Esperey seen French; he had met Wilson, the Deputy Chief of Staff. Unlike Murray, Wilson represented the francophile, co-operative section of opinion at British G.H.Q. Greatly impressed by the dynamic personality of the 5th Army Commander, General Franchet d'Esperey, he had – in all good faith – given his agreement to the proposed offensive. But afterwards he had had second thoughts: "Perhaps I have said too much?" Hence his telegram to Gallieni: "The Field-Marshal is not yet returned, etc."

*Sir W. S. Churchill; *The Great War*, Vol. 1, p. 170.

When, therefore, Sir John French returned to G.H.Q. after his tour of inspection, he had found on his desk, first, the letter from Joffre, dated September 2nd, declining French's offer to halt the British Army at the Marne, and suggesting, on the contrary, that it should withdraw behind the Seine; second, a report on Gallieni's visit and on his request that the British Army should take part in the attack on von Kluck; and, third, Wilson's agreement with Franchet d'Esperey's proposals. Faced with this mass of contradictions, Sir John's cheeks had flushed an even deeper red than usual.

"Hold up the orders drafted by General Wilson."

The bombshell arrived at French G.H.Q. at 22.00 hours in the form of a telegram in quite unequivocal terms from Colonel Huguet: "In view of the continual changes (in plans) the Field-Marshal commanding the British Expeditionary Force prefers to study the situation more fully before deciding upon his course of action." In other words, the problem was no nearer solution than before.

At this moment of crisis Joffre (in my view) showed the real quality of a Commander-in-Chief. No angry protest (none at least was ever recorded); no recrimination. "The only thing to do (for it was already late at night) was to send an officer to Melun with the orders that had already been prepared for the Field-Marshal, which would themselves explain the degree of importance I attached to his co-operation with our plan. I selected Major de Galbert, who was particularly well-informed of my intentions, to carry out this mission."

Eleven hours later, at 9.30 a.m. on September 5th, a haggard and almost distraught Major de Galbert got out of his car outside the boys' school of Bar-sur-Aube.

"Mon Général, I was unable to make contact with anyone there."

"No one at all?"

No English officer, in any case. The sergeant of the guard and the orderly officers had evidently thought that this Frenchman must be out of his mind if he imagined that they would wake Sir John – or Sir Archibald for that matter – at half-past two in the morning. But one of the N.C.O's had gone off to wake Colonel Huguet, who said:

"My dear fellow, the fact is that opinion here is by no means favourable to a resumption of the offensive. But, of course, I will pass on this copy of General Joffre's orders."

To whom did he hand it, and when? Joffre listened to de Galbert's report and (as always) said nothing. He had gone late to bed and risen early. He had just written to Millerand, asking him, once again, to bring pressure to bear, through diplomatic channels, on Field-Marshal French.

"Mon Général, the only person who can deal with them is yourself."

The only person. Joffre was not a man to find fault with a remark of that kind. Why should he? It appears, in any case, in capitals in his own account of the incident, and suggests a curious need of self-assertion on Joffre's part. One wonders if this man, who finally achieved such immense popularity, suffered at times from a secret inferiority complex.

"Very good," said Joffre. "I am going to Melun myself. Have a telephone message sent at once to Field-Marshal French."

The historic meeting took place that same day at 14.00 hours, not at the Melun school but in the Louis XV Salon of the Château de Vaux-le-Pénil, where Sir John was staying. A long deal table occupied the centre of the room (in almost comical contrast with the eighteenth-century furniture and the mirrored doors). The French and British officers – all standing – faced each other across it. Joffre took off his képi, put it on the table, and began to speak. His voice was usually toneless and his delivery slow; but, to everyone's surprise, he displayed on this occasion an unwonted, simple eloquence, punctuating his phrases with short gestures of the forearm. He explained the situation in every detail; the opportunity that must be seized at any cost; and why British co-operation was absolutely necessary. An interpreter translated, sentence by sentence. French – not tall, but trim and impeccably dressed – leaned on his hands over the table, watching Joffre intently, with a sort of fascinated curiosity.

"This is the moment of supreme decision," concluded Joffre. "My orders have already been given, and whatever happens, the French Army is committed up to the last man. I cannot believe that the British Army will refuse to fight at our side. The judgment of history will be severe upon you if you hold aloof."

One felt that Sir John needed no interpreter to understand the sense of the words. Joffre then stepped forward and brought his fist down on to the table.

*"Il y va de l'honneur de l'Angleterre, Monsieur le Maréchal!"**

Major-General Spears's version (for the benefit of English readers, no doubt) was: "Monsieur le Maréchal, c'est la France qui vous supplie!"† All the French eye-witnesses, however, support the other version, and I am inclined to agree with them, for they also state that at that moment, the Field-Marshal's face flushed red. He must indeed have blushed deeply if his heightened colour was so noticeable; and why should he have blushed at all if the remark were no more than a pathetic entreaty? There can be no doubt that Joffre's exclamation was a sincere and deliberate appeal to the honour of a gallant soldier; an appeal which no man – French least of all – could ignore. A tense silence followed. Then two tears rolled, with historic solemnity, down the rubicund cheeks of the Commander-in-Chief of the British Expeditionary Force. He tried to say a few words in French, but abandoned the attempt, and turned to Wilson: "Tell him that we will do everything we can." Wilson, the champion of Anglo-French co-operation, eagerly took his cue: "The Field-Marshal says: 'Yes'."

Murray, unmoved and unconvinced, could keep silent no longer: "But the British forces are at present ten miles behind the positions laid down by Order No. 6. They cannot go into action at 6 a.m.; certainly not before 9 a.m.

Joffre shrugged his shoulders. "That can't be helped. I have the Field-Marshal's word, and that is good enough for me."

"Shall we have tea?" asked Sir John, in French.

Two hours later the three cars from G.H.Q. were hurrying back to Châtillon-sur-Seine their new headquarters. Where would the next one be? Further north, or further south? Just before dark, Joffre stopped the convoy to give the drivers a rest. The sun had just set in an immense red glow of unusual splendour, filling the sky from west to east. The little group looked on in silence, impressed, notwithstanding, by a spectacle that seemed to them like a significant omen; of good, or ill.

*"The honour of England is at stake, Field-Marshal!"
†"Field-Marshal, France begs this of you."

8

THE DEATH OF CHARLES PÉGUY

As THE shells landed in the village the houses seemed to explode in a whirl of smoke and flame. A ceaseless thunder of gun-fire came from the French and German batteries on either side.

The men rushed into the assault, breathless as much with excitement as from sheer fatigue. They seemed, somehow, to realise that this was a fight to the death. The dead, indeed, already lay by dozens in the stubble, in the beetroot, and in the ditches by the roadside. The wounded, propped up against the round corn-stacks, called in vain for help from the men hurrying past them. There were dead and wounded, too, lying in the streets of Iverny and Penchard.

The yellow-turbaned Chasseurs of the Moroccan division had their knives out. With knife and bayonet, in the gardens of Penchard, they crept like tigers through the orchards and along the sheltering walls. When the Germans of the 4th Corps troops saw these men charging across a thousand yards of open ground they were so astonished that for a moment they hesitated to turn their machine-guns on them. The survivors of that charge were now at the Germans' throats. *"Couper cabèche,"** they said. Each was determined to collect at least one German helmet.

The Moroccan Brigade under General Ditte was fighting alongside the 5th Group of reserve divisions (under General Lamaze) of the 6th Army. It was made up of veterans of the Moroccan Guard; fierce, stubborn fighters, when well led. Their African sun was, surely, no hotter than this; and their light khaki uniforms seemed almost to sparkle in it. The shrill, exotic music of their *nouba†* never ceased throughout this bloody engagement, punctuated by sharp, brief orders and hoarse, strangely incomprehensible shouting. One wondered

*Pidgin French: "Me cut his head off."   †Moroccan regimental band.

how their lungs could stand the strain of such a pace. On the immediate left of the Moroccan troops was the 276th, the leading battalion of the 55th Reserve Division. They had just reached the outskirts of Villeroy. The slight upward slope ahead of them was bare of cover and swept by withering fire from artillery and machine-guns; but they must cross it some-how. The 56th Division was in action farther north, somewhere near Saint-Soupplets. From the high ground at Penchard German officers watched the long lines of French troops advancing one behind the other under heavy shell-fire. On both sides fresh battalions were being flung into the battle.

This, however, was September 5th, not the 6th, which was the date at which the French High Command had finally decided to launch the attack. While the guns roared and blood was flowing on the plains of Brie,* Joffre was still holding forth in the Louis XV Salon at the Château of Vaux-le-Pénil, trying to persuade the British Commander-in-Chief to join forces with the French.

The officers bringing the orders for the attack from G.H.Q. had just reached their respective destinations or were still on their way. But, like a restive animal, the battle had broken loose from all their calculations and all their orders. The 6th Army was intended to strike the first blow against von Kluck's exposed flank; but in order to ensure that it would be ready to cross the Ourcq river on the evening of the 5th, or early on the 6th, Gallieni had asked Maunoury to move his troops off during the morning of the 5th. These troops, coming from the west, had simply marched into the 4th German Army Corps moving south.

The 276th Infantry Battalion had started from Vémars at seven o'clock in the morning, marching east with the whole of the Lamaze group. The men were saying, "Things look better today." They were glad to have finished with the retreat and to be moving forward again. "We knew we were fighting for Paris and defending our own homes." At Thieux, at ten o'clock in the morning, the two divisions (the 55th and 56th) and the Moroccan Brigade had marched in ceremonial order past General Lamaze. The divisional wireless station had been set up in a field near by.

*About thirty miles east of Paris.

The weather now had settled into a period of cold nights and days of blazing heat. At Nantouillet the 276th had been given a ten-minute halt. The men lay down in the meagre shade offered by the walls of the houses; but one officer, with fair beard and unmistakable pince-nez, was seated on a stone – in full sun – as if he enjoyed the self-imposed discomfort of it. It was (of course) Lieutenant Charles Péguy, reading a letter from home. When the ten minutes were up he told his men: "We stop and eat at Villeroy."

Ah, that's more like it. These days we know when and where we're going to get our grub.

Exactly at noon the battalion came to a narrow lane between hedges, near a farm called La Trace. Villeroy was just across the fields; they would soon be there. But at that very moment the first German shell came over. They heard the warning drone of it, distant, then louder and nearer; and then the crash. Some wag shouted: "They're giving us an appetizer!"

But the fun was short-lived. The next shell was a direct hit on the ammunition wagons of the battalion 75's, concealed behind a row of poplars. The detonation that followed sent up a grim mass of dark-blue gunner uniforms, shapeless and dis-membered; and what had been a team of horses . . . .

"Battle order! By sections in fours!"

The greatest battle as yet known had begun. German shells came over fast; but the French 75 batteries were now in action, firing incessantly. Shirt-sleeved gunners quickly passed up the ammunition, the gun was laid, an officer raised his arm to the ready. Fires could already be seen burning at the outskirts of Monthyon, where the German batteries were in action. The scene was filled with crude colour and brilliant light, like an old print in a child's story-book.

The 276th was slowly making its way across broad fields of freshly-cut oats. Sheaves were still standing, line upon line, in open order, like the fighting men amongst them. Now and then a bursting shell would set the stooks alight and they would blaze into a sudden, yellow flame. As the warning drone of shells grew louder, Péguy's clear voice could be heard, above the din, still cheerful and reassuring: "Get down! Get down! And cover up!"

And the men would lie flat on their faces, pulling their

packs up over their heads. The company halted, just short of
Villeroy, near a well, in a kind of sunken lane. From there
one could hear the Germans at Penchard and Neufmontiers,
keeping up a fierce defensive fire against the Moroccan
Brigade. A counter-attack from a flank had saved the German
guns. The German riflemen were picking off the French
officers, and the Moroccans, leaderless and out-numbered,
broke and drifted back.

The rising ground in front of the 276th was under a constant hail of shrapnel and machine-gun fire.

"19th Company, advance in open order. Forward!"

Objective: the high ground at Monthyon. Captain Guérin
and Lieutenant Péguy, revolvers drawn, walked side by side
on the right of the line.

"No firing without orders; there are Moroccans in front of
us. Pass it on!"

Luckily, the shelling was less heavy now. The German
batteries must have taken some pretty severe punishment.
But, as the 276th came over the rise, the bullets whistled
louder than ever.

"Watch your alignment!" shouted Péguy.

Yet another field of oats, but, this time, uncut. It was five
o'clock now.

"Move to the left, towards the road! Behind that bank. Halt!"

Ah; at last. "Thank God we're out of those bloody oats!"
And then (after a moment's reflection): "Well, we're still
alive!" There they were, crouched behind the bank, safe, it
seemed, as any man could be. But the bullets whistled loud
just above their heads.

"Range, five hundred yards. Rapid fire!"

They could just see the Germans, well hidden behind some
bushes along a small stream. But they were no easy mark in
their grey-brown uniforms.

Lieutenant Péguy went up and down behind the line of men,
running from one to the other, busy and eager, giving help or
advice, as if they were at practice. And (of course) he stood
upright; with more than half his body exposed.

"Look out, Sir, it's pretty hot here!"

Not for protection, but because he was out of breath, Péguy
leaned for a moment against a roller from one of the near-by

farms. Between the distant trees they could catch a glimpse, now, of Germans leaving their positions and hurrying back up the hill.

"They're off! They're clearing out!"

In their excitement the men thought no more of whistling bullets or whining shells. They saw Captain Guérin make a sign to Lieutenant Péguy; saw Péguy brandish his revolver and heard him shout: "En avant!"

He himself was the first over the bank. The men followed him, crouching low, their rifles at the trail.

"Hell! More beetroot!"

Captain Guérin, limping from his old wound, had dropped a little behind the leading files. He limped a few steps farther, and they saw him fall at the foot of a tall tree. Killed outright.

"En avant!"

They were advancing at the double now, on a downward slope, but under the raking fire it seemed interminable. Two hundred yards; a halt for breath, then another three hundred yards. All that, no doubt, was laid down in the Manual for Infantry, but no text book had pointed out (in suitably forceful language) what amazing targets these men presented on that forward slope in the brilliant light of a summer's day; incredible targets indeed; for these were the Infantry of France, in their blue greatcoats and red flannel trousers. Even the bravest amongst them must have felt like the very small prey of a very large hawk, ready to swoop.

"Lie down!" ordered Péguy. "Rapid fire!"

Rapid fire – with one hundred and fifty rounds left per man. They still had to get to the bottom of the slope, and then climb up on the further side. How many of them would reach the top? Lieutenant Péguy remained standing, directing the fire through his field-glasses.

On his left, a short distance away, was Lieutenant de la Cornillière, also directing the fire of his platoon. He also was standing upright, raising and lowering his field glasses with his gloved hands. Yes, La Cornillière always wore gloves. A rather dressy person, La Cornillière. Every man in the company heard his last order: "Range, five hundred yards. Rapid fi –"

Death most rudely cut him short, and he lay there now, just like any other dead soldier. Except for the gloves. His sergeant-

major (named Legrand) could not believe his eyes. He took
two steps forward; then dropped, shot through the head. ·

And now Lieutenant Péguy was the only officer left standing.
"Keep on firing!" he cried.

During a battle men often feel that so long as they go on
firing no harm can come to them. For a time the infantrymen
of the 19th had the same impression; and they were shooting
like men possessed; with a sort of grim fury. But gradually the
longing for some kind of protection became overwhelming.
Some of them put their rifles down and scratched at the
ground with their bare hands in a ludicrous, breathless search
for any kind of cover.

There were many dead and wounded in the company now.
The dead gave little trouble, but the wounded groaned and
cried in a distressing manner. Shrapnel was bursting only
six feet above the ground; and many of the men had lost – or
thrown away – their packs; their only protection.

"I've got no pack, Sir!"

"Nor have I, Sir! At this rate we'll all be done for soon!"

> *Heureux ceux qui sont morts pour leur âtre et leur feu*
> *Et les pauvres honneurs des maisons paternelles**

"Their fathers' homes" were not far away from these men
from Paris and the Brie plains ("from Crécy and Voulangis",
Péguy had said) who made up the 19th Company. More than
half of them were to meet their death in their own familiar
countryside, some of them on their own fields, in their own
gardens. Meanwhile, Lieutenant Péguy, crazily standing
upright under a rain of bullets and splinters, was probably
not thinking just then of his own prophetic lines. It is far more
likely that Charles Péguy, the perfect officer of reserve, having
reached the climax of his third vocation – Socialist, Christian,
Officer – was simply thinking that his obvious duty was to go
on standing upright. ("Lie down, Sir, lie down!" they shouted.)
Lie down? Certainly not. One must give these chaps the
impression that a man without fear is invulnerable.

"We've lost our packs, Sir! We'll all be done for!"

*The opening lines of one of Péguy's most famous poems.

"Happy are they who died for their fireside and their hearth
And the humble honours of their fathers' home"

"Never mind. I've got no pack either. Keep on firing!"
(*Tirez toujours.*)

"*Tirez toujours*" were the last words he spoke. With a bullet
through his head, Péguy "fell on his side with a half-stifled
groan".

So Péguy is dead, and Captain Guérin is dead, and Lieutenant de la Cornillière is dead, and many, many more. And now
they are but blue and red shapes lying still, amongst the beetroot and the stubble. Just so many ordinary, good-natured
Frenchmen; so many others who might have been men of
brilliant genius or great saints, who knows? Their names will
never have a place in history. That is true of them all; but of
Péguy first and foremost; for this was the Massacre of the Best;
a terrifying price to pay for national survival. They mentioned
him in despatches: "An officer of great moral qualities. Displayed conspicuous gallantry in acutely critical circumstances.
Was killed by a bullet through the head while leading his men
to the attack." And on the 6th Army front the battle went on.

General Hache, commanding the 3rd Corps, looked even
more unwell than usual. His face was ashen, his voice trembling
and ill-assured. He looked as if he had been bludgeoned into
semi-consciousness.

"It is madness" (he quavered) "to attempt to attack tomorrow.
The men are half-dead with fatigue and short of food. There
will be a mutiny. There is hardly any ammunition left. Morale
is at a low ebb, even amongst the officers. I have just been
obliged to replace two of my divisional commanders. The
troops should be withdrawn at least behind the Seine so that
they can be rested and taken in hand."

"The Germans will give us no time to do that. The attack is
ordered for tomorrow morning. The Commander-in-Chief
expects the 5th Army to do its duty. And so do I."

"But that is absurd. The people at G.H.Q. are crazy. We are
heading for disaster."

Franchet d'Esperey, Lanrezac's successor, fixed his keen,
dark eyes on this defeatist general.

On September 3rd, in the office where Lanrezac was handing
over command to Franchet d'Esperey, the telephone had
begun to ring. Hély d'Oissel, Chief of Staff of the 5th Army, took

up the receiver. "Yes, Sir. No, Sir. I think you ought, at least, to try, Sir. We are expecting the 18th Corps to make an effort."

"Who is it?" d'Esperey had asked.

It was General de Mas Latrie, commanding the 18th Corps, and he was saying that his troops were at the end of their tether and must be rested. Franchet d'Esperey had grabbed the receiver: "Hello, Franchet d'Esperey here. I have just taken over command of the 5th Army. I will not have you question my orders. You have no choice; you sink or swim."

Franchet d'Esperey, with his heavy-jowled face, his square jaw and his toothbrush moustache was a holy terror. He had not always been so – to his friends at least – but, since the war, he had become increasingly unapproachable. His colleagues – and his subordinates in particular – went in awe of him. British officers (with whom, nevertheless, he was on quite good terms) called him Desperate Frankie. Strangely enough, his ruthless methods were successful, in establishing his authority over the formations under his command.

Such was the man whose sharp, dark eyes were riveted on the defeatist general in front of him. He looked quite ready to wring the man's neck, sack him angrily on the spot. But Franchet d'Esperey knew that the attack was timed for the next day. In the 5th Army during the past three weeks three corps commanders out of five, seven divisional commanders out of thirteen and a similar proportion of brigade commanders had been replaced – not to mention the army commander himself. One must draw the line somewhere.

Keeping his temper under control, Franchet d'Esperey pointed out that the situation was not so hopeless as it might seem, and that things might not go so badly, after all. His view was that the 3rd Corps was quite able to play its proper part in the attack, in spite of the pessimistic attitude of the Corps Commander. After all, his two divisional commanders bore the names of Pétain and Mangin.

"That men should be prepared to fight to the last is neither surprising nor unusual; it is counted upon, in fact, in establishing any plan of operations; but" (wrote von Kluck) "that men who have been retreating continuously for ten days and are lying about half-dead with exhaustion can pick up their arms and go into the attack with bugles blowing is something that had never entered into our calculations, never been taught as even a remote possibility in our military schools." General Hache was gravely mistaken – as, indeed, were many others – in thinking, first, that his troops were not in a fit state to fight; and, second, that they would resent and protest against the order for a counter-offensive. It would have been reasonable, nevertheless, to expect them to do so, and any honest historian should be extremely cautious in accepting much that has been written about the "Miracle of the Marne". It is clear, however, from the evidence of men who took part in the battle itself that, with rare exceptions, the order for the counter-offensive was well received by all ranks. Nor from a psychological standpoint is this in any way surprising.

In the first place, these men had had enough of this seemingly endless retreat. To move away from danger is a normal reaction, a human instinct of self-preservation, but, sooner or later, men get tired of finding themselves in a constant state of inferiority. Quite apart from any feelings of patriotism or personal honour, there is an urge to recover one's self-respect, a secret desire to come to terms with oneself. This desire found its satisfaction when the retreat was halted.

Secondly, the order to resume the offensive meant, for a few hours at least, the end of forced marches and relief for tortured feet. Prosaic as it may seem, it would be unreal to under-estimate the importance of this factor. In 1914 the troops were not transported in tanks or troop carriers; they covered every mile of the retreat on foot. Many men who took part in it have told me: "We felt that anything would be better than these interminable marches." Among the worst sufferers were the middle-aged reservists in the divisions composing the Vala-brègues Group. These – according to medical reports – were taxed almost beyond the limits of human endurance, and for some days they were in a state approaching complete demorali-sation. But they *rejoiced* when (the retreat ended) they were ordered to dig trenches instead.

Both Mangin and Pétain, when they took over command of the 5th and 6th Divisions respectively (their predecessors having been removed "to Limoges") had been at pains to conceal their concern at the low morale of their troops. These men had obviously been incompetently handled at Charleroi, where they had been sent into action under very heavy fire over ground completely devoid of any cover. Their subsequent conduct seemed to suggest that their morale had been shattered by that experience. On September 5th, however, at 12.30, when Pétain had learned that the retreat was at an end, he had gone on horseback to announce the news personally to his battalions; and the men had enthusiastically cheered him. Mangin had had an equally rousing reception. "Anything" (they said) "rather than this endless marching."

For the cavalry, the counter-offensive meant, first, the resumption of reconnaissance work. All patrols necessarily began before dawn. But the horses were quite immune to psychological factors; they could not know that the retreat was over and that the hardships they had endured now had a new meaning. No orders could inspire the weary, unshod animals, incapable, for the most part, of moving faster than a walk. There was therefore no hope of relieving their sufferings, which, in fact, tended to increase.

The orders for the counter-offensive also fell heavily upon the administrative services responsible for the supply of equipment, rations and ammunition. On the assumption that the retreat would continue, the captain in charge of these services in the 9th Army had been working for forty-eight hours at a stretch (with three hours' sleep) organising the evacuation of food, ammunition and vehicles to the area south of the Seine. Then Colonel Weygand, Chief of Staff to Foch, told him: "We attack tomorrow."

The captain got into a car and went off into the night in search of his supply columns. Hundreds of other Service Corps officers that night were scouring the dark roads in every direction, hunting for vehicles that they knew to be loaded with precious stores, now urgently needed by the whole army. Drivers, in a state of semi-torpor after two weeks' continuous retreat, were shaken out of their sleep and given urgent new orders which, with much eye-rubbing, they did their best to understand. It is almost frightening, after any detailed study of the records available, to realise the vast scale and appalling complexity of the operations involved in this counter-march of the impedimenta of a great army. It was, indeed, a remarkable achievement, rarely acknowledged by the historian.

9

"AT THE OUTSET OF A BATTLE"

THE NIGHT of the 5th–6th September had been quiet along the whole front of the 5th Army from the source of the Grand Morin to Provins. Men were asleep around bivouac fires; in an almost Napoleonic setting. The wheat-stubble smelt fresh and clean in the night air. Sentries moving to and fro would suddenly stop on their beat, listening intently; but little was to be heard. Just a shot or two, now and then, in the far distance. Patrols, no doubt.

A group of cavalrymen passed, just before dawn, leaving an odour of horse and leather and an impression that they could travel neither fast nor far. Nevertheless, reports came in a little later that the ground was clear of Germans, at least up to four miles in front of the troops.

The enemy positions were discovered, however, between eight and nine o'clock, by leading patrols of the advancing infantry. The Germans were in strength on a curving line running from west-south-west to east-north-east, based on the commanding position of Montceaux-les-Châtaigniers. Although a small town of only 400 inhabitants, Montceaux was perched high on the western spur of a plateau overlooking the plain to the south. Through their field-glasses the French officers could see, on the highest point of the crest, the sturdy and squat grey-walled church, its slate roofs and low, square steeple, with a Gothic window that must be an excellent observation post. La Ferme des Châtaigniers – or Chestnut Farm – was a long, strongly built homestead, east of the town. This natural fortress was almost certainly bristling with rifles, machine-guns and even a field-gun or two. East and west of it the green and brown earth was scarred with trenches. The 18th Corps had been ordered to capture this position, and a preparatory attack had been made on the village of Saint-Bon,

to the right of the main objective, by the 6th Division of the
3rd Corps under General Pétain.

Philippe Pétain had been a subaltern in the *Chasseurs à pied*,
a graduate of the Ecole de Guerre and – according to his
commanding officers' reports – an officer with a brilliant
future. Pétain was no believer in last-minute improvisations.
He had ordered his units to prepare a definite starting line
for the attack, and, at the same time, a line to fall back on,
if need be. He had sited his artillery on low crests from
which they could give effective support to the attacking
infantry.

But the Germans also were well provided with artillery
cover. In spite of the comforting bark of the 75's behind them,
the leading waves of the 6th Division were somewhat daunted
by a line of 105 mm. shells in front of them. Pétain, watching
his men go in to the attack, realised what was wrong. On
parade the day before they had enthusiastically cheered him;
but the after-effects of the long retreat from the Sambre to the
Meuse were now as heavy a handicap as the absurd packs
they were carrying. The attack, nevertheless, must, somehow,
get started.

Thirty years later the American, General Patton, wrote: "If
you want troops to advance, get out in front and lead them."
Nearly all the generals in the French Army would have been
killed during August and September 1914 if they had adopted
this principle. But – at this moment of crisis – Pétain evidently
thought it necessary to do so, to give the men the confidence
and dash they lacked. He therefore walked forward through
the ranks of the leading brigade until he reached the wavering
front line and beyond it. Then, several yards ahead of them,
he went straight on towards the barrage of 105 mm. shells.
The men followed at once, rallied round their General, and
went steadily forward.

By nine o'clock Saint-Bon had been taken and Pétain gave
the order to dig in. "The artillery will now move forward and
cover the next phase, which will be an advance in the direction
of the Champfleury farm. This position will be attacked under
cover of Hill 105, which is a screen against enemy observation
from that side." The plan succeeded. The farm was plastered
by the guns, then attacked at its most vulnerable point, and

captured. The divisional artillery then switched to the railway line beyond, on the outskirts of Montceaux-les-Provins.

At 14.45 hours a bayonet attack by three battalions captured the railway. Pétain was then ordered to co-operate with the 18th Corps in the assault on the fortified position of Montceaux-les-Châtaigniers.

The bombardment of Montceaux-les-Provins by the French artillery began at 16.30 hours, and was carried out by a concentration of three divisions of 75's (including Pétain's division), and a heavy artillery group (of 120 mm. Bacquet guns), making in all a total of 125 guns, each firing between three and four rounds a minute, the 75's using incendiary shell. The effect on the small town was certainly impressive. I have seen photographs, taken a few days after, with a caption, typically worded for boosting popular morale: "Under the heavy fire of our 75's the houses literally fell apart. As usually happens, the appalling impact of exploding shells caused fires, which totally destroyed the town. All that was left was a twisted, pulverised mass of farm implements and household goods."

The result, in fact, was far less satisfactory. Montceaux Farm, a natural fortress dominating the road to Villiers-Saint-Georges, was neither destroyed nor even hit. It was left standing, intact, amidst the ruins, and its machine-guns were still raising spurts of dust on the road.

But there was nothing for it. The 123rd Infantry must get across that road somehow, for the orders were that the position had to be carried. Even an infantryman, however, is not expected to walk straight into machine-gun fire if he can help it. He can at least make use of a few simple lessons; he can crouch behind a friendly mound of earth, or crawl along a ditch or behind a hedge. He can move in groups, or by twos and threes – or even alone. But, when all is said and done, there will still be that cursed road to cross, with no cover at all. The problem was, how?

The same question was being asked at that very moment by the infantry of the 11th Brigade of Pétain's division, who were faced by the problem of crossing the bare, rising ground between them and Chestnut Farm. This morning's work had been easy money compared with this. However accurate and heavy the artillery preparation, it can never destroy all opposition, and sooner or later the infantry would have to advance under machine-gun fire.

They had certainly noticed, however (although they could not tell why), that the shelling had ceased. They owed their protection, in fact, to an aeroplane that Colonel Estienne, commanding the artillery of the Pétain division, had acquired, on mobilisation, *in exchange for an ammunition waggon*. This curious deal had been made with another artillery commander, who, like many others of his kind in 1914, had no faith in aeroplanes. But this primitive aircraft – the only one in the 6th Division – had succeeded in spotting the battery of heavy artillery in action 500 yards north of Montceaux, and the 75's had subsequently knocked it out. Now there were only machine-guns firing from Chestnut Farm and Montceaux. *Only* machine-guns!

Soldiers on leave from the front during the Great War were, generally speaking, disinclined to enlarge upon the dangers of their daily existence ("no need to upset the family"); but I remember, as a small boy, how their faces darkened if the sinister "coffee-grinders" were even mentioned. A nest of machine-guns was more difficult to locate and destroy than a whole battery of artillery; two of them could easily wipe out an entire company; and yet it was extremely rare, in any attack, not to find oneself faced with these deadly weapons. In any case they were used with grim effect against the French infantry during the final capture, just before dusk on September 6th, of the hedge-hog positions at Montceaux and Chestnut Farm. In the 11th Brigade alone, 600 men were killed.

At his H.Q. in the Château de Flaix, General de Maud'huy, commanding the 18th Corps, was anxiously awaiting the result of this battle, which (he thought) had already lasted long enough. At 20.00 hours a message arrived from General Marjoulet, commanding the 35th Division: "We are holding the southern outskirts of Montceaux."

Maud'huy's reply to the liaison officer who brought the message was short and sharp: "That is not what I want," he said. "I shall not come back to my command post at Le Houssay until I am told that the whole position has been captured."

Maud'huy, a native of Metz, detested Frenchmen from the

south, whom he considered poor fighters and responsible for all the misfortunes France had ever suffered. It happened that the 18th Corps (of which he had taken over command only a few days previously) was part of the peace-time Bordeaux garrison and was almost entirely made up of men from that district. Mas Latrie, the previous commander, was a native of Bordeaux, a brilliant cavalry officer, but his spirit had been broken by the retreat. Maud'huy regretted leaving the division he had commanded in Alsace and was inclined to be prejudiced against the men of his new command.

General Comte de Maud'huy was a type of officer utterly incapable of understanding how a man of spirit could follow anything but a military career. At the age of nine he and all his family had left Metz, for Metz had become a German city. In order to ensure that the tragedy of Alsace-Lorraine should never be forgotten, he had made a solemn vow never to enter a place of entertainment – theatre, concert-hall, or café – until the flag of France should fly once again over Lorraine. He was a devout Catholic, and had taught his children to follow the example of such men as Bayard and du Guesclin,* and above all, never to tell a lie, "for lying is the act of a slave".

Such was the man, then, who was now awaiting, in a château behind the line, the issue of the battle for Montceaux-les-Provins; but during a night attack at Morhange, he had gone up to the front line with his men. German machine-guns were busy, but Maud'huy had shouted, "Come on, follow me!" To die for his country was the most enviable fate Maud'huy could imagine.

He was known for his humanity and generosity. He had the common touch, too, and would distribute quantities of cigarettes and tobacco to his men. He was by no means unpopular with them. That night, therefore – on September 6th – his 35th (Bordeaux) Division, who had been fighting all day for possession of the vital spur, gave ample proof to their aristocratic general that they were by no means at the end of their tether. By 23.00 hours he was informed that Montceaux-les-Provins was completely clear of the enemy.

*Pierre du Terrail Bayard, 1470–1524. The famous soldier "sans peur et sans reproche".
Bertrand Chevalier du Guesclin, 1320–1380 app. Constable of France. A hero of the Hundred Years' War.

The fight for Montceaux-les-Provins, which was a mere episode in the main battle, provided an interesting demonstration of the progress being made in tactical ideas by certain French commanders since the beginning of the war. Artillery preparation and support, selection and organisation of rallying-points, phasing of the various stages in the attack, even aerial observation, were all brought into play during this action. Lieutenant Spears, the British liaison officer with the 5th Army, was evidently impressed: "It is hardly too much to say that, when they fought in the latter half of August, the troops though well disciplined, knew less than nothing. The little training they had had served but to bewilder and confuse them. Yet, in a fortnight of unparalleled disasters they succeeded in so altering and improving their methods that their tactics became at least equal to those of their opponents. No people but the French – the most adaptable and intelligent race in the world – having started so badly, could, in so short a time, have learnt so much."* One would like to think that this flattering comment could have been applied more generally; but (as will be seen later) many commanders still used the traditional, haphazard methods of attack – perhaps in certain instances because no other was possible – and they often paid a heavy price in casualties without achieving any material result.

From the strategical point of view, however, the most important action of the day was being fought on the extreme west of the battle front, where the Army of Paris and Maunoury's 6th Army were advancing abreast in a northerly direction with the object of turning the flank of the German 4th (Reserve) Corps, which was covering the right wing of von Kluck's army.

By nine o'clock the first series of objectives laid down in the previous day's orders (on a line running roughly north from Meaux) had been reached; Penchard, Monthyon, Saint-Soupplets, Pringy and Chambry were in French hands. The area was littered with derelict guns, vehicles, arms and equipment. Hardly able to believe their eyes, the troops of the Paris Army were (above all) astonished at their own swift success. German medical orderlies were awaiting their arrival, silently pointing to the Red Cross on their armbands. Their wounded were in the Monthyon Church (the last French steeple Péguy

*Major-General E. L. Spears: *op. cit.*, p. 432.

had looked on before he died). Other Germans, either slightly wounded or quite unhurt, asked nothing better than to surrender, and did so with visible relief. After a retreat that had seemed endless, this, indeed, was a sight worth seeing, and there were broad smiles on French faces everywhere. Even the red trousers of the infantry and the exotic uniforms of the Zouaves and Moroccans looked less travel-stained in the bright sunlight, in colourful contrast to the drab *feldgrau* of the discomfited Germans.

At nine-thirty, however, a distant rumble of guns was heard, and German shells came over thick and fast. Fields and villages just captured went up again in columns of smoke, flame and flying debris. The whole German line was ablaze with machine-gun and rifle fire; for von Kluck had seen the danger and was reacting quickly. In view of its effect upon the subsequent progress of the battle, his manoeuvre is worth a moment's close study.

"A general must press on continuously and relentlessly" (wrote Marshal de Saxe) "when pursuing a retreating army. Any manoeuvre is good that achieves this object; prudence and restraint are useless." This principle had led the ambitious von Kluck to disobey – with calculated deliberation – von Moltke's order of September 2nd requiring him to move in echelon behind the 2nd Army. Instead, he had driven on without even slackening speed. On September 4th he had sent his impertinent reply to the effect that the G.H.Q. Instruction "could not be carried out", and he followed it with another, confirming his intention to continue marching south, "attacking the enemy wherever he could be found". His only concession to G.H.Q. was to leave his 4th (Reserve) Corps north of the Marne as cover for the German main body against possible attack from the Paris side.

On September 5th, having been informed of the movement of French formations by train from east to west (to form the 6th Army), von Moltke had bluntly ordered: "The 1st and 2nd Armies must remain on a front east of Paris." But von Kluck again refused to give way. "I consider it unwise to interfere with the movement of the 1st and 2nd Armies. I propose to continue the pursuit as far as the Seine, and then to invest Paris." Joffre would have choked with rage if any of his generals had dared to make such an answer.

Von Kluck, however, had not lost his head. He was one of the cleverest generals in the German Army and had brilliantly out-manoeuvred his opponent, Mackensen, during the Imperial manoeuvres of 1912. When he heard, on September 5th, that the 4th Reserve Corps had been attacked from the west his reaction was swift and effective. The greater part of his army was then marching south. He immediately ordered the 2nd Corps, the nearest formation available, to counter-march and come to the aid of the 4th Corps, threatened by the French attack. But this manoeuvre was far more difficult for the 2nd German Corps than it would have been for French troops. The country in the rear of von Kluck's army had practically no workable railways, the roads were inadequate and the population hostile. Certain commentators have suggested (quite wrongly) that von Kluck's manoeuvre was a somewhat belated gesture of obedience to orders from G.H.Q. Von Kluck, in fact, was acting entirely on his own initiative, to protect his flank and his communications at all cost; and he acted with characteristic vigour and speed. First he brought back the 2nd Corps; then other corps as the threat became more serious. Finally, every corps in the 1st Army, then facing south, was turned about and marched in column across the front of the British Army, which – alas – was all too slow in following suit.

But all these manoeuvres, movements and plans were not to be revealed as yet. The soldiers lying flat on their faces under shell-fire on the 6th Army front, or seeking a scrap of friendly cover from bursts of machine-gun fire, certainly had no inkling of them; nor (in fact) did their officers or even the staff themselves, who – for their part – knew only that heavy shelling was reported somewhere. But the orders were to advance; and to keep on advancing; for the attack on the 1st German Army's flank had hardly begun.

In order to cover his defensive manoeuvre, von Kluck brought every available gun into action; and he sited his heavy artillery out of range of the French 75's. The ground in front of the 6th Army was covered with the dense, grey smoke of bursting 105 mm. shell; but the French infantry must advance through it somehow. Time after time, in the course of the day's fighting, waves of French infantrymen would walk,

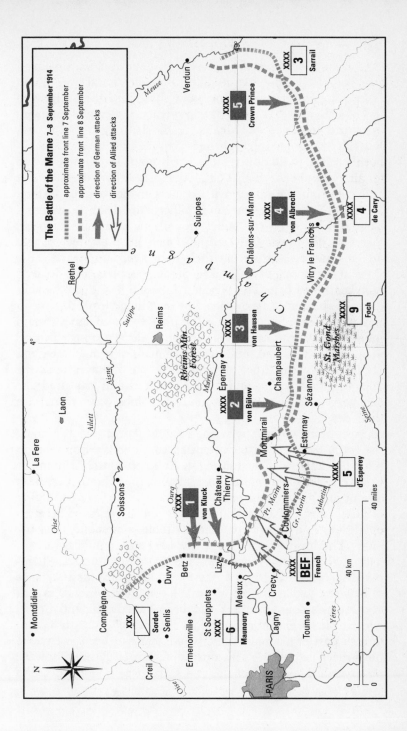

run or stumble forward, bayonets gleaming, bugles blowing –
a typical Déroulède* picture. The lines waver and break; and
re-form again, getting thinner and shorter as they approach
the objective. At Marcilly the survivors of Péguy's regiment
cross the bullet-swept Meaux road, shouting: "Come on,
Paris!" At regular intervals one of those officers who so stub-
bornly refuse to lie down under fire is made to do so once and
for all by a bullet or shell. The 246th is ordered to take Vareddes
and goes into the attack with colours flying, drums beating.
Within half an hour twenty of its officers are dead. Lieutenant-
Colonel Chaulet, with bullet wounds in arm and shoulder,
takes off his tunic and leads his men in a bayonet charge
fifteen hundred yards from their objective.

At about noon, having taken Saint Soupplets, the Zouaves
attacked Chambry. The German infantry had dug in under
cover of the cemetery overlooking the village from the north-
west. (A cemetery could often be used as an effective strong-
point.) The Germans had dug trenches, thrown up earthworks
along the walls and built emplacements for machine-guns.
Under heavy fire from the cemetery the Zouaves took the
village, lost it again, and finally attacked and captured the
cemetery itself. The grass around the tombs was strewn with
their dead.

Except for two pauses, at noon and at four in the afternoon,
the costly 6th Army attack went on continuously from 9.30 in
the morning until eleven at night. At 20.00 hours, Lieutenant-
Colonel Dubujadoux led his Zouaves in a final, desperate
assault on the German positions.

The Church of Neufmontiers was full of wounded. Urgent
operations had to be performed without anaesthetic – on the
altar. The losses of the 6th Army were never published.

By nightfall the French were holding a line through Chambry, Marcilly-Puisieux and Acy-en-Multien, a modest advance
of between two and three miles. What mattered most was that
von Kluck's counter-attack had been halted. His 2nd Corps,
which had been called back in support of the 4th Corps,
formed part of his main body, whose task had been to envelop
the French left wing. This operation, however, must now be
postponed. The recall of the 2nd Corps was a first indication

*Paul Déroulède. Poet and Politician 1846–1914. Author of *Chants du Soldat.*

(and indeed the beginning) of the general retreat of the German armies; but, at the time, no one was aware of it. Von Kluck was asking himself the question: "Can I quickly dispose of this Paris Army and then throw my whole weight upon that French left wing?" while Gallieni was wondering how long the Paris Army alone could hold on without support. According to the directives issued by Joffre and the undertaking given at Melun by French, von Kluck should have both Maunoury's 6th Army and the British to contend with. But what were the British doing?

On that same morning French had issued a stirring proclamation to all ranks, calling upon them for a supreme effort. No one doubted the intention of the British Expeditionary Force to carry out these directives, but the operation of turning about was being carried out at an appallingly slow speed.

General Mangin, commanding the 5th Division, spent the greater part of the day watching the battle through his fieldglasses from the top of the church tower at Escarde; Franchet d'Esperey's observation post was a small hill at Point 200. "A magnificent battle scene," he observed.

To the south-west, Montceaux-les-Provins, on its high hill, was burning like a torch, with a yellow and red flame in the clear sky, a long trail of black smoke drifting from the summit. From Courtacon to the forest of Le Gault, the whole countryside was dotted with burning villages: Courgivaux, Esternay, Retourneloup, Châtillon-sur-Morin, and many others. Here and there, squatting low amongst their fields, great farms, too, were smouldering, in strange, indifferent isolation.

From the batteries of 75's in action on slope or crest would come the intermittent flash of gunfire; and the two generals could clearly see whole divisions manoeuvring, company by company, the assault waves moving forward – so slowly it seemed at a distance – towards German positions as yet unbroken.

A magnificent battle scene, undoubtedly. But what the generals could not see through their field-glasses were the grim details of the hand-to-hand fighting amongst the burning ruins of Montceaux-les-Provins or in the shattered streets of Châtillon-sur-Seine.

The 5th Army was made up of the 18th, 1st and 10th Corps.

In the 18th was Pétain's division – already seen in action – and Mangin's division. The 1st and 10th were reserve corps. It was the 5th Army that was now contending with the main body of von Kluck's forces, of which the left wing was engaged with the Army of Paris to the west. Von Kluck had so far only brought back his left wing. At about 17.00 hours Mangin, from his post on the church tower, had seen a hail of shells descend upon Courgivaux, already in French hands. Very soon after, a number of red-trousered infantry began to stream out of the place. Within a few minutes, Mangin himself was amongst them, ordering them back. These men were from a regiment that had had practically no food for forty-eight hours. Like many others they had been caught up in the vast operation of the retreat and the sudden counter-march. But that evening they went back and re-occupied Courgivaux.

Coming out of the wood at Près-du-But, the infantry had crawled for some two hundred yards under machine-gun fire from a point above them. Bullets tore into the sandy earth around them, and sometimes into the bodies of men already killed. Gunners of the 2nd Division, in action on the edge of the Loge forest, at Gond, had been spotted by the Germans. In a very short time, more than two-thirds of their guns and wagons had been knocked out; and the losses in men were equally heavy. The 73rd Regiment, also, had been blocked by terrific gunfire at the edge of the Gril d'Arcan wood; but this time it was from French 75's; an unfortunate mistake.

General Mangin spent some time that evening following the interrogation of German prisoners in the dimly-lit courtyard of the school at Escarde. The Germans there would certainly not have guessed that this general, in his well-brushed uniform and shining field-boots, had been in the thick of the fighting an hour or so earlier. The French soldiers around, however, knew this, and were asking themselves: "How does he do it?" Under interrogation, the listless prisoners gave these answers:

"The French attack took us by surprise. We were supposed to be resting today."

"We were all in; we had marched sixty-five miles in forty-eight hours."

"We had had nothing to eat for two days. Our supply column could not keep up with us."

Prisoners are always inclined to make the most of their hardships; a natural (and, indeed, prudent) attitude. But some of the tougher-looking amongst them had probably found plenty to drink – *manu militari* – without worrying about their missing supply wagons. Away to the east, in the Champagne country, the roads were strewn with empty bottles, and a fair number of the prisoners had been picked up dead drunk. But, in the main, the prisoners being interrogated in the school playground at Escarde gave no sign of over-indulgence, either in food or drink. They looked as haggard and as famished as the French themselves, and they bit hungrily into the slices of bread they were given; gulped their mug of wine with evident relish. After that, their one idea was to sleep.

These men – like the French – had suffered a mental shock, but of a completely opposite kind. It seemed quite contrary to the natural order of things, incomprehensible (and, in a way, intolerable) that what seemed easy prey should suddenly turn on them, showing their teeth. They had also been some-what demoralised by a succession of quite contradictory orders; "Forward, nach Paris!" they had been told; but then the promised delights of Capua* had been snatched away, with the warning: "The French armies must first be destroyed." A disappointing business indeed.

One hundred and forty miles away, in the Luxembourg girls' school, Helmuth von Moltke, Chief of Staff of the German Armies, was standing in the cloak-room-passage that served as an absurdly inadequate office for his Operations Branch. He was reading – for the second time – the latest message intercepted by the G.H.Q. radio station from von Bülow's 2nd Army to the 3rd Army, under von Hausen: "Certain units of the 1st and 2nd Armies are engaged in stubborn fighting on the Morin Gap. It is highly important that the 3rd Army should intervene quickly to the east of Fère-Champenoise." What was the exact meaning of the words, "stubborn fighting?" Which units exactly were engaged? Why had neither von Kluck nor von Bülow telegraphed direct to Luxembourg?

Colonel Tappen, however, the head of the Operations Branch, refused to be unduly concerned: "If they have not

*Hannibal's winter quarters in Italy (215 B.C.).

telegraphed, your Excellency, it means that the situation cannot be very serious."

Not entirely reassured, von Moltke looked at the map, the same map on which, three weeks before, the arrows had shown the German armies launched on a vast encircling operation that would engulf the whole of the French forces. The grandiose plan had already been modified on September 2nd ("von Kluck will pass to the east of Paris") in order to avert a serious threat to the whole front; then again, on the 5th ("The 1st and 2nd Armies must remain on a front east of the capital"), in order to avert a threat coming from Paris. Was it possible that the French, already beaten (as they obviously were) could suddenly become dangerous again in the same theatre in which they had been ignominiously defeated? Anything was possible with the French. After Charleroi there had been that unpleasant thrust at Guise. But perhaps after all it was no more than another similar convulsion?

"No doubt whatever, your Excellency. With the French in their present state..."

At 20.00 hours Lieutenant-Colonel von Werder, chief of the Operations Branch of the 3rd Army, asked Colonel Tappen to come to the telephone to receive an urgent message.

"Hallo; the 30th Brigade have just found on the battlefield at Frignicourt, south-east of Vitry-le-François, an extremely important French army order. I have a copy here and will dictate it to you. It is in French."

"Very good. Read it out slowly, please."

"Here it is: 'September 6th. Order from the General Officer Commander-in-Chief: At the outset of a battle upon which the whole fate of our country depends, all ranks should remember that this is no time to look back. Every effort must be concentrated on attacking the enemy and driving him out. Any troops unable to continue their advance will hold on, at all cost, to the ground recovered and fight to the last man rather than give way. In the present circumstances, no weakness can be tolerated. Signed: Joffre.' Shall I read it again?"

"No thank you; no need. I quite understand."

10

THE MARSHES OF SAINT-GOND

THIRTEEN HUNDRED years before the Great War began, a barefooted monk was making his way along a rough path on the banks of the Petit Morin river. It certainly had no such name at the time, nor had the monk himself any idea whether it had a name or not. His humble ambition was to follow the river to its source and there build himself a hermitage. Hundreds of simple, devout men were to be found, in those days, wandering over the sparsely-populated countries of Western Europe. The monk in question never found the river's exact source, for the river was fed by the overflow from a great expanse of bog and marshland.

A depressing region, in all conscience, of heath and poor grass, chalky mud and bog, punctuated here and there with meagre groups of ash and alder; lonely and forbidding. But the heart of the wandering monk was suddenly uplifted, and he said: "I will build a monastery here."

We know that the monastery was duly built, and that its founder was Saint Gond. But for many centuries after the Barbarian Flood, all trace of it was lost. Then, one day, other monks came, cleared away the briars and brambles from the ancient ruins and built a humble priory. Of this, all that remained in 1914 was a Norman entrance-gate and, at a little distance, a tumble-down house. Here lived an elderly priest, well-known in the district, the Abbé Millard, who passed his days between his learned books and his kitchen-garden.

The country around had remained unchanged, lonely and depressing, even under the blue sky; and its name had a somewhat sinister ring: the marshes of Saint Gond. A line of poplars marked the bed of the Petit Morin, but even the hottest summer of the century had not dried up the marshes.

The only way to cross them was by jumping from hummock to hummock, with the risk of slipping in up to the waist; but they were quite impassable for any kind of vehicle. This, then, was the terrain that formed the greater part of the battle area of the 9th French Army.

The 9th Army had been formed from units taken from the 3rd and 4th Armies, and was now holding the front between the 5th (Franchet d'Esperey) and the 4th (de Langle de Cary). Its commander was General Foch; its mission was defined, in Joffre's General Instruction No. 6, as follows: "The 9th Army will cover the right of the 5th Army by holding the southern exits of the Saint-Gond marshes and by moving forward part of its forces on to the plateau north of Sézanne." As the 5th Army was under orders to attack, Joffre's Instruction meant that Foch also must attack with his left, and hold on elsewhere. One look at the map was sufficient to show Foch that his task was by no means easy.

Both north and south of the marshes the ground rose in a ring of hills, dominating the marshes by some three hundred feet. No commander, therefore, could cross the marshes unless he held the high ground at either end. To the west of the marshes was a thickly-wooded, undulating plateau. Together, the marshes and plateau formed an ideal defensive position, but it was precisely over this ground that Foch must attack. The right of his sector, on the other hand, was the western edge of the flat, bare Champagne country – "*La Champagne pouilleuse*" – that had always been the broad highway of enemy invasion. This, however, was the ground Foch must hold.

General Foch's father, a civil servant, had been christened Napoleon. Ferdinand Foch was born at Tarbes on October 2, 1851. The headmaster of his Jesuit school had noted on the boy's report: "A geometrical brain. Has the makings of a Polytechnician." A "geometrical" brain, perhaps, but surely something more. Foch, a devout Catholic, was also an enthusiast, and as an officer he had formed a cult for the offensive. "Attack, attack, attack" (he preached) the will to conquer sweeps everything before it." As an instructor at the Ecole de Guerre he would quote Joseph de Maistre*: "A battle is only lost when it is thought to be lost," and Foch would add: "As

*Philosopher and writer (1753–1821) Catholic and Royalist.

defeat is the result of moral causes, so also victory can be born of moral causes; and one may, therefore, say that a battle won is a battle in which one refuses to admit defeat!" Foch, no doubt, never imagined that his pupils – and particularly Colonel de Grandmaison – would later develop these principles to a point of absurdity; and, as the commander of the 20th Corps when war began, he himself had to taste the bitter fruits of the doctrine of "*l'attaque à outrance*".

Foch, however, had had no hand in the "Regulation upon the conduct of large formations", nor in the famous Plan XVII. He had never disdained what may be called "safety measures" in military techniques. Above all, as he grew older, his unquestionable belief in the attack became tempered by a no less unquestionable sense of realism. His famous dictum: "What is the problem?" (*de quoi s'agit-il?*) was another proof of his constant desire to establish the facts of any situation.

He was not so much unsociable by nature as indifferent to – or unaware of – social obligations. Anyone who approached him before ten on a particular morning would be abruptly dismissed, simply because he had decided that he would be in a bad humour all that day. He was autocratic, he hated lectures and conferences, preferring always to think things out for himself and make his own decisions; once made, he announced them in sharp, clipped language that was almost unintelligible to many. As time went on, this trait became more marked. By the greatest stroke of good fortune, however, Foch was to meet Weygand.

On August 28, 1914 (before Foch had taken over command of the 9th Army), Joffre had asked him to come to G.H.Q. The note ran: "General Foch will be accompanied by Colonels Devaux and Weygand," for Joffre wished these two officers to join Foch's staff. Leaving Joffre's office, Foch had met them, and asked:

"Which is the senior of you two?"

"I am, Sir," replied Weygand.

"You shall be my Chief of Staff," said Foch.

Weygand, lieutenant-colonel of Hussars, had no Staff College diploma. Within a few days he had learnt to discern every shade of meaning in Foch's obscure, almost incoherent forms of speech (which even alarmed some people, who thought he was mad); Weygand would then interpret them in perfectly clear language. He had quickly become absolutely indispensable to his chief. When pressed for details or explanations, Foch, with an impatient gesture, would interrupt the speaker: "See Weygand about it." Even generals would be given the same reply. Foch called Weygand his "Encyclopedia".

The 9th Corps formed the left wing of Foch's army, and it was this left wing that was to attack on September 6th. Its commander, General Dubois, had sent out his first order: "The Moroccan Division will capture Congy, if necessary by a night attack, and consolidate the position." Congy is on the north side of the marshes.

Like General Ditte's Moroccan Brigade in the 1st Army, the Moroccan Division was composed of native troops. Its commander, General Humbert (who wore a monocle), was preparing to pass the night on a bale of straw at the village of Broussy-le-Grand, south of the marshes, when General Dubois' order reached him. He arose from his bed, adjusted his monocle and read the order carefully. When a general receives an order he invariably dictates another. So Humbert sent for his A.D.C.

"Take this down; for the Blondlat Brigade."

Two hours later the Moroccans of the Blondlat Brigade, who had already reached Bannes (a village on dry ground in the middle of the marshes), set off again over the treacherous expanse of swamp. It was two o'clock in the morning; the sky was brilliant with stars. The Moroccans moved forward in complete silence, as if they were hunting their prey. (It was not by pure chance that the corps commander had picked on these men for the opening attack.) The only sound to be heard was the occasional dull thud of a man falling, the squelching noise of someone heaving himself out of the morass; very rarely, a clink of arms.

The mud itself was almost warm, but the night air was cold. At four o'clock, before dawn, the leading battalion came out of the marshes and reached the villages of Coizard and Joches. No sound, and no Germans in sight. An hour later, in the first glimmer of dawn, the main body of the brigade also emerged from the marshes and set off on the road up towards Congy.

Suddenly, the Moroccans were blinded by the glare of German searchlights, and brought, almost at once, under heavy rifle and machine-gun fire.

The searchlights had been set up on each side of the road and were sweeping across it. Dazed and confused, the Moroccans were mown down without knowing where the firing was coming from; nor, of course, could they see, beyond the searchlights, the trenches from which the Germans were firing. Then the German field-guns opened up.

In the meantime, General Humbert was setting up his command post at the Château de Mondement, which stood on one of the high points overlooking the marshes from the south. It was an unpretentious building, in rustic style, but, for a brief period, the Château of Mondement was to become world-famous.

A round tower on its north-west side housed the dining-room, of which the window commanded a view of the marshes; General Humbert thought it would make an excellent observing station.

He shared this room with the whole of the Moroccan divisional staff; maps were spread on every table, except on a side-board, well-stocked with food and drink by the thoughtful owner of the château, M. Jacob.

Through his field-glasses the General could clearly see the German shells bursting on the road to Congy, beyond the marshes. No shells were falling in Congy itself; the Germans, therefore, still held it.

But shells now began to fall around the château, and M. Jacob, his family and the Curé of Mondement took refuge in the ground-floor room, below the dining-room. One of them would raise a trap-door from time to time, to ask news of the battle.

At 9.20 General Humbert learned that the Blondlat Brigade had been halted and that the Germans had thereupon occupied Toulon-la-Montagne, east of Congy. The German artillery was keeping up an intense, incessant barrage.

At 10.30, a message was received from General Dubois, commanding the 9th Corps: "The Moroccan Division must overcome enemy resistance at Congy at all costs." The last three words were underlined.

Having received an order, General Humbert dictated another. On this occasion, Humbert drafted it himself, not without difficulty and much rubbing-out: "A general offensive is now begun. Its success depends upon the efforts of each and everyone to move steadily forward." The Blondlat Brigade must "persevere in its attack on Congy. Immediate action is required". The liaison officer had hardly left the room with this message when heavy shells began falling on the château. Cracks appeared in walls and roofs; the servants' quarters and outhouses were soon ablaze.

"Tell M. Jacob and his family to take refuge in the cellar. We are moving across to the church."

But very soon the church itself came under fire. General Humbert came back to the château and went on observing the battle from a point outside the tower. Shells were dropping uncomfortably close. Baur, the chief divisional medical officer, sitting under a tree near the general, was also observing the battle. A tearing explosion was heard; the tree split in two, and Baur lay dead beneath it.

So they went back to the church; then back again to the château, and back again to the church, to and fro several times. During one of the journeys a shell burst among the general's escort, killing horses and wounding their riders. Even the cellar protecting M. Jacob and his family showed signs of collapse as broken masonry fell from the roof. The unfortunate M. Jacob (who had a weak heart) died a few days later.

The order to press on with the attack on Congy reached the Moroccans of the Blondlat Brigade at a time when each of them was wondering how many more minutes – or seconds – he could hope to survive under such shell-fire. Their only hope was to withdraw to the marshes and go to ground in the mud.

General Humbert was not entirely surprised, for what he could see from his uncomfortable observation post made it quite clear that his infantry, in their present plight, would be wiped out completely by the German batteries in position near Villemard, overlooking the marshes from the north-west. General Humbert therefore dictated another order, in fact he dictated two orders; the first was to the Blondlat Brigade to the effect that they should attempt no further advance; the second was to the divisional artillery, calling for vigorous counter-battery action against the German guns. But the French batteries were fewer in number, had less ammunition, were not so well sited, and included fewer heavy guns than the German.

The 77th Infantry Regiment of the 17th Division, fighting on the right of the Moroccan Division, had been ordered to re-capture Toulon-la-Montagne, which had been lost early in the day. They set out at 11.00 hours from Bannes, whence the Blondlat Brigade had started five hours before. Crossing the marshes now was a very different problem, first, because it was broad daylight and, second, because the whole area was under shell-fire. Although the going was heavy the men made little complaint, for the mud, although it hindered their progress, gave them protection. The shell-bursts produced enormous spouts of mud and water, but their explosive effect was smothered and the splinters did little damage.

The situation changed, however, when the men reached the northern side. The German artillery and machine-gunners had no further need of searchlights; they could clearly see the French infantry struggling out of the morass and plodding heavily on to the open road. It was not until 16.000 hours that the 77th received their order to withdraw; in the meantime they had lost one-third of their numbers.

Foch had established his command post in the town hall of Pleurs, about eight miles south of the marshes. He himself and all his staff there were complaining bitterly of their lack of information regarding the enemy's movements.

At an air-race he attended in the east of France, in 1910, Foch had been unimpressed: "Flying, you must understand, is merely a sport, like any other; from the military point of view it has no value whatever." (Napoleon himself had been equally sceptical of the future of steamships.) Today, however, Foch was wondering why his aeroplanes had not yet arrived.

On September 5th, at seven in the morning, two squadrons of Blériots allotted to the 9th Army had been drawn up on the aerodrome at Belfort. The twelve planes were fully equipped and manned; they were also provided with motor-drawn trailers for transport by road.

The fragile machines of those days had to be handled with great care. Exposure to the cold night air or to rain would cause their wood and canvas to stretch; over long distances, therefore, they were usually dismantled and transported in closed containers.

On this occasion, however, there was no time to lose. The station commander, Captain Zarapoff, set off from Belfort by road with the supplies and equipment while the pilots took off with their machines for the aerodrome at Mailly. One pilot, however, was killed while taking off, and two others stayed behind to bury him. Nine aeroplanes therefore eventually landed at Mailly. Their speed was sixty miles an hour, and they carried petrol for two and a half hours' flight; their armament: one carbine.

Captain Zarapoff arrived at Mailly at ten-thirty that night. The sergeant of the guard covered him with a revolver: "Who are you? What's the pass-word?"

The Blériot pilots, who had already arrived, were standing in the darkness by their planes, puzzled and somewhat perturbed: "No one here was expecting us, and no one has any orders for us."

"Well, I have," said Captain Zarapoff. "When I got to Chaumont I was told that our rendezvous had been changed. You're going to Méry-sur-Seine."

Wandering about the camp were two hundred gunners, without officers or N.C.O's. No one knew where they had come from, nor where they should go.

"The Boches are coming!" (they said). "They are only twelve miles away." Just then one of the station officers came up with a message for Captain Zarapoff: "The aeroplanes must leave for Troyes." So now it was Troyes.

"The Germans are not there yet," said Zarapoff. "Take off at dawn. Have you got enough petrol?"

"I shall want five litres or so," said one of the pilots.

There was not a drop of petrol at Mailly, at least so the station-officer said. In the light of two oil lamps the lost gunners gathered round, listening to the discussion.

Second-Lieutentant de Serre (the pilot who was short of petrol) said: "Surely there's a grocer in Mailly?"

Yes, there was one; they got him out of bed, and he produced a five-litre can of petrol from the back of his shop. De Serre paid for it out of his own pocket.

He then took off from Mailly at 5 a.m. on September 6th, in

thick mist, flying at one hundred and fifty feet and taking his direction, to begin with, from a railway (a favourite method of aerial navigation at the time). Having lost the railway he landed in a field and looked at his compass.

"Right. I think I know where I am. Off we go."

There was no map in the plane (one can't have everything), but de Serre picked up Arcis-sur-Aube and flew low along the road to Troyes. "I shall probably see the aerodrome," he thought. But he saw nothing, passed over one village, then over two more. "Perhaps I've gone wrong. I'd better land." Some peasants came running up: "But Troyes is over there, Monsieur l'aviateur. This is Vendeuvre. *You are French*, aren't you?"

Troyes was twenty miles to the west, twenty more minutes flying through the mist. De Serre dared not look at his petrol-gauge. At last a ghostly town appeared below, fairly large, apparently. "This must be it; but I can't see any aerodrome. Well, anyhow, I'm going down."

It was not Troyes, but Barberey, five miles to the north. Second-Lieutenant de Serre finally landed at Troyes at nine o'clock, having taken four hours to cover thirty odd miles.

"Well, you're the first arrival," said the station officer. "But where are the others?"

The others (less one) arrived between two and six in the afternoon, having had equally intriguing adventures on the way. One, however, flying too low over wooded hills, unfortunately crashed. Merely a sport, as Foch had said.

Since ten o'clock that morning the 9th Army Commander had had nothing but bad news. The enemy seemed to be in strength along the whole front and their shelling was extremely heavy. Two battalions of the Grossetti Division had fallen back in front of Villeneuve, west of the marshes. Once they had been halted, however, and suitably admonished, they re-formed and seemed furiously annoyed and surprised at their own behaviour. The explanation was simple enough, although no one seemed to realise it at the time, so common had it become now to see haggard and weary faces everywhere. These two battalions were composed, for the most part, of young soldiers recently called up, who had been fighting and marching for the past two weeks. On the average they had slept but three hours in twenty-four; on the night before the attack they had had no sleep at all, nor any food next day.

General Dubois, the 9th Corps Commander (author of the order: "The Moroccan Division must overcome enemy resistance at Congy *at all costs*"), now realised that it was impossible to expect any further advance for the present. To order these men to attack was not merely unrealistic; it was even dangerous, because the survivors of these fruitless attacks would become incapable even of remaining on the defensive.

"Ring him up," said Foch to Weygand.

There was no question, this time, of the legendary "Attack! Attack! Attack!" Foch's order, transmitted by telephone, was that the 9th Corps "must in any case take up a definitely defensive position", and his orders for the next days were "to use the infantry sparingly, the artillery to its utmost capacity, and to consolidate strongly any ground gained".

Weygand had hardly finished telephoning this message to Dubois when a runner reported: "Saint-Prix has just been evacuated by a regiment of the 42nd Division."

Saint-Prix was on the road to Sézanne at the extreme western limit of the marshes. From that point the Germans, advancing through the woods, were beginning to reach the southern exits. In such circumstances a purely defensive policy was inadequate to deal with what might be a dangerous development. Weygand telephoned once again to Dubois.

A crack regiment always pays dearly for its fighting reputation. Half an hour later the Blondlat Brigade was ordered to re-capture Saint-Prix. At dawn they had been half blinded and severely mauled on the road to Congy; for four hours thereafter they had grimly held on, just short of the deadly road itself, before being given permission to withdraw into the marshes. The battalion strength had been reduced from 600 to 400 men, now almost at the limit of endurance; and one half of the officers had been killed.

The Tirailleurs of the Cros Regiment set off in single file, under shell fire, along the western edge of the marshes, creeping under cover of hedge and ditch, running from spinney to spinney.

"Move in small groups," ordered Major Fralon, "if not we shall all be for it."

They re-formed in Botrait Wood, just to the west of Saint-Prix. On a slope beyond its northern edge was a large farm: Montalard. Were the Germans holding it – or were they not? The question was quickly resolved, for the first ten men out of the wood were shot down by rifle and machine-gun fire.

"All right, come on! Use your bayonets!"

Moroccan troops will *always* follow their officer's lead. But to their astonishment the firing from the farm had ceased. The Germans were moving out.

War sometimes produces such unexpected good fortune, once in a while, but rarely twice in succession. The battalion had just left the farm on its way to Saint-Prix when a burst of machine-gun fire blew tiles off the roof.

The mound they had occupied was being swept by machine-gun fire from the Poirier Crest (or Poirier Signal), a ridiculously unimportant feature, which, during the next few days, was to acquire a sinister reputation almost equal to that of Mondement Farm. Within a few minutes two hundred men and six officers, including their commander, Major Fralon, had been wiped out by fire from the Poirier Crest. Saint-Prix was not taken. But the Moroccans dug themselves in on the mound south of the farm.

On the eastern side of the marshes, the 65th Infantry Regiment, whose objective was Morains-le-Petit, were met by a hail of bullets and shells as they emerged from cover. This they were prepared for; but they were also confronted by a strangely tragic spectacle. A number of men and women came running towards them, waving their arms and shouting, many of them being shot down as they ran: "Don't go to Morains! The Germans are there! The Guards!"

The Devil himself could not have terrified them more. The 2nd Grenadiers – the Emperor Franz Regiment – were holding Morains; on their left the 4th Grenadiers – the Augusta Regiment – were holding Ecury; both regiments, it was true, were in the Guards Division. The Guards Army Corps, under General von Plettenberg, formed part of the 2nd Army under von Bülow. The men of the 65th Infantry knew nothing of these famous regiments nor of the formations they belonged to; but they were duly impressed by their name: the Guards.

"Forward!" said Colonel Balagny. "In open order."

The leading waves reached the southern edge of the village; but the Guards had their gunners as well as infantry. Intense shell-fire and flying masonry made the place untenable, and the men of the 65th fell back. The 64th, who had attacked Ecury, were also driven back into the shelter of the woods. The shelling went on; Ecury and Morains were now burning fiercely. Shells tore into roofs and windows, as smoke and flame burst from them. The ruined walls of houses were left standing, strangely still in the glow of smouldering fire.

On the right of the 9th Army was the 4th, under Langle de Cary, and, on its right, again, the 3rd, under General Sarrail. The vast battle – as yet without a name – raged from the outskirts of Paris to Verdun, while the two remaining armies (the 2nd, under Castelnau, and the 1st under Dubail) held a defensive front in Alsace. The battle had opened in the west; and what was happening in the western sector, from Meaux to the St Gond marshes, was, strategically, the most important of all, and would continue to be so; but the whole battle could be lost if any part of the eastern front gave way; and there were certain alarming signs that this might happen.

The 4th Army had had to turn about and face an enemy that was hot on its heels. September 6th had, therefore, been a day of crisis, with an advance on the left and withdrawal on the right; the heavy pressure of the 3rd German Army (von Hausen) and of the 4th (Duke of Wurtemberg) was being held; but no more than held.

General Sarrail (3rd Army) had been ordered to attack the German left flank in a manoeuvre more or less symmetrical with that of Maunoury against the German right flank. The plan had attractive possibilities, but Wurtemberg's left wing and the Crown Prince's Army had forestalled it by attacking with forces at least double those of the French. The 5th French Corps, on the left of the 3rd Army, under pressure of greatly superior numbers, had been forced to give ground, leaving the famous Revigny Gap uncovered.

Joffre's historic order: "At the outset of a battle . . ." had been telephoned to the H.Q. of each army at nine in the morning. The confirmation in writing reached them at various times in the course of the day. Duly copied by the orderly clerks, it was included in the mail with a number of other miscellaneous orders. In certain units, and with varying degrees of solemnity, it was read out to the troops, but this was impossible in others already engaged in the fighting. For many of them there could no longer be any question of looking back, or forward, for that matter; their eyes had closed for ever.

In Paris troops had been marching all day through the city. At 15.00 hours a communiqué had announced that "troops in the forward defence positions had been in contact yesterday with enemy forces on the Ourcq river, apparently covering the south-eastern movements of the main German right wing". That was all. But popular rumour had produced a whole spate of more exciting news: two Germans, disguised as British officers, were said to have found their way into the capital, but they were so astonished by the morale of the Parisians that they had telegraphed to Berlin to the effect that the German armies must now retreat; Turpin, the inventor of Melinite, had brought out a new, incredibly powerful explosive called Turpinite; soldiers from the front line had seen with their own eyes whole companies of entrenched Germans wiped out by a single shell; 500,000 Indian soldiers had landed at Marseilles, while the first battalions of a contingent of 300,000 Cossacks had arrived from Archangel at the Gare de Lyon. Countless Parisians, of course, had seen and spoken to them . . . . "They are going to march tonight along the Boulevard St Michel, on their way to the Gare du Nord."

From six o'clock that evening crowds had gathered along the pavements of the Boulevard St Michel and the Boulevard de Sébastopol. Some people waited patiently until late at night, but no Russians had appeared.

In the Champs-Elysées a few tardy citizens halted in their evening walk to listen to the guns, away to the east; a strange, distant thunder in the starlit night.

THE PARIS TAXIS

THE LAST of the Marne Taxis stands in the dim corner of a passage under a stairway at the far end of the courtyard of the Invalides Museum in Paris. An ancient, faded brown, hearse-like vehicle, brooding over the past; as if spellbound by its own romantic story. I had seen, as a child, specimens of the motor-cars of those days. I thought I could remember, later, what the taxis of 1914 looked like; but I was mistaken. I had to go back and look again at this ghostly contraption with its tiny engine, its high, gawky body, blissfully ignorant of the laws of aerodynamics. It seemed even more archaic than a four-wheeler.

Its story is, indeed, romantic. France invaded, Paris threatened; and suddenly the taxis are called in to carry a whole army to the front; the outcome swings for a time in the balance; and the Germans are routed.

"The Marne?" people say, "Oh yes, the taxis . . . ."

One heard the remark often enough. But on the last occasion someone added: "My brother was there; he rode in one of the taxis."

And I asked: "Do you think I could see him?"

No; I could not see him; nor could I see his grave. He had been reported missing and his family had made heart-breaking efforts to find his body; but they had failed. I began to wonder how many were still alive who had taken part in the operation.

There were still a number, thank God, but what I had heard rather discouraged me from continuing my search.

I should have liked, also, to meet one of the taxi-drivers. But the men who took part in that historic episode were all much older than their passengers. Of the twelve thousand Paris taxi-drivers, seven thousand had been called up; all that remained were the old stagers and a few army rejects. None is

alive today to tell the story of their trip along the Nanteuil-le-
Haudouin road. Luckily, however, Major Henri Carré, a
veteran of the 1914 campaign, had kept a detailed record in a
little book published just after the war. No copy of it is to
be found today; but, as a child, I often heard other details of
that memorable expedition.

The story begins in Gallieni's office in the Lycée Victor-
Duruy. The general had sent for the Army Transport Officer
and was talking with him and other members of his staff. It
was eight o'clock in the evening of September 6th. Gallieni
said: "The 7th Division must be moved up to the front line at
once." The first half of the division was in billets at Pantin.*
The battalions concerned had been transferred from the 3rd
Army and had endured the purgatory of the interminable
train journey from Sainte-Menehould to Paris. Near Troyes
some of the trains had taken twenty-four hours to cover six
miles. The railway system was choked with Belgian troop-
trains, British ambulance-trains, civilian evacuees and wounded.
The infantry of the 7th Division, packed into trucks and
coaches, had been stranded on sidings for hours in the scorching
sun, listening to the groans of the sick and wounded parked
in other trains alongside them, while harassed and dog-tired
railwaymen walked up and down the track.

The second half of the 7th Division was due to arrive on the
7th. Gallieni had spent the day poring over his large maps,
receiving telephone messages and listening to reports from
liaison officers. He could not know, as yet, that Maunory's left
was on the point of giving way, but he knew that German
resistance was stiffest on that section of his front; his aeroplanes
reported that the 2nd German Corps had turned about and
was marching quickly north.

The Army Transport Officer said: "The 7th Division will
be moved up by rail, one half at a time."

"Why only half?"

"We are short of rolling stock."

"Very well, use motor transport. Move one brigade by rail
and the other by road."

"But we have only two hundred and fifty motor vehicles with
Army drivers."

*A northern suburb of Paris.

"Why not use taxis?"

Now the taxis were already, in a sense, on active service. A certain number of them were kept in the garages for half the day by rotation, ready to move anywhere at any time under orders from the military authority. They had already been used to move the Marines to Pierrefitte.

"Requisition *all* the taxis," said Gallieni, "and use them to move the 14th Brigade, I want the first convoy to leave tonight."

The troops concerned were not stationed in Paris itself. The taxis would have to leave empty, pick up the men in their barracks or billets in the suburbs and then drive them up to the front line. Five minutes after Gallieni had given his order the Transport Section sent out its first instructions by telephone to the Prefecture of Police: "Give orders to the police to have all taxis – without exception – returned to their depots. Instruct the taxi companies by telephone to arrange to have all their vehicles supplied with petrol, oil, and, where necessary, tyres, and then sent immediately to the Esplanade des Invalides."

The first of them began to arrive at about ten that night on the vast open space in front of the Invalides.

A few officers, municipal guards and police were hurrying about in the darkness. "Territoriaux" carried lamps to guide the taxis to their places as they arrived. The esplanade gradually filled with a solid, dark mass of strange vehicles.

"There should be at least one N.C.O. accompanying every fifty cars and an officer for every hundred and fifty; but there are not enough to go round. Second-Lieutenant La Chambre will lead the first convoy."

"Very good, mon capitaine: which way do we go?"

"An officer from the Transport Division will tell you that. He should arrive at any minute now, and will catch you up. In the meantime, get moving."

"Very good, mon capitaine: but – where to?"

"To start with, make for La Villette; and halt there at the *Octroi.*"*

The column moved slowly off in a seemingly endless line, including the hundred and fifty taxis of the standing reserve and the first hundred of those requisitioned that evening. Their speed was hardly impressive. Lieutenant Lefas, of the Transport

*Where duties were levied (at that time) on certain commodities entering Paris.

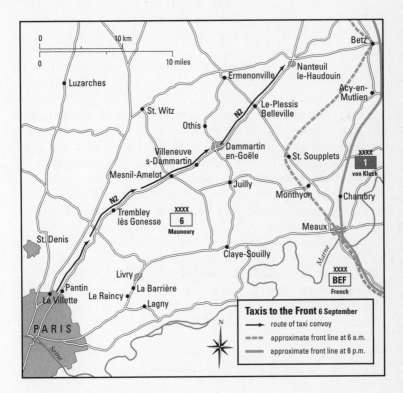

Taxis to the Front 6 September

→ route of taxi convoy

---- approximate front line at 6 a.m.

···· approximate front line at 8 p.m.

Division, joined the convoy in his car at the Place de la Concorde. He had been given verbal orders ("no time to put
anything in writing, the Governor is on the rampage") to
conduct the first convoy to Tremblay-les-Gonesse. "You will
be given further orders there. Strictly secret."

The weird procession caused some surprise amongst the few
people abroad at that hour. An elderly taxi-driver in oil-cloth
cap and gray dust-coat, asked: "What's going on here?"

Lieutenant Lefas stopped his car and said: "You're requisitioned. Military Governor's orders. Fall in behind the
column."

"All right. But what about the fare? By the clock, or so
much for the trip?"

"By the clock."

The old man climbed into his seat and clicked his flag down.
As soon as they had left the *octroi* at La Villette they found
the road obstructed by barriers of felled trees and upturned
carts. Lieutenant Lefas had to argue with the guards at every
halt. It was a cold night, and the "Territoriaux" were crouched
around their lanterns, in scanty bivouacs, warming themselves – as the atmosphere suggested – with red wine. The
leading vehicles reached Tremblay-la-Gonesse (twelve miles
from Paris) at two in the morning.

The little town was dark, and as silent as the grave. The first
cars to arrive parked in the square outside the Town Hall;
others roamed through the streets, looking for an open space,
the drivers losing their way (and their tempers) cursing each
other in the general confusion. Lieutenant Lefas, having been
told: "You will get further orders there," searched through the
empty streets, knocked at doors, but found no one. The
village had been evacuated. A window opened at last on the
first floor of the Town Hall.

"What do you want?"

"I'm coming up!"

Seated at a completely bare table in an empty room,
Lieutenant Lefas found a duty officer from the staff of the 1st
("Territorial") Division.

"Have you any orders for me?" asked Lefas.

"What orders? No, I've no order. What are you doing here
with all these cars?"

"I've been ordered to bring them here."

"A written order? Have you got it there?"

"No."

"You ought to have a written order."

"Well, anyhow, I suppose I can use your telephone?"

"Yes, if you want to."

"Hello Paris, is that the Transport Division? We're at Tremblay- what are the orders?"

"What? You have no orders?"

"No, I was supposed to get them here."

"And you haven't had any?"

"Of course not – if I had I shouldn't be ringing you!"

"All right; we will telephone the 6th Army, and call you back."

The convoy had apparently got away too quickly for the slow-moving staff machine to keep up with them.

By now the streets of Tremblay were packed with waiting taxis, some of the drivers dozing in their seats, others un-ashamedly asleep inside. Some walked up and down, but the night air was chilly and conversation languished.

At three in the morning, in a chorus of creaking brakes and minor bumps, a second convoy halted just outside the village. Two hundred and fifty vehicles of all shapes and sizes, large and small, a few twenty-four-seated char-a-bancs, and even a sprinkling of racing and sports cars. Gallieni's peremptory orders had roused the Army Transport Depot to turn out every vehicle in the place. Meanwhile Lieutenant Lefas was sitting in the office on the first floor of the Town Hall, waiting for orders.

At 4.20 the telephone rang: "Conduct all your vehicles on to the main-road to Nanteuil, between Dammartin and Mesnil-Amelot, in the vicinity of Villeneuve-sous-Dammartin."

"Very good. And what must I do then?"

"Wait for further orders."

"From whom?"

But the speaker at the other end had already put his receiver down. The huge fleet of four hundred vehicles slowly dis-entangled itself from the streets of Tremblay-les-Gonesse, formed up in column on a secondary road, reached the main National Road No. 2 and turned right. Every village they passed through had been evacuated. The leading vehicles reached Dammartin-en-Goelle, eleven miles from Tremblay, at seven in the morning.

"Draw up under the trees, and wait."

Under the trees? Ah yes, the drivers began to understand what was going on. They looked up at the clear, morning sky; a convoy of this size must be uncomfortably visible from the air. The *Taubes* had already dropped a few bombs on Paris (although no one knew how many) and might well be tempted to have a little target practice. The idea of being attacked from the air was too new as yet to be terrifying, but it made the men feel uneasy. As usual, the barrack-room lawyers began to air their views.

"No objection to being requisitioned; that's fair. But they've no legal right to bring us all this way from Paris. And no grub since last night. I say, what's that? Guns?"

Yes, it was gun-fire – but a very different sound from the distant rumble they had heard from Paris at night. Here it was definitely nearer, and more distinct; an intermittent thunder that made you jump; very unpleasant. How far were those guns away? And what was the range of heavy artillery? Supposing a *Taube* spotted the convoy and warned the German gunners? Meanwhile, officers went up and down the column looking very unconcerned, very reassuring, even friendly.

"You would have to travel as far again" (they said) "before you could even see the smoke of those shells."

The drivers noticed, however, that, amongst themselves, the officers were not quite so cheerful. They also had questions to ask. What would happen if these civilian drivers were captured by the enemy? This business of using non-belligerents for a military operation was extremely tricky (their scruples might be thought somewhat naïve nowadays). But another sound – more familiar than the rumble of guns – now made them all turn their heads: the clatter of horses' hoofs.

"The Dragoons!"

Two squadrons of Sordet's cavalry division were on their way up from the south. But what had happened to these troopers and horses to reduce them to their present, pitiable condition? The men's faces were drawn with fatigue and lack of sleep; the horses were scraggy and listless. They had been almost continuously in action during the fighting around Liége; they had then made their way, during the retreat, on a wide circular detour that had brought them to the western approaches of Paris; and now they were marching up to the front again. But, tired as they obviously were, they carried themselves well, with their lances in rest and the pennants fluttering. And their general himself was leading the column. The taxi-drivers gave them a cheer: "Vivent les Dragons!"

Their arrival created a useful diversion. The taxi-drivers began to feel less lonely, less exposed to unknown dangers. A company of cyclists went by soon after; and they, too, looked drawn and travel-stained, pedalling away as if in their sleep on their quaint, low-geared machines. So the taxi-drivers gave them a cheer too: "Vivent les cyclistes!"

A few other cyclists arrived; but these were sappers, and an officer was with them. They put a foot to the ground and the taxi-drivers gathered round: "Suppose you're blowing up the bridges?"

"That's all we've been doing so far, replied the officer, but that's finished. Now we are advancing and we shall have to rebuild them." (This chap's optimistic, evidently; that's good.) Other squadrons of cavalry went by, a whole division of Dragoons; and Cuirassiers; several batteries of 75's; detachments from the entrenched camp of Paris; all marching at a good pace up to the front; but the artillery moved on past them. The taxi-drivers were impressed:

"Well – this is something like!"

They could still hear very distinctly the sound of guns away to the north-east; but by now the taxi-men's morale was fully restored. Guns? Well, what of it? The French have got guns, too, haven't they? It was now eleven o'clock, and the sun was hot.

"Here come the rations!"

They gave a cheer for Lieutenant Lefas, who had succeeded in drawing rations from the depot at Mesnil-Amelot: tinned meat, army biscuits and wine. (Some of the older men found the biscuits rather hard for their liking.) A half-barrel of wine was produced; but no glasses or bottles, nothing to drink from; and the officers forebade them to search the houses around. Some enterprising person discovered two hundred empty bottles in the local Mairie; but, surprisingly enough, more than twenty drivers declared they drank nothing but water.

"Where do you expect us to get water from? The main supply has been cut off, and there is no one here; all the houses are empty."

Luckily there were wells in the farms near by. So, having eaten and drunk, the taxi-drivers, now in philosophic mood, settled down to await events. At about one o'clock a closed car drove up, and an officer appeared: "6th Army staff. Where is the officer in charge of the convoy? Oh, there you are, Lieutenant. Listen –"

The orders were that they should not move beyond Dammartin, where they were at present. Nothing more? Nothing more. Some of the old soldiers, who had forgotten the joys of military service, began to learn once again that, in any well-ordered army, patience – or the art of waiting – was as essential as good discipline.

There arrived (at last) a third convoy, led by a general in his car, and consisting of lorries loaded with six hundred rations of meat, wine, coffee and chocolate. Once the rations were issued, however, the taxis had to move off; for General Laude, Director of Transport Services, had also brought orders, of which the first was that they should turn round and go back.

From Dammartin, therefore, they returned to a point near Livry, some thirty kilometres distant, where they were to pick up the 104th Infantry and bring them back to a position behind the front line.

The 104th had been in billets at Villemomble since the evening of the 6th. On the morning of the 7th their officers were given large-scale maps of the Paris sector. At 14.00 hours they were told to have their troops ready to be picked up by taxis at the village of La Barrière, between Livry and Le Raincy, on the road to Meaux.

Under cover of dusk the regiments lined up alongside the long column of vehicles. To these infantrymen, who had survived the ordeal of an almost interminable journey in railway goods-wagons, a ride in a taxi seemed too good to be true. A night to be remembered.

As soon as it was dark the convoy moved off. There was no moon, and lights were forbidden. The drivers strained their

eyes to see the car immediately ahead. Moving more or
less at the same speed, the taxis could keep together; but
behind them was a nondescript collection of vehicles, including
lorries, char-a-bancs, limousines, and even sports cars, and
some engines quickly became over-heated, for the pace was
dead slow. The night was hideous with grinding gears, screeching
brakes, sudden stops and minor collisions; but the long cater-
pillar moved bravely on, and the soldiers slept, blissfully
unperturbed while they journeyed back to the deserted
villages of Tremblay-les-Gonesse and Dammartin.

Lieutenant Lefas' car broke down at Dammartin and the
convoy halted. With the rations, however, General Laude had
also brought breakdown lorries, mechanics and tools, and the
experts got quickly to work. Meanwhile, with a rumble and
roar that filled the night air for miles around, another convoy
almost exactly resembling the convoy transporting the 104th
debouched from the road leading to Gagny and came to a
sudden and noisy halt, throwing the whole column into
grinding confusion. A harassed and visibly perplexed brigadier-
general got out of the leading car: "Where is this place,
Nanteuil-le-Haudouin?"

This convoy was carrying the 103rd, the sister regiment of the
brigade to which the taxis had been allotted. Duly informed by
Lefas, the brigadier-general got back into his car and the column
slowly disappeared into the night. Lefas' car was now in action
again, but there was further delay, for other vehicles now
needed attention. A group of strange figures emerged from the
darkness and moved towards the column: "Got a spot of grub
you could give us?"

Soldiers, apparently; but a queer-looking lot. No packs, and
no arms. Wild-eyed, apparently exhausted, and visibly scared.

"What the hell are you chaps doing here?"

An officer came up: "Where have you men come from?"

"The front line. We're looking for our friends."

The usual answer. Even front-line troops are not all heroes,
and these men certainly looked as if they were at the end of
their tether. There was no time to deal with them; but someone
gave them some bread.

"The Prussians are coming," they said. "We were fired on
at Plessis station."

"It's not true. You're lying, and you know it. Get to hell out of here."

Le Plessis was only five miles farther on. These deserters must not be allowed to start a panic. If the Germans were in Le Plessis other French troops would be falling back, and the news would have filtered through somehow. It was past midnight now, and all the repairs were finished. The convoy moved on.

There were no Germans at Le Plessis. The infantrymen of the 104th Regiment reached their destination that night just south of Nanteuil, and the officer-guides were there to meet them.

On the night of September 6th only a few belated Parisians had seen the departure of the convoy to pick up the 104th Brigade. The requisition of the taxis required for the 103rd took place during the following day, September 7th, and was a more spectacular affair.

Policemen all over the city were blowing their whistles and raising their batons: "Requisition. Go back to your garage."

"But, look here, I've got a fare."

"Never mind. Your fare must get out."

The fare was a lady, and she put the window down, protesting: she was going to the station, she had luggage, she was unwell, she was going to visit her old, dying mother or a soldier in hospital. But there was nothing doing, orders were orders, and she had to get out. Or the fare was an elderly gentleman with a ribbon in his buttonhole, who thought he was being ill-used ("I shall make a complaint"), but had to get out, nevertheless. Parisians of that generation still remember these and hundreds of other similar incidents. When the convoy eventually made its way – in daylight this time – through the streets of Paris everyone in the crowd thronging the pavements knew that the taxis were going to take troops up to the front line. Within a week it was being commonly reported that the taxis "had been going through all day; more than ten thousand of them". Thus was the legend born.

All schoolchildren had to learn by heart the official slogan posted everywhere: "Do not talk; take care; the enemy is listening." Spy mania is an inevitable war-time phenomenon. It invariably produces unforgettable examples of collective stupidity and even of collective cruelty; and it goes hand in hand with the most flagrant indiscretions, resulting in astonishing disclosures of the most secret military movements.

Thus it was that from September 4th onwards – forty-eight hours before the 103rd Infantry Regiment detrained at Pantin station – the place was crowded with mothers, wives, fiancées and friends, all well aware that certain troops whose homes were in Paris were travelling from the east and would arrive at Pantin on their way to another sector of the front. Most of them even knew which regiments were expected.

The 103rd duly arrived and marched off at once towards their billets at Gagny. They were followed throughout the five miles of the journey by an extraordinary procession of an almost equal number of women who had barely succeeded in catching a glimpse of their men at the station and were now anxiously determined to speak to them, embrace them, hand over parcels. Officers and N.C.O's had no little difficulty in keeping the men in step, or even in line.

On the 7th the soldiers of the 103rd, in billets at Gagny, saw the distant column of taxis on the road. They thought at first that their womenfolk were on their way back; but, alas, the taxis were empty.

Under the conditions of army life, personal disappointments, however keen, are often short-lived. When the men were ordered to prepare to leave they heard the surprising news that the taxis were intended for them; and their delighted reaction quickly drove away sombre thoughts of the girls they had left behind them. Rumour was quickly busy amongst the more simple-minded: The Germans had been defeated in a great battle; they had lost one hundred thousand prisoners (two hundred thousand, perhaps), and the 103rd was being sent to guard them; the war was to end shortly, the Germans had asked for an armistice, and part of the French army was to leave in motor transport to occupy German territory. Et cetera.

A general appeared (it's Gallieni!) and was loudly cheered. They could not hear what he was saying, but he was smiling and talking to people around him; another proof that things were going well. Gallieni apparently asked one of the aged drivers if he was scared of shell-fire. The old boy saluted smartly and replied: "Mon général, we'll go anywhere we're wanted."

It was a mild September night, and the men of the 103rd slept as soundly as their comrades of the 104th had done, inside the ramshackle vehicles. There were long halts, minor collisions, innumerable jolts, which sometimes roused the sleepers (what on earth are we doing here?), but they arrived at length and got out on to the road about a mile south of Nanteuil. A regiment of cavalry was waiting there; the troopers, dismounted, standing by their horses. The 104th spent the rest of the night in a small wood near by. The empty taxis were sent back to Gagny to pick up another contingent; and so they completed their two journeys.

In all, the "Marne Taxis", together with a small number of other vehicles, transported five battalions of infantry, a total of four thousand men, from Sevran-Livry and Gagny to a point near Nanteuil-le-Haudouin; a distance of some thirty miles. The numbers carried and the distance covered were modest enough by comparison with the scale of the armies and distances involved in a battle upon which the fate of France depended, but every local effort, every act of courage, and every sacrifice along the whole of the vast front carried its own weight in the final issue. Above all, the 7th Division was flung into what we now know to be the crucial point of the battle. If the Army of Paris had been over-run and defeated, the situation would have been radically changed. The legend that has grown up around the exploit of the Marne taxis is therefore amply justified; more so, indeed, than that of Roncesvalles,* which, by comparison, was a minute incident of negligible consequence.

By the night of September 7th/8th the greater part of the operation had been completed; but some of the taxis had been delayed by breakdowns, others had lost their way. During the morning of September 8th a number of drivers could be seen in a heroic effort to make up for lost time, careering madly along the roads, sometimes two or three abreast, in a cloud of dust, a roar of over-taxed engines and disintegrating coach-work. They brought their meteoric course to a grinding halt at Nanteuil, which had now become an almost chaotic mass of troops of all arms, some having arrived by rail, some by car,

*Where the rearguard of Charlemagne's army was cut to pieces by the Gascons in A.D. 778.

some on foot. Regiments of dust-laden cavalry emerged like statues from the general confusion. Fortunately for all concerned, the age of the bomber-plane had hardly begun. A solitary aeroplane marked with the German black cross appeared and was greeted at once by a fusillade of rifle fire, producing complete pandemonium. But everything comes right in the end (as Gallieni had foreseen), and he himself was already reporting to Joffre that the 7th Division was in position and ready for action.

Lieutenant Lefas, the leader of an expedition that many a general might have handled with less skill, was awarded a well-deserved mention in dispatches. In the citation the historic procession was described as the "famous convoy of taxi-automobiles". It is worth noting that the drivers were also awarded a collective mention in these terms: "The General in charge of Transport of the Entrenched Camp of Paris noted with the greatest satisfaction, during a personal inspection on the night of September 7th, the keenness and devotion to duty displayed by the drivers of the taxis. In spite of the physical strain involved, no accident and no untoward incident has been reported. The General expresses his thanks to all concerned."

Needless to say, when the drivers arrived back in Paris they immediately became objects of popular curiosity. Where had they been, what had they seen, what had they been doing? How could they refuse to reply to all these questions? And if, in the telling, the narrator waxed somewhat lyrical, who should blame him? The story he was embellishing was, nevertheless, an integral part of the whole memorable operation.

The taxi-cabs had worked on the meter. The clerks in the garages recorded the figures registered, added them up, and the drivers drew their money. They were, in fact, paid twenty-seven per cent of the amount shown on the meter, which was the lower tariff applicable "to loads of over three passengers". Some of the meters registered one hundred and thirty francs and a few centimes; equivalent (in those days) to about five pounds sterling.

12

THE PRUSSIAN GUARD COMES TO A HALT

IT SEEMED too good to be true; and, at times, they could hardly believe it. But the troops were actually advancing; and not just by a few hundred yards, dearly paid for in blood and sweat, nor even by a mile or two. Whole regiments, divisions and army corps, almost the entire 5th Army, were actually moving forward.

Early on September 7th, in light mist and fine weather, the Germans had attacked at Montceaux and Courgivaux; but the attempt was unconvincing and was clearly little more than a rear-guard action. The 18th and 3rd French Corps had quickly gained the upper hand. In almost every other sector the advance, begun at dawn, was continuing unopposed.

The men moved cautiously towards the first hazards ahead (and noticed that their officers did the same). A halt would be called and a patrol sent out before approaching a copse, a line of trees, a ditch or a silent, shuttered farm. But nothing was found. The Germans had vanished into thin air. "They've beat it and gone home," said the soldiers (in a more picturesque French idiom). "The war's over." Even the less credulous among them were convinced that a great victory had been won; and they could not understand why they were forbidden to sing as they marched.

Now and then, however, a few shots were exchanged and small isolated German detachments were rounded up; a half-section, here and there, putting up a show of resistance before surrender. Some Uhlans, caught by surprise at a crossroads, had barely time to turn before a volley unhorsed them, and the French soldiers eagerly pounced on their showy helmets; rare and treasured trophies. A German ambulance would be captured; "Kamerad!" said the drivers, as they raised their hands; and sometimes French wounded would be found inside.

There was no sound of gun-fire from the north, but in the east a distant rumble could still be heard. Rumours of a great victory drifted back over the advancing troops, growing louder with every mile they covered. The officers themselves began to feel elated, more especially as reliable reports were coming in to the effect that French aeroplanes had observed an enemy column ten miles long, marching north-east on the road from La Ferté-Gaucher to Saint-Barthélemy; and another, five miles long, with its tail at Montalivet and its head at Montmirail. And many others. The Esternay region was clear of the enemy.

At 11.40 an order was sent out by Franchet d'Esperey to all units: "The enemy is in retreat along the whole front. The 5th Army will make every effort to reach the Petit Morin river (at Montmirail) tonight." Now the victory was official. The Army Commander had used the magic name – Montmirail – like a trumpet-call, echoing Napoleon's victory there in 1814.

"Along the whole front" meant, of course, the front of the 5th Army. Neither men nor officers knew, as yet, that they were advancing, as it were, into the void, von Kluck having ordered his troops back from the south-east to meet the attack launched by the Army of Paris. The manoeuvre was now in progress that would eventually bring each of his army corps on to a front facing west.

On the right of the 5th Army the 10th Corps had moved forward after an artillery concentration upon the La Gondine trench, occupied by the Germans, along the edge of the forest of Le Gault. On reaching their objective the French infantrymen had found five hundred German bodies lying, seated or crouched in a dreadful confusion of crumpled and lacerated flesh. Some amongst them were still breathing; some were still clutching a staff or rifle to which a square of white cloth had been fixed. The French had, in fact, seen these white flags being waved above the trench; but several other groups of Germans had already abused the white flag by shamming surrender and then opening up with their machine-guns at the last minute. The French artillery had, therefore, continued firing until no sign of life could be seen.

So the 5th Army continued its advance through the stench and litter of the battlefield. Although the troops had marched so long and so far before and after Charleroi, they carried them-

selves well, and morale was high. Most of them believed that,
even if fighting still had to be done, the war would soòn be
over.

*　　　　*　　　　*

"The truth is, Monsieur, that nothing could get that idea
out of our heads. On mobilisation, people had said: 'Back for
Christmas'. During the retreat we could think of nothing at all,
we just went on and on. And now we were marching north
again, our tails were up; we even thought that it was only a
matter of days before it would be over. Just imagine; on
September 7th, my regiment never saw a single German or
heard a shot fired all day! All we heard was a rumble of gun-
fire, away on our right."

*　　　　*　　　　*

For the past twenty-four hours, however, the 5th Army
Commander had understood the meaning of that distant
gunfire. Foch's 9th Army had been engaged in bitter fighting
around the marshes of St Gond. At midday Franchet d'Esperey
had ordered his right-hand (10th) corps to slow down their
advance in order to support the 9th Army. The remainder of
the 5th Army had continued its pursuit of the enemy.

On the night of September 7th every man in the 5th Army
slept soundly, protected only by a light screen of sentries.
General Mangin, who had a taste for comfort, stayed at the
Château de Joiselle, which had been left intact by the 9th
German Corps. He slept (under the impassive gaze of an
equestrian portrait of Napoleon) in the room occupied on the
previous night by Duke Gunther de Schleswig-Holstein, the
Kaiser's brother-in-law. To be lodged in a château is the
acknowledged privilege of any general on active service.
Maud'huy, well ahead of his own advancing troops, had
reached the château of Saint-Martin du Boschet that night.

"Thank God, I can see some lights, so the place is not
deserted. We will sleep here."

The first door opened on to a drawing-room filled with
German wounded, lying on the floor. The medical orderlies
had sprung to attention.

"Bad luck! Never mind," said the 18th Corps Commander,
and shut the door again. "I suppose there's a barn somewhere?"

And he, with the whole of his staff, slept on the straw. At ten o'clock next morning, September 8th, a message from G.H.Q. arrived at the 5th Army H.Q. at Romilly: "The general situation is good. The German offensive has been halted along the whole front, and on the left we have made notable progress." G.H.Q. were not yet aware that, beyond the marshes of St. Gond, the right of Foch's (9th) Army had been driven in by a German attack of unprecedented violence.

General von Hausen, commanding the 3rd German Army, had been unwell for some days. Neither he nor his doctors, however, had realised that he was sickening for typhus. Throughout the day of September 7th, he had suffered violent attacks of dysentry, and his Chief of Staff was therefore somewhat perturbed when the general declared, late in the afternoon, that a vigorous offensive must be mounted at once, regardless of the possible losses involved.

"I feel tired," he admitted, "but I'm not finished yet. Von Kluck, on our right, is being attacked by troops from Paris, and is now exposed to a flanking attack by French forces coming from the south. It is vitally important that we should open a breach in the centre of the French front. I shall, therefore, attack. But I must be supported on my right, and also covered against possible attack on my left. Take down messages for von Bülow and the Duke of Wurtemberg."

The troops earmarked for the attack, as agreed between the three army commanders concerned, included the 1st and 2nd Guards Divisions of the 2nd Army and the 33rd and 23rd Reserve Divisions of the 3rd Army.

"The attack will be made at night," said von Hausen. There will be no artillery preparation. The approach will be carried out in complete silence. A few short, heavy salvoes of artillery will be used as a signal to the leading waves of infantry. The first assault will be made at bayonet-point. In order to ensure that only cold steel is used, all rifle-bolts will be removed.

"The Guards will never accept such an order," said the Chief of Staff. "They would look upon it as an insult. We cannot give detailed orders to the Guards; they belong to the 2nd Army."

"You can, at least, give the orders to the Saxon Regiments."

The French positions were guarded only by sentries, but main guards had been posted in the front line. Fog came down that night in an inky cloud, punctuated only by a few fires still burning in the darkness around.

The men of the 116th and 19th Regiments of the 9th Army, holding the line opposite Normée and Lenharrée, were asleep in their bivouacs, their equipment laid aside, while the guard kept watch. At three o'clock they were suddenly awakened by the first German salvo. A minute later, before they could scramble to their feet, they were being pinned down by German bayonets.

What followed, during the first shock of the assault, more resembled a massacre than a battle. In the glow of the fires still burning in Lenharrée, the outposts of the 19th had barely time to see shadowy figures wading across the Somme, in water up to their waists.

"Who goes there?"

But the sentry was dealt with before he could raise the alarm. N.C.O's were shouting: "Shoot! Shoot, for God's sake!" but their men had no time to raise their rifles before they were overwhelmed. A few shots were fired at random, many of which hit their own comrades. The official regimental histories of the incident refer to "vigorous, although necessarily last-minute resistance", but the vigour displayed was (more accurately) a despairing attempt to kill before being killed.

More officers died from bayonet wounds during this attack than during any previously recorded engagement. In the darkness and confusion officers and men were merely ghostly figures, without identity; and groups of men began running terrified and breathless towards the rear. A few minutes earlier they had been fast asleep. It all seemed like a nightmare.

But the nightmare went on. One group of survivors had herded together under some trees, listening. They could hear the Germans firing now, on their right and left. And even from behind them.

A few units held their ground until (in the official version) they were "cut down where they stood". The survivors, out-flanked on one side or other – if not on both – had no choice but to make their way as best they could towards the rear.

Certain other units – the 62nd for example – found themselves in a gap between two attacking German columns and
were able to retire in good order, guided by the sound of the
firing on right and left.

Two groups of artillery had bivouacked more than a mile
south of their guns, which (they thought) were in a safe
position behind the front line. As soon as the first German
salvoes came over they rushed to man their guns, but were
stopped by the stampeding infantry.

"To hell with your bloody guns! The Boches have got them
already!"

As a matter of fact the guns were still there, and the major
commanding one of the groups had time to have the breech-
blocks removed. The guns were recaptured two days later.

*   *   *

"My regiment was the 32nd, 18th Division. The division
wasn't in the front line, it was in reserve near Connantre,
just east of Fère-Champenoise. We were bivouacked there, in
the middle of the woods. We had piled arms and laid down,
dead tired, I assure you. Being in reserve we had nothing to
worry about, and we slept like logs; so much so that even the
shelling didn't wake me; which is saying something. Someone
shook me and I woke up, heard people shouting and running
about everywhere. I had taken off my rifle and all my gear.
Never found them again. But I found myself amongst a lot of
chaps all running, but I didn't know where to, and I saw a lot
of men shot down on either side of me. I heard firing too,
and even heard the Boches shouting behind me."

*   *   *

That morning the 32nd Regiment of Infantry lost six hundred men and fifteen officers. And yet their division (the 18th)
was in reserve more than two miles behind the 22nd Division,
which was holding the front line. Nothing so far had equalled
the ferocity and momentum of this German assault.

A battalion of the 114th Regiment, however, entrenched
along the edge of a wood south of Normée had not been taken
by surprise and was impudently holding out against a battalion
of the 4th Guards Regiment. At dawn the German artillery

opened fire on the trench; the 75's quickly retaliated, but the
fog had upset their calculations and the unfortunate French
infantry came under the combined fire of large-calibre German
howitzers and French 75's, using incendiary shell. None of the
runners got through to warn the French batteries; but the
survivors of the battalion succeeded later in making their
escape to the rear.

Whole companies, battalions and regiments were now
moving back through mist and fine rain. The Germans were
still coming on; but now they made no attempt at concealment.
Above the crackle of rifle-fire the French infantrymen could
plainly hear the shrill music of fifes and drums, growing louder
and louder.

General Eydoux, commanding the 11th Corps, had been
awakened by the first German salvoes and had made his way to
his command post at Fère-Champenoise.

"But what are all these fellows doing here? Where are you
going? And where are your officers?"

The men were retreating in disorder along the road; in
stony silence. But some would stop and tell their story. They
had been caught in their bivouacs; the Germans had come over
in hundreds; the Guards – giants, all over six feet.

"Fall in there!" said the general. "You're under the major's
orders now. Follow on behind him."

It was a disagreeable task for staff officers to round up these
stragglers and get them into some kind of order, especially as
they either took little notice or pretended they could not hear
what they were told. Once a group had been formed, however,
the worst was over; others joined in, and the ranks re-formed.

General Eydoux telephoned a report to the H.Q. of the 9th
Army: "Very heavy shelling at 3.00 hours on Morains, Ecury
Normée and Lenharrée. German attack began at 4.30. The
11th Corps is holding all its positions. The 8th Division is
ready to counter-attack."

The general's main preoccupation was to placate Foch, the
impassioned believer in offensive tactics and in the importance
of maintaining morale. An hour later, in fact, a liaison officer,
also bursting with optimism, arrived from H.Q., bringing most
encouraging news. It was unfortunate, of course, that the 9th
Army had had to meet such a heavy attack, but elsewhere the

French were definitely in the ascendant. Maunoury and the British were advancing, and Franchet d'Esperey was ready to deliver a vigorous thrust against von Bülow's flank.

"So long as you can hold on here, Sir, all will be well."

Optimism – like defeatism – feeds on itself; but not on reality. At 7.30 hours General Eydoux sent a further message to the Army Commander to the effect that the 11th Corps and the 18th Division had re-formed on the line Saint-Georges Farm – Connantre; the 18th Division had been ordered to mount a determined offensive. "I have every reason to believe that if this attack, which will be carried out by fresh, well-disciplined troops, is pressed home with due vigour, we shall be able to re-occupy practically all our original positions."

A striking example of wishful thinking. Neither from his Army H.Q. nor even from his command post at Pleurs (to which he had just gone forward) could Foch have seen that these "fresh, well-disciplined troops" were still drifting back like ships in distress, scuttling for shelter.

Foch knew nothing of what was happening; and this exasperated him. Owing to bad weather, aeroplane observers who had taken off at dawn had seen nothing; and the roar of their engines prevented them from hearing gun-fire. The only message received was at 5.00 hours, reporting the attack. Foch had sent out his interpreter, Lieutenant André Tardieu, in search of information. He returned from his wanderings at eight o'clock, just after the arrival of General Eydoux's remarkable message. Tardieu's report, however, was something quite different. When he heard what had happened to the 22nd Division Foch exploded: "What? troops caught napping in the *second line*? It's intolerable!"

His anger, however, in no way obscured his quick appreciation of a situation that was obviously critical. The enemy was certainly making a determined attempt to break through. And the 9th Army alone would not be able to withstand it.

"Ask de Langle what the 4th Army can do to support my right. Use the telephone."

The 4th Army could no nothing. The direction of its attack was not north-west, but north, and it was impossible to make any change for several hours.

"Call up Franchet. If he could attack with his right in

conjunction with our left, it might lessen the pressure on our right."

Franchet d'Esperey agreed. He ordered the right-hand (10th) corps of the 5th Army (which had already been standing-to in expectation of an attack on the previous day) to give the most vigorous support to the attack to be made by the 42nd Division (on the extreme left of Foch's army). An *attack*. Foch, in difficulties, had decided to attack. His reaction was character-istic. But he was not attacking just anywhere. Not in that sector where things were going so badly. He would be quite happy if he could, at least, hold on there.

"Tardieu, go and see Eydoux again. Tell him he must hold on. On no account must he give ground at Fère-Champenoise."

On paper, Eydoux was still holding on; but not on the ground. At 12.30 hours the liaison officer who had had such •an enthusiastic tête-a-tête that morning with the 11th Corps commander arrived back at Foch's command post in a very different state of mind. Fère-Champenoise had been lost, and the 11th Corps were falling back behind Connantre and even further south. Since dawn they had retreated nearly eight miles.

Foch was at lunch with all his staff when the news came.

"The enemy is losing men, too," he said. "And getting tired. They can't go on chasing the 11th Corps indefinitely. Especially as they know their right is beaten."

On the German right, the 5th (French) Army, which had been in action since September 5, was having to meet ever-increasing opposition from the German forces brought up from the south with the avowed object of wiping the Army of Paris off the map. Von Kluck's was the strongest, numerically, and the best-equipped of all the German armies.

*   *   *

"Their artillery was terrific. I was in the 298th. We had held on all day at Nogeon Farm, under heavy shelling. When we had had enough of it we tried making a sortie, at first with the idea of moving forward; then, later, in an attempt to withdraw. But the machine-guns opened up on us each time, and we couldn't move. We could see the villages on fire all around us. The French would attack one of them, and take it; then they would be driven out again by the German artillery and the Germans would come back. This happened several times. There was continuous fighting everywhere."

"I was in the 42nd. I saw our second-lieutenant hit three times in a few seconds. The first bullet severed his revolver-belt, the two others hit him in the right knee and the left thigh. Almost at the same time another second-lieutenant, just out of St Cyr, was hit. We propped him up against a straw-stack, but just then a shell hit it, and it caught fire."

"I was a second-lieutenant of Zouaves, in d'Urbals' battalion. D'Urbal was a giant; over six feet. At the attack on Etrepilly he went forward with just a walking-stick, smoking his pipe. He absolutely refused to lie down. 'A French officer isn't afraid of Germans,' he said: and, a second later, he was shot through the head. We had a feeling we must follow the example of men like that. Major d'Urbal's body was left lying where he fell, and we couldn't go and fetch it until next day. No one was strong enough to carry him, so we laid him across a horse's back and returned to Barcy like that. It was a queer sort of funeral procession, with bullets flying round us all the time."

*　　*　　*

There and elsewhere the casualties amongst regimental officers were as appalling as ever. The officers refused to lie down under fire, and the men hated digging themselves in. It was no question, then, of the deep trenches used later, but merely of funk-holes for protection during an advance. All official histories and other records confirm that French troops often found themselves fighting against an enemy they could not see, because the Germans were not above using their entrenching tools. During an assault the Germans – like the French – would charge over open ground, with their fifes playing and kettle drums beating; but between the assaults they took cover more readily and more efficiently than the French.

From the reports upon the fighting on September 8th, it becomes apparent, however, that in some units the officers were able to persuade their men to dig in and organise defence positions. The Zouaves, for example, who excelled in attack, and who had taken and re-taken the cemetery at Chambry after a series of bayonet charges, had dug trenches amongst the graves and cut loop-holes in the walls; and although the

German guns firing from Vareddes had more or less wrecked these improvised defences, the Zouaves had made good use of their trenches in wearing down the strength of the German attacks.

Many officers were reluctant to order their men to dig themselves in because they had been trained in the belief that the bayonet charge (with bugles blowing) was the only honourable method of infantry attack. Describing the battle of the Ourcq river, a German staff officer wrote: "The French fight like demons. They will advance under heavy fire and seem prepared to sacrifice their lives quite cheerfully."

In contrast to the tactics used during the early days of the war, the French artillery was now learning to prepare and cover an infantry attack; but the problem of spotting enemy batteries still presented a grave problem. On September 8th the 56th Division had been held up by a heavy barrage, and the officer commanding the French 75's had sought help from the aeroplane observers. The only machine available took off and circled boldly – and dangerously – over the battefield. As he passed over the French batteries the observer, having no other means of communication with the ground, threw out a written message to the gunners.

It was during this battle that a certain gunner officer (whose subsequent career was to prove as meteoric as it was brief) distinguished himself in a most unusual – and most unorthodox – manner. His name was Colonel Nivelle. The 63rd Reserve Division, on the left of the 6th Army, had lost most of its officers and was now in a precarious situation. The line was wavering; groups of men were beginning to fall back. Colonel Nivelle rode forward at a smart trot, leading a few guns of the 5th Regiment. They went ahead of the infantry, came into action at top speed and opened fire on the advancing Germans at twenty rounds a minute and at fifty yards range – with considerable effect.

Von Kluck, meanwhile, was making a personal tour of his Army front. On September 8th he had moved his H.Q. to La Ferté-Milon "in order to be nearer the scene of operations". As the convoy of H.Q. staff cars was passing close to a camp occupied by the German flying corps they saw it being attacked by French cavalry. The staff officers immediately got out of their cars, drew their revolvers and prepared to put up a fight. There was a long pause, while the battle rumbled on in the distance. But the French troopers finally moved off without having seen the little groups of generals and other important persons deployed for action.

The 4th (regular) German Corps, back from their positions south of the Marne, had now been launched against Maunoury's left wing. Their arrival more than counter-balanced the French reinforcements brought up by taxi. This French left wing was beginning to give way; the Germans had already re-captured Betz; and the 14th Division was falling back. Maunoury sent a warning message to Gallieni: "After three days of continuous fighting with all available forces already engaged, the 6th Army must give up hope of opening a breach in the enemy flank-guard; unless, of course, the German command makes a colossal blunder." Within the hour Gallieni arrived in his car. The road was congested and the last part of the journey had been over a villainously bumpy track; but Gallieni betrayed no sign of the pain he had endured.

Maunoury had established his H.Q. at Saint-Soupplets, a few miles behind the front line, in the house of a local doctor. Two captured German flags hung from the balcony.

"I have come to put your mind at rest," said Gallieni at once. "You are up against three German Army Corps, at least, and your advance has been checked. But don't worry . . . . "

What mattered was that the Army of Paris should pin the enemy down in the west; von Kluck would soon have the British Army to cope with and even part of the 5th Army. If the Germans were pushing so hard in the west it was because they realised their weakness elsewhere. Their losses were heavy, and their men were getting tired; they could not keep up the pressure much longer.

Gallieni, in fact, was repeating Foch's words, in an effort to reassure those around him; and (perhaps) to reassure himself. He was also echoing what Joffre himself had just said, by telephone, to Castelnau, who was seriously talking of evacuating Nancy. Army commanders all along the line were saying the same thing to their corps commanders, who, in turn, were passing it on to their divisional commanders until the oft-repeated refrain eventually reached regimental levels: "If they're pushing so hard here, they must feel they are beaten somewhere else." But, as a matter of fact, the Germans had advanced everywhere. Nevertheless, the private records of German fighting men clearly show that the statements made by Gallieni, Foch and Joffre were not entirely incorrect.

*   *   *

"Richter, Captain of artillery, 4th (regular) Corps, 1st Army. On the morning of September 7th our battery was in action south-east of Trocy. Five or six hundred of our guns were in position there like a circle of steel surrounding the crest that commands the approaches to Paris. We had begun firing, and the din of the guns put fresh heart into us, made us forget how tired we were. But, soon after, the French began shelling us, probably with 4.8 inch guns. Four shells would come screaming over together – each at a different pitch; then you felt the earth shake as they exploded; and the splinters would fly. Many of the men were praying as they served the guns.

"At midday, under the baking sun, we were given orders to change position. But moving about in the open was more terrifying than being shelled where we were. The teams drawing the guns and ammunition-waggons set off quickly along the road leading to the village of Etrepilly, down in the valley. When we got there we came under shelling from a flank, and, what is more, we began to hear bullets whistling around us. A column of French soldiers were advancing along the valley, and we were ordered to open fire on them. But we were being fired on ourselves and we could not find out where the shelling was coming from. At six in the evening we were told to go back to our original position; so we turned about and made for Trocy.

"Next day we began to suffer the pangs of hunger; we had had literally nothing to eat for eighteen hours. In the morning each officer and man received a lump of army bread about as big as your fist and half a glass of red wine; that was all. The weariness and exhaustion we had almost forgotten the day before came back and weighed us down; the news, too, was bad. The French Turcos had surprised our troops in a night attack at Etrepilly and had absolutely slaughtered them.

"French shells began to come over again. During the afternoon a direct hit on one of the guns of the 4th Battery sent up a mass of smoke, metal and dismembered bodies. Captain von B. telephoned to the general's Command-post and asked: 'May we move to another position?' (This time it was we who were asking.) But the orders were that we must hold on to Trocy and not move. Three other guns were knocked out. I remember I could not get the horror of it out of my mind when I lay down to sleep on the bare ground, having had nothing to eat since that morning."

"Captain Wirth (also of the 4th Corps). So we had crossed the Marne again and were marching north. We could hear the noise of the battle ahead of us, and the bridges being blown behind us to prevent the enemy attacking from our rear. We had just reached our billets that night when some troops came along who had been fighting in the front line all day. They were trudging wearily along, haggard and hollow-eyed, looking straight ahead with a grim, almost frightening look in their eyes; hardly uttering a word. Their faces were covered with sweat and dust, their uniforms dirty and torn, sometimes blood-stained. I got out what was left of my rations and gave it to them; and they snatched at it hungrily."

"Lieutenant Wilhelm Harloff, 90th Infantry Regiment, 17th Division, 9th Corps. Nothing can compare with the marching record of the 17th Division. We were on the left wing of the 1st Army, and during the counter-march we had to make a wide detour behind the lines in order to move up in support of the right wing up in the north. We left the vicinity of Esternay on the evening of the 7th and arrived at eleven that night at Guillauche, near Fontenelle. Nearly twenty miles. We were so tired that, without realising it, many of us lay down to sleep on a dung-heap. At three in the morning of the 8th we were up again, and off we went. Some French aeroplanes flew over us. At eleven in the morning we went through Château-Thierry, a pleasant town, but badly damaged by shell-fire. At one in the afternoon we had a ten-minute halt in a field; then set off again in the dust and heat. We had another ten-minute halt near La Ferté-Milon, then another six hours' march, three hours' sleep, and started off again. We finally arrived in our battle positions after having covered twenty miles in thirty-two hours, with seven hours' sleep. A record, surely. As a special honour we became known as the Kilometer Division."

"I was a second-lieutenant in the 178th Infantry, still some-times called the 13th Saxons, in the 3rd Army. I took part in the attack before dawn to the east of the Saint-Gond marshes. My regiment was not in the leading assault-units, so we arrived in front of Lenharrée at daylight. The town was on fire, standing out against a misty sky, streaked with red; like blood. A wonderful sight. The French advance-guard had put up a good defence at first, but could not stand the strain. And now the Red Trousers were running away in complete disorder, all along the line. Our task was to go in pursuit of them and round them up in the woods and spinneys where they were hiding. The French dead were lying in hundreds all along the railway line. Many French soldiers surrendered when we caught them. But in spite of this success we were longing for a rest, for we were dead-tired after the previous day's fighting and all the marching we had done before."

"Captain Kutscher, 10th Reserve Corps. We attacked on the same day and in the same sector, but on the west of the St Gond marshes, and rather later; at two in the afternoon, in fact, when the Guards had just come to a halt. The real reason was that they were fighting on empty stomachs; and we were no better off ourselves. All we had to eat on the day before was some fruit we shook down from the trees . . . ."

*　　*　　*

When the Guards had just come to a halt. Most unfortunately, I have been quite unable to put my hand on any diary belong-ing to a fighting soldier of the Guards Corps (2nd Army). The officers and men of this crack regiment were so filled with their own conceit that they probably thought that anyone keeping a diary was slightly suspect, an intellectual snob, even a pacifist. It is, nevertheless, quite evident, from all official and unofficial records of the battle of the St Gond marshes, that at 13.00 hours (according to French accounts) the Guards came to a halt; stopped dead.

At three in the morning these men had swept everything before them; they then had to continue their advance under fire from the French guns, and in blazing sun. "In open order, advance! Halt! Lie down! In open order, advance!" And so on, time after time. But for the most part these crack troops were no better fed than the other regiments in von Bülow's army, and they had marched just as far. The tremendous strain put upon them that day had over-taxed them, and they were exhausted. Every time they stopped the men would fall asleep. At 13.00 hours – no reinforcements having arrived – the Guards finally came to a halt.

This halting of the Guards on September 8th at 13.00 hours did not, however, bring the fighting to an end; nor was it a turning-point in the battle; military commentators failed even to attach any great significance to it. It is difficult, however, not to see in it a clear indication of underlying factors that explain the progress and final issue of the immense struggle.

It is easy to lose oneself in a detailed study of figures, of the hundred-and-one episodes in the battle, of artillery pre-parations, attacks and counter-attacks, of local advances and withdrawals; and to overlook the essential fact that each and every engagement was being fought by men who – on both sides – were short of food, footsore and physically exhausted. The Battle of the Marne, which was to decide the fate of France, was fought between men who, in times of peace, would have reeled under the physical strains imposed upon them. They were able – for the most part – to endure them because the heat of battle and the sense of danger released latent reserves of physical and moral stamina; or because (like the Guards east of the St. Gond marshes) they would fall asleep after long hours of fighting. They endured – or they died – but they did not collapse.

No sooner had the Guards halted than the two army corps on their right (as Captain Richter observed) launched an attack against the 9th French Corps under General Dubois, who had also been ordered to attack. General Eydoux's 11th Corps, which had just suffered a serious set-back and was precariously re-forming, had also received the same order.

Foch felt, at this stage, that if he had ordered these hungry and exhausted men merely to hold their ground they would give way. He conceived it his duty, as Army Commander, to ignore the critical condition of his troops, for the only altern-ative open to him would be to order a general withdrawal.

It was three in the afternoon. The exhausted men were taking what cover they could under the heavy shell-fire, while the enemy were filtering through the woods east and west of the marshes. Their only consolation was that the weather had deteriorated into thick mist and rain. But the shelling now seemed to be decreasing and the attacking Germans were handicapped by the rain. A short respite seemed possible. It was at this precise moment that liaison officers arrived from H.Q. with orders to attack. The harassed battalion and company commanders, unwashed and unshaven, soaked to the skin and covered with chalky mud, read the orders, shrugged their shoulders, stuffed the paper into their pockets and wondered, with a grim smile on their faces, if the whole of the H.Q. staff had gone mad.

Nevertheless, a little later some companies and battalions began to move forward; but not all, for many units could do no more than hold on, while others were forced to give way. But the attack went in.

Fighting from tree to tree in the dripping undergrowth of the woods, French and Germans stalked each other in Red Indian fashion. The Germans, astonished to meet resistance where none was before, slowed down their advance and hid themselves – like the French – amongst the trees.

In the open country beyond the woods the French infantrymen could be seen on the move again, bugles sounding the charge, while the men jog-trotted heavily but doggedly into the attack. The lively tempo of the bugles made a pathetic contrast with the slow ambling gait of the weary, pack-laden infantrymen, but they charged, nevertheless – as best they could. Their objective was Pear-Tree Ridge (La Crête du Poirier), which they had already captured once that morning; but the German heavies had driven them out, and a new assault was now being made on the sinister ridge by a battalion of Chasseurs, who were at half their normal strength after the previous day's fighting. They were now under the command of a second-lieutenant, their only surviving officer. But, once again, the few bold spirits who set foot on the ridge were met by a storm of shell; the place was untenable.

By the end of the day all units on the 9th Army front were under orders to hold on at all cost to positions then held, and to prevent any penetration by the enemy south of the marshes. *South* of the marshes? So the 9th Army had fallen back? But their front was still intact. No irreparable damage had been done.

In his first report, sent to G.H.Q. by telephone at about 20.30 hours, Foch did not reveal the stark reality of the situation. He admitted that the 11th Corps had fallen back, but he gave an over-optimistic picture of the situation on his left wing. In certain particulars ("the 9th Corps made some progress in the direction of Saint-Prix") his account was, in fact, untrue. It seems incredible that a man of such intellectual and moral integrity could be guilty of a lapse of this kind. The circumstances, therefore, deserve close examination.

For my own part, I believe that Foch, at that moment, was, primarily, anxious to be left in peace. What he wanted least of all was a telephone call from G.H.Q. saying (in effect): "So things are going badly on your front. What are you proposing to do about it?" Foch wanted to be left in peace because he was in process of elaborating one of the most interesting manoeuvres of the Battle of the Marne. In a simplified (but distorted and quite inaccurate) version, this manoeuvre later became famous: "My right is driven in, my left is falling back. Excellent. I attack with my centre." The true version, however, was quite another story.

The essential rôle of a general during a battle is to study the map; and to think. Studying the map on the evening of September 8th, Foch could see that his right was certainly driven in, and (just as certainly) that his left had fallen back. But his centre was by no means invincible; it was not protruding proudly beyond the discomfited wings on either side. And, even if it were so, the centre was in no position to attack for, by so doing, its two flanks would be in the air.

His front formed, in fact, a slightly undulating line, with no pronounced salient. What was the answer? Should he attempt to resume the offensive along the whole front, attacking in every sector at the same time? That was what Joffre had tried to do on a grand scale at the beginning of the war; and we saw what happened. On that same day, September 8th, Foch himself had given orders to attack all along the line; but, in the circumstances, that was merely another way of saying: "Hold

on everywhere." What was required now was a tactical
manoeuvre; an attack at a selected point with forces superior
to those opposing it. But at which point? And with what forces?

"The all-important thing, tomorrow, is to debouch from
La Fère-Champenoise."

Why La Fère-Champenoise? Did Foch know that it was the
point of junction between von Bülow's and von Hausen's
Armies, and therefore vulnerable? Possibly. Was his information sufficiently exact to tell him that the German front just
south of La Fère-Champenoise formed a slight salient that might
be attacked from a flank? Possibly. But I must, in all honesty,
admit that I have failed to discover any clear and precise
answers to these questions. Foch himself apparently thought it
unnecessary to give reasons for his decision; and, in any case,
it matters little. What interests us is the manoeuvre itself and
the point selected for it.

There remained the question of the troops he should use for
the attack. They must be the best available; men who had
retained their fighting qualities in spite of what they had
endured during the past weeks. Foch thought: the 42nd
Division. But could he risk withdrawing it from its present
position on the west to his front? Yes, on condition that
another unit be found to replace it.

"Take down a message for General Franchet d'Esperey."

Foch was asking (in effect) if the 5th Army could place its
right-hand army corps at his disposal so that he could withdraw his 42nd Division for use elsewhere.

Within half-an-hour the answer came by telephone: "The
10th Corps, that is to say, two regular divisions and the corps
artillery, is placed at General Foch's disposal for twenty-four
hours as from midnight."

The 5th Army's self-denying gesture on this occasion has
been acknowledged by all military historians; and rightly
so. "Desperate Frankie", the Holy Terror, had his good
points.

"Right," said Foch. "The 42nd Division will withdraw from
its present positions and move along the Army front in readiness
to attack at La Fère-Champenoise tomorrow. The left of the
11th Corps and the right of the 9th Corps will attack at the
same time and at the same place."

General Weygand asserts that Foch never uttered the famous words "My right is driven in, etc." According to General Gamelin it was André Tardieu, the brilliant and impulsive young second-lieutenant-interpreter, who (thinking he was correctly interpreting Foch's words) used the phrase in a telephone message to G.H.Q. He was greatly excited at the time, for he had been one of the admiring group of staff officers to whom Foch had disclosed his plan.

General Grossetti, commanding the 42nd Division (powerful build, short beard, gruff manner, a fire-eater) was asleep, fully-dressed, on a bale of straw in a barn at Chapton Farm when, at about ten o'clock, the liaison officer from Army H.Q., Captain Réquin, appeared with a written order from Foch. A quarter of an hour later, after a characteristic explosion of rage, Grossetti was busy dictating his preliminary orders for the move.

Since September 5th, G.H.Q. had been installed at Châtillon -sur-Seine in a large building that had once been a Franciscan monastery. The Commander-in-Chief was housed in a château near by. As at Vitry-le-François and Bar-sur-Aube, he would still sit for hours each day astride on a chair, staring at a large map; and saying nothing.

On his map the French front now appeared as a huge arc, broken by a breach on the left. There was also a breach in the German front, immediately opposite, between the 1st and 2nd German armies. Von Kluck had executed a masterly man-oeuvre in bringing back his entire army on to a front facing the Army of Paris; but the result was to create a gap between the 1st and 2nd Armies. According to all the information available, only a cavalry screen was reported in the gap; in other words, it was wide open to attack, if only Joffre could sweep into it with the necessary men and guns.

The 5th Army was moving forward into the right-hand section of the gap; but its own right wing was being held back by its obligation to support the sorely-pressed 9th (Foch) Army. On its left, facing the German gap, was the void created by the all-too-slow advance of the British forces. The latest messages from Joffre to the British G.H.Q. were at that moment being filed by one of the secretaries.

September 7th – "The continuation of the British attack would facilitate the operations of the 5th Army. The British forces will endeavour to secure a foothold beyond the Grand Morin, the Petit Morin and the Marne, successively."

September 8th – "The rôle of the British Army is to make a flanking attack against the forces opposing the 6th Army."

September 8th – "It is desirable that the British Army should, as soon as possible, occupy positions north of the Petit Morin and Marne rivers in order to prevent the enemy from making a stand behind these obstacles."

September 8th – "It is vitally important that the British forces should be in position to advance north of the Marne by tonight. The German forces opposite the British sector are now attacking the 6th Army."

September 8th – "The British forces, after having crossed the Marne between Nogent-l'Artaud and La Ferté-sous-Jouarre, will engage the left and rear of the enemy now located along the Ourcq river."

The British Army had set out early on September 6th from the line Hautefeuille-Pézarches-Vaudoy, marching with their long, swinging stride, and whistling "It's a long way to Tipperary." No enemy was to be seen. The liaison officer from Conneau's Cavalry Corps had told them: "The villages and woods are empty. All you will find are a few stragglers." Near Frétoy, however, they had met something more interesting than stragglers: three squadrons of the 1st Dragoon (Guards) Regiment covering the German retreat. They were engaged at once and driven off by famous British cavalry regiments; the 9th Lancers and 18th Hussars. After that, except for a few shots exchanged on approaching Coulommiers, they had met no opposition whatever.

An astonishing spectacle awaited them in the town. The streets were so thickly littered with empty bottles that neither vehicles nor cavalry could move along them; the horses would have broken their legs. Squads of men had to be detailed to clear the streets. According to the inhabitants, the last Germans who left were so drunk that they could hardly stand.

The country beyond Coulommiers was thickly wooded. Drunk or sober, Germans might still be found hiding there; but the British were taking no chances. By nightfall they had halted a little beyond Coulommiers, astride the Grand Morin river.

By dawn on the 8th no further advance had (as yet) been ordered, for French was still undecided. "There was the certainty that the passages of the Marne opposite my left flank between Changis and La Ferté-sous-Jouarre would be strongly guarded, and that our advance at this point would be difficult. A large force of German heavy artillery had been reported in the loop of the river near Vareddes."* Sir John had proved – on more than one occasion – that he was by no means faint-hearted; his troops had already fought (and would continue to fight) with outstanding gallantry; but Sir John must always remember the secret instructions he had been given at the outset; he could hardly have forgotten them for it was only six weeks ago: "Every effort must be made to ensure that losses in men and equipment be reduced to a minimum."

The British troops, however, moved off fairly early in the morning of September 8th, still marching with their long swinging stride, still whistling "Tipperary". If they saw a patrol of French cavalry (or knew that one was about) they would even attempt a somewhat shaky version of the "Marseillaise", for on one or two occasions already their khaki uniforms had been mistaken (in bad light) for the German *feldgrau*, and they had been fired on. No German was to be seen, however, until they reached the south bank of the Petit Morin. The bridges and fording-places were guarded, but the Germans there gave themselves up after a show of resistance. Having crossed the river, the British found a few Germans at Orly-sur-Morin and Buitron; but they, too, showed little fight. Four hundred prisoners were taken. These very weary Germans seemed glad to be picked up (as it were) by the smart, well-groomed, well-fed British Expeditionary Force; and the Tommies gathered a rich harvest of *Pickelhauben* and other souvenirs.

By nightfall on September 8th, however, no unit of the British Army had reached the Marne. "The enemy are continuing their retreat northwards," noted French in his diary, "and our Army has been successfully engaged during the day with their rear-guards on the Petit Morin, thereby materially assisting the progress of the French Armies on our right and

*Field-Marshal Sir John French, *op cit.*, p. 124.

left, which the enemy have been making great efforts to oppose."* It must be remembered, however, that French was writing history (or was, at least, preparing to do so) for the benefit of British readers, who would have resented any suggestion that the British Expeditionary Force had not greatly distinguished itself in a venture of which by no means all Britons (as yet) approved.

For Joffre, astride his chair in front of the map in one of the rooms of the one-time Franciscan monastery at Châtillon-sur-Seine, the British Army was no more than a pencilled line. Yesterday it had been oblique; today it was horizontal, but it was moving all too slowly northwards. And all the other French armies – eleven hundred thousand strong when war began, but Heaven knows their number now, we shall know that later! – were represented in similar fashion by pencilled lines; for these totally abstract symbols were the indispensable tools of a Commander-in-Chief.

The conditions under which the battle had begun were such that what was happening on the right of the front was determined by developments on the left; and it was most certainly on the left that the issue would be decided, so long as the German pressure could be held on the rest of the front.

On the right of the 9th (Foch) Army, the 4th Army under de Langle de Cary, was holding – with partial success – heavy and repeated thrusts from von Hausen. Between Foch and de Langle de Cary a gap some twenty-five miles wide was being closed, or at least masked, by the 9th Cavalry Division. Joffre had just sent out the order: "The 21st Corps of the 1st Army (General Dubail) on the Alsace front will be withdrawn from the line and placed at the disposal of General de Langle. (Joffre alone, as Commander-in-Chief, could give such an order.) The 21st Corps would therefore be able to fill the gap, in part at least, and all that was necessary thereafter was to give the order to the 4th Army Commander: "Hold on at all costs." And this, too, was the kind of order that only a Commander-in-Chief could give.

The 3rd Army, under Sarrail, lay on a line swinging north from the right of Langle de Cary's 4th Army up to the great bastion of Verdun, which was still quite unsubdued by the

*Field-Marshal Sir John French, *op cit.*, pp. 131–132.

German onslaught. Facing Sarrail, the Crown Prince was making every effort to break through the Revigny Gap. Having again studied the map, Joffre had just sent this message to Sarrail: "What matters most are your centre and your left wing. Do not think yourself under an obligation to hold on desperately to Verdun. Never mind if your communications are cut on that side. But *on no account* give ground on your left." Sarrail, as it happened, was standing firm on his left; nor was he giving up Verdun (had he done so the war, later, would have taken a very different course.) And, on the right of the French front, from the Vosges to the Meuse, Castelnau and Dubail, too, were now holding on. All these generals were holding on, which meant that every officer, N.C.O. and man was holding on, in spite of shells, machine-guns, rifles and bayonets; or, if forced back, they were willing to go forward again, each one hoping that, whoever was hit, he himself would survive. Without that hope no army at war could be kept together.

The vast front was ablaze from end to end. Joffre was now certain that the issue would be decided, the battle won or lost, during the next four or five days; in a week at most. Won, or lost? Won. Joffre was saying so and he thought so. In the early days of the war he had been utterly convinced that by attacking in every sector at once, "*toutes forces réunies*", he would sweep the Germans before him back to Metz. He had, himself, in fact, been driven back almost to the Seine; but had remained unshaken. And, later in the war, before every offensive he planned, (none of which was to succeed), he was incapable of imagining that he could fail. Why, therefore, should he think so, now?

13

VON MOLTKE FEELS THE STRAIN

"WE KNOW next to nothing; and the little we know is quite appalling."

General Helmuth von Moltke, Chief of the German General Staff, was pacing moodily up and down the corridor-cloak-room of the Luxembourg girls' school, the absurdly-inadequate office of the Operations Branch of the *Oberste Heeresleitung*. He seemed overwhelmed. The time was nine o'clock on the morning of September 8th.

In the office with him were Colonel Tappen, in charge of the Operations Branch, Colonel von Dommes, also of the Operations Branch, and Lieutenant-Colonel Hentsch, Head of the Intelligence Branch. From time to time the bulky figure of their chief would stop for a few seconds in front of the map: then resume its pacing, like a caged animal. Tappen and von Dommes looked worried; Hentsch, inscrutable.

"Your Excellency," said Tappen, "the 6th Army is, admittedly, making only slow progress in Lorraine, but it is preparing to make a further attack on Nancy as soon as its heavy artillery arrives. In the centre, the 4th and 5th Armies are heavily engaged, but there is no reason to despair of a successful issue."

The Chief of the General Staff impatiently shrugged his shoulder: "What does Lorraine or the centre matter to me? The crux of the situation is on the right."

Von Moltke raised his arm and put a finger on the map: "Don't you see this gap? Nearly twenty miles wide! And it is not between two armies but between Marwitz's cavalry and Bülow's right. Even if Joffre were a fool he would not miss his chance. And Joffre is no fool."

"Von Kluck," answered Tappen, "has certainly left troops behind on the Marne to support Marwitz's and Richthofen's cavalry. In any case, if he is successful on the Ourcq, it will be easy for him to drive out any enemy forces who had ventured into the gap. The British seem hardly to have got the bit in their teeth."

"How do you know? the latest telegram from Richthofen to Bülow was intercepted an hour ago. His cavalry have been attacked south of the Petit Morin, and are now withdrawing northwards. So the British are on the move."

"That a cavalry corps should withdraw is hardly a matter for alarm, your Excellency. The cavalry are very tired."

"That is not what alarms me. It's Bülow's telegram, this morning. He says he has been able to hold his positions *up to the present* against superior enemy forces."

"All commanders, your Excellency, say they are up against superior forces. It's just a form of words, to cover themselves."

"I know that. But what of the last part of his message? 'Owing to heavy losses, the 2nd Army's fighting strength is now reduced to the equivalent of three army corps'. Three army corps! I doubt if you realise what that means."

The Chief of the Imperial General Staff sat down in front of the map, leaning slightly against the wooden table. His face was drawn and set, as if he were witnessing some tragic scene, a shipwreck or a great fire. He went on talking incessantly, in a low, tired voice, raising his arm at times towards the map.

"It is bad enough to be held up in Lorraine or in the centre. I can accept that. But, this gap! Don't you see that, if von Bülow is out-flanked, he has no reserves left? Three army corps! He will have to withdraw north-east; and then what will happen? The gap will widen. As for von Kluck, he is caught between two stools. If he stays where he is, he will be all alone, cut off from the other armies. If his attack succeeds he is too near the entrenched camp of Paris to exploit it. He will be obliged to keep part of his forces in reserve to meet the attack of the French and British troops advancing northwards. And so?"

No one answered. They all realised that von Moltke wished to pursue his train of thought to its logical conclusion. All staff officers are familiar with such situations. Many commanders indulge in a habit of thinking aloud, and sometimes a gleam of light appears . . . .

"One ought to throw another army in *there;* the 7th Army.

But it is at present, too far north; it would take four days
to get there. We might, of course, borrow some troops from
the left wing in Lorraine. If so, it is useless to continue the
attack on the Grand-Couronné de Nancy, where we have been
squandering men and munitions for God knows how long. We
might, for instance, take the three regular corps from the
Crown Prince of Bavaria; why not?"

"He will only agree to it under protest, your Excellency,"
said Tappen. "But it is one way out. Nevertheless, before
doing so, it might be advisable to await further news as to
what is happening on our right wing."

Von Moltke started, as if waking from a dream, and looked
at Tappen: "Yes, that's true, we know nothing! It's terrible!"

At this precise moment, Maunoury's troops, grimly holding
their ground under the heaviest bombardment since the war
began, were making an almost desperate effort to beat off
von Kluck's divisions. Further to the right, the British were
cautiously moving forward; on their right again, a part of
Franchet d'Esperey's 5th Army was definitely gaining ground;
but the remainder was still held up in order to support Foch's
9th Army, in grave danger of collapse. On the rest of the
French front the line just held; but only just. And the Chief
of the German General Staff was saying: "We know nothing,
it's terrible!" and fearing the worst. Perhaps the worst (for him)
was his incredible lack of communications and liaison with the
front; the O.H.L. was receiving only the most meagre reports
and they arrived so late that, by the time they were received,
Moltke's decisions had already become ineffective. And this
had been going on since the beginning; nothing had been
done to remedy it.

"Your Excellency," said Tappen, firmly, "I think one of us
should go at once and find out exactly what is happening on the
Ourcq and on the Marne; and make your decisions known to
the Army Commanders."

"You are right," said von Moltke, with apparent relief.

"Your Excellency," said von Dommes, "I await your
orders."

"No. I think Lieutenant-Colonel Hentsch is the obvious
choice. He has already seen General von Kluck and he is well
known to General von Kuhl, the Chief of Staff."

"As you wish, your Excellency," said Hentsch.

At this point the discussion took a somewhat surprising turn. Its interest lies – paradoxically – in its sheer lack of interest, for the three men – von Moltke, Tappen and von Dommes – rambled on, exchanging vague suggestions as to what might happen on the right wing, what von Kluck might do, what von Bülow could do. Then they turned to the eastern sector and hazarded guesses as to possible action by von Hausen and the Duke of Wurtemberg, whose operations were being hampered by the developments in the west. The whole conversation drifted aimlessly on, no definite opinion being expressed, and no conclusion reached. Tappen and von Dommes seemed to have become infected not so much by von Moltke's pessimism as by a kind of inertia, as a result of which, after vaguely considering suggestions put forward they would shake their heads and relapse into puzzled silence. Tappen and von Dommes were thinking, perhaps, that it was useless to make any decision until von Moltke's messenger returned with the information they lacked. Hentsch, however, said nothing.

The scene must, indeed, have been surprising; and not without its grim humour. Three weeks earlier the staff officers of the O.H.L. had been strutting around, clicking their heels, expanding their chests, flashing their monocles and loudly voicing their views to all and sundry, in characteristic – and usually peremptory – fashion. And now three of them (including the Chief of the General Staff) had sunk to this listless, idle chatter, leading nowhere.

The meeting ended at length, and Tappen departed to draft the order to Ruprecht of Bavaria calling for the transfer of part of his troops elsewhere. Hentsch went downstairs to warn two captains of his staff to be ready to accompany him. As usual, two cars were to be used; one being in reserve. They would leave in half an hour. Then Hentsch went up again to the first floor and asked to be received alone by von Moltke. Their conversation lasted one hour.

If one knew what then transpired, it would put an end to forty years of conjecture and controversy as to where and when the issue of the Battle of the Marne was, in fact, determined.

In his manuscript report dated September 15, 1914, Hentsch summarised in *two short lines* the instructions given him by the

Chief of the General Staff. He firmly maintained this same statement at the court of enquiry set up – at his own request – in 1917. No one contested his evidence at the time, and Hentsch was completely exonerated. In 1920 Generals Tappen and von Dommes caused a stir by jointly asserting that Hentsch, in 1914, had exceeded his duties, and that his mandate had been less extensive than he claimed. But how could they know (not being present) what orders Hentsch had received from his chief? Their protest, in any case, had come to nought.

Not having been present ourselves, we can only examine the events subsequent to the Moltke-Hentsch tête-a-tête, and draw our own conclusions.

Hentsch left von Moltke's office a little after eleven on the morning of September 8th. As he was getting into his car he met von Dommes, with whom he exchanged a few banalities, without any reference to his conversation with the Chief of the General Staff, a moment earlier. Tappen and von Dommes were perhaps under the impression that Hentsch had been told to find out, on the spot, what exactly was the position along the whole front, and to make his report. And no more. Was he also expected to "inform army commanders of the decisions taken by the Supreme Command", as had been suggested during the talk between the four of them? It is impossible to answer with any certainty. No one, it seems, not even Tappen himself, showed any particular thirst for further knowledge at the time.

Hentsch had gone; he had been gone an hour. Von Moltke, back in his office, looks through the papers on his desk; but his mind is elsewhere, and he knows it. All his worried thoughts are concentrated on Hentsch and his mission. What shall we hear next?

"Your Excellency, here are two messages."

"What, already?" (Of course not; it's too soon yet). These messages had been intercepted by the G.H.Q. wireless station, and the first was timed 10.35 hours: "To 1st Army from 2nd Cavalry Corps (von Marwitz). Enemy column moving along road from Coulommiers towards La Ferté. Am now on the north bank of the Marne."

The second was timed 10.45: "From 2nd Army to 3rd Army. Urgently request vigorous action by the three Kirchbach divisions to relieve right wing. Enemy seeking to envelope right wing 2nd Army. No reserves available."

"No reserves available; Bülow sounding the alarm again!"

The French are at least fighting in their own country, their communications and transport are easy, and they can draw supplies from their depots. But how can one cope with these German armies, miles away from their base? Moltke wishes he need not re-read the messages, for worse is to come: the enemy is not only advancing between the 1st and 2nd Armies; he is also threatening Bülow's right and seeking to turn it. It is clear – abundantly clear – that Bülow will be forced to withdraw his right wing.

Withdraw? Can one even imagine oneself proposing withdrawal to the Emperor? Von Kluck's counter-march from the south could be called a "manoeuvre", but what of this? Bülow is threatened with envelopment and must pull back his right because, beyond that right, there is no possible support available. There is only the gap; and that gap is becoming an obsession, a thorn in the flesh of this heavy, sick body of his.

The day drags on, adding acute impatience to von Moltke's mental discomfort. Will Hentsch think of telephoning? Will he be able to? (for the German telephone lines are being constantly sabotaged by the French civilian population).

16.00 hours. A call from Hentsch: "The situation is good on the 4th and 5th army fronts. The 4th Army reports that the attack made by the left wing of the 2nd Army was successful." To Tappen (who took the call) von Moltke says: "Hentsch said nothing more?"

"No, your Excellency. But what he says is not too bad."

"You really think that Bülow's left could make a successful attack, when his right is outflanked?"

"Why not, your Excellency? Bülow's left is the Guards Brigade!"

The Guards. Yes, to be sure. Pity they were not Bülow's right. And why does not Bülow change them over?

"One other matter, your Excellency. His Highness, the Crown Prince of Bavaria, is asking if you will see him."

"Yes; I'm not surprised."

Heaven preserve one from having Royal Highnesses to command. They behave in the most off-hand manner, they never reply to letters, never send in reports and are constantly complaining. The hefty Rupert, with his enormous moustaches, has no doubt come to protest against having troops taken from him.

No. The news has not yet reached him. He has (as yet) only received an order calling upon him to transfer six ammunition columns to the Imperial Crown Prince.

"In other words, I am being told to call off my attack on Nancy!"

Yes, my dear Royal Highness. That's exactly what it does mean. But will Moltke say it as bluntly as that? No. Moltke is aggressive, but weak-minded, and he now lets himself get embroiled in a long discussion of the previous exploits of the 6th Army; then, suddenly tiring of the argument, he gives way. The attack on Nancy may continue, but on condition that, in certain (purely hypothetical) circumstances, etc. etc. And so Moltke gives his weakness a semblance of authority. But after all, it matters little; all that matters is to have news of Hentsch.

20.00 hours. An officer brings a message from 3rd Army: heavy losses; von Hausen has thrown in all his reserves, but he will go on attacking tomorrow to *drive the enemy back*. So von Hausen had lost ground? Ten minutes later, a radio message (at last) from Hentsch states: "Situation and impression 3rd Army entirely satisfactory."

"'Entirely satisfactory' sounds quite good, don't you think, Tappen?"

"Certainly, your Excellency. Very good indeed."

Watching him closely, some of his colleagues are beginning to notice a change in von Moltke. The man's vitality seems to be impaired; his moral fibre snapped or, at least, sagging. He now finds it difficult to believe that news can be good, and even good news fails to remove his visible anxiety. Von Moltke comes for a moment into the Operations Room, asks a few vague questions, hardly listens to the replies and then retires to his own room. Half an hour later he comes back.

If only he need not look at that map. This column, reported this morning on the road from Coulommiers to La Ferté-sous-Jouarre, where is it now? How can it be stopped? By Marwitz's cavalry? Ridiculous. Of what use is cavalry against rifles, machine-guns or artillery? And is there only one column? There may be several! This column would certainly not advance alone, leaving its flanks exposed; there must be other enemy columns on its right and left, Heaven knows how many! And they are pouring into that gap . . . .

In his anxious state, his imagination was running riot. No one ever knew – least of all von Moltke himself – at what precise point this began, for one must remember that his career as a soldier had been thrust upon him; it had always been a crushing burden upon the nephew of the great von Moltke. It would be a mistake, however, to imagine that he was mentally unbalanced. As a private citizen, doctor or artist, he could have been happy and successful. But the responsibilities he had inherited – unwillingly in a sense – had broken his spirit.

Midnight on September 8th. And, now, one in the morning of September 9th. The staff officers are still at work in the cloak-room corridor of the Operations Room. Ten past one. An officer from Signals brings a radio message from Hentsch,* timed 23.30 hours, sent out by the 2nd Army transmitter. Tappen reads it, and is silent for a moment or two.

"Find the duty A.D.C. If the Chief of Staff is not asleep, see that he gets this message."

Von Moltke is not asleep. He is still seated at his table, beginning a letter to his wife, to whom he writes almost daily.

To picture Moltke's state of mind, we need only look over his shoulder as he sits, alone in his office, writing, on the evening of a day that had left the fate of France still undecided:

"I cannot find words to describe the crushing burden of responsibility that has weighed on my shoulders during the last few days and still weighs upon me today. The appalling difficulties of our present situation hang before my eyes like a dark curtain through which I can see nothing. The whole world is in league against us; it would seem that every country is bent on destroying Germany, once and for all."

Meanwhile, one hundred and twenty-five miles away, Lieutenant-Colonel Hentsch was asleep in a French house; sleeping the sleep of the just, although, an hour before, he had

*The message from Hentsch read: "Situation serious, but not desperate, on the left wing of the 2nd Army."

opened flood-gates that would bring disaster to the German armies on the Marne.

His two grey cars had arrived at 16.00 hours at Varennes, H.Q. of the 5th Army. Hentsch had immediately asked to be received by the Crown Prince.

"I have come on a mission of information," he said. "And I have the honour to communicate it, first, to your Imperial Highness. Based on the latest reports received, the situation, as we understand it at the O.H.L., is as follows. . . ."

The Crown Prince had listened carefully to Hentsch's exposé. "As I understand it," he answered, "the situation is by no means unsatisfactory; but our initial successes and our swift advance have come to a temporary halt. Is not that so? Very well; report to the Chief of the General Staff that the 5th Army is ready to continue its advance. We still have ample means at our disposal, and our morale is excellent."

The answer given, an hour later, at the Duke of Wurtemberg's 4th Army H.Q. was no less optimistic. At 18.00 hours Hentsch had arrived at the 3rd Army H.Q. at Châlons-sur-Marne. The Saxon General, von Hausen, still plagued by violent attacks of dysentery, still had no idea that he was, in fact, suffering from typhus. But he was even more optimistic than either the Imperial Crown Prince or the Duke of Wurtemberg: "I intend to split the French front wide open. I am now going to draft my orders for tomorrow. I was even going to send a copy to Luxembourg."

Hentsch, with due respect, had expressed his approval, but had hardly dared to congratulate von Hausen upon his diligence in reporting his plans to Luxembourg; this was an extremely unusual concession on the part of a German army commander. At 19.45 hours the two grey cars arrived at Montmort, twelve miles south of Epernay, and drew up in front of the verandah of the large house where von Bülow, the 2nd Army commander, had established his H.Q.

"I am really extremely sorry, but His Excellency is not in."

The A.D.C. treated this lieutenant-colonel with the peculiar deference due to an emissary visibly invested with the Olympic power and authority of G.H.Q. Bülow, the veteran of eighteen-seventy, always declared that he was an old man (at sixty-eight) and that he was tired and ill; but he was out and about all day.

"Ah, there is his car. You haven't had long to wait."

"I have just got back from my advanced command post at Fromentières. The news is bad. A panic has occurred somewhere near Champaubert, at the junction of the 10th Regular and the 10th Reserve Corps. It seems that the enemy stormed into the breach. I am going there, now, to see for myself what happened. I am leaving in five minutes, when I have looked through a few papers. Would you like to come with me, Hentsch?"

As a matter of fact, nothing – or very little – had happened. There had been an attack, but it had been quickly countered. Bülow should have been pleased, but he still looked gloomy. Coming back in the car with Hentsch, he had complained incessantly about his right wing. He seemed querulous and dispirited:

"My right is really very weak. It is giving way and completely in the air. There is an eighteen-mile gap between it and the 1st Army; and not a word, naturally, from von Kluck. He is supposed to be under my command, but he completely ignores my existence. You are staying the night at Montmort, of course. You must dine with me.

Dinner was grim. Bülow, whose conversation was never very amusing, continued to complain of von Kluck's behaviour. His Chief of Staff, General Lauenstein, took pills during the meal, ate little and drank nothing. And Hentsch remained silent.

The conference took place immediately afterwards, since this was the object of Hentsch's visit. But this time it was Bülow who at once monopolised the conversation. On a large map opened on the table he pointed out the gap between his own and von Kluck's armies; the gap that was now von Moltke's nightmare. He showed the red arrows representing the enemy's army corps. The British Expeditionary Force appeared to be shooting, rocket-like, up from the south, as if French's troops, in a mad rush, would soon be arriving in Montmort itself.

"If I had any reserves I could send them in *here*. But I have none. Once the enemy crosses the Marne my right wing will be in grave danger. And what about von Kluck? He will not be able to hold on indefinitely in front of Paris. Even if he wins a few minor battles there, he will be caught between two fires."

Hentsch still kept silent; he had no comment, for he agreed
with every word.

"The French attack against von Kluck's flank," Bülow
continued "was now producing its logical – one might say
even mathematical – consequences."

"A message, your Excellency, from the 13th Division."

Bülow looked up quickly; the 13th Division was covering the
right of the Army front. This report stated that it had just
been severely shaken and was falling back. Lauenstein plotted
on the map the details given in the message. The gap, the
nightmarish gap, had grown even larger; by some eight miles.

"It may be wise to consider the possibility of the 2nd Army
withdrawing to new positions."

It was Lauenstein who had made the remark. Although his
name was seldom mentioned later, General Lauenstein was
the first to suggest (in so many words) an unconditional
withdrawal; a withdrawal, that is to say, in the near future,
without waiting on events. He had looked steadily at von
Bülow as he spoke.

"There is no other solution," Bülow had answered, watching
Hentsch.

Even an army commander is conscious of the prestige of an
emissary invested with the authority of G.H.Q. This lieutenant-
colonel had (so far) described his mission as purely informatory;
but surely he could express an opinion? He would, no doubt,
reply that a decision to withdraw was a serious matter; that it
would be wise to refer it, first, to Supreme Command, and in
the meantime, Bülow must hold on at all costs. Or he might
say: "In view of the circumstances I will go and see von Kluck
at once, and then come back and inform you of the situation
on the 1st Army front; so that you can judge the position for
yourself."

Very calmly, Hentsch had replied: "Withdrawal is the
logical solution. I have been given instructions by the Chief
of the General Staff covering the possibility of a withdrawal by
the 1st and 2nd Armies. I have full authority to co-ordinate
their retreat. It should be carried out in such a way as to
ensure that the wings of the two armies, which are at present
some distance apart, will operate their junction at Fismes.
And the gap will thus be closed."

Von Bülow had by no means appeared to be shocked. On the contrary he had seemed relieved. So G.H.Q. had provided for every eventuality? Everything seemed perfectly simple, perfectly natural; as if this withdrawal were in the nature of things; a possibility that could be foreseen, even at the outset of the campaign. Bülow and Lauenstein had immediately begun preparation of orders for the following day; withdrawal of the 13th Division and the 13th (Reserve) Corps. It was to be clearly understood that the withdrawal applied only to the right wing; the remaining units would go on fighting, and even continue to attack.

Bülow was considered an able tactician, but one wonders how long he imagined he could continue to withdraw his right while advancing with his left. Did he realise he was starting, as it were, a chain reaction, which – even if nothing worse happened – would postpone indefinitely all hope of a German victory? But von Bülow, most probably, was concerned above all, for the fate of his own army; and in this he followed the pattern of all German army commanders. As for Hentsch, he had already gone to bed.

14

THE MESSENGER OF DEFEAT

DURING THE rainy season the marshes become impassable.
First, the dried-up cracks between the hummocks disappear;
then the whole area takes on an appearance of uniformity, a
kind of humid richness, somewhat like ill-tended pasture-land.
But woe to him who ventures thereon. For centuries the
monks of St Gond had known all too well, that, once the
rains had come, it was folly to put a foot outside the narrow,
paved path that led to safety. There were times even when
parts of the causeway itself would be sucked into the morass.

It was early September, and autumn not even begun. But on
the night of September 8th/9th heavy rain was falling. The
men of the 9th Corps, in bivouac or on guard, were drenched to
the skin. Their uniforms, once stifling in the hot sun, now
clung, sodden and heavy to their half-frozen limbs; but the
officers told them cheerfully: "This rain is a good thing." It
was turning the marshes into an impassable barrier, a grave
for guns and even for infantry. So let the kindly rain come
down! Never mind if we shiver.

An infantry bivouac, in September, 1914, had to be seen to
be believed. I never saw one myself, but I have in front of me
a few "coloured" photographs – crudely coloured by hand, I
imagine – that give a realistic impression of what one looked
like. The caption reads: "Our soldiers of 1914 under the trees;
our front-liners, worthy followers of their glorious ancestors of
the Empire." The men can be seen, seated, lying down,
propped upon an elbow, some standing; all looking straight at
the camera. Some are smiling, some serious. ("I wonder if I
shall still be alive when she sees this?") The wood-fire seems
minute.

On the night of September 8th/9th the rain had put out the
smouldering fire and the men were lying on the bare ground,

with no covering but a rain-soaked blanket. The unfortunate Africans of the Moroccan Brigade were also there, in their scanty linen uniforms. They had had no hot meal for three days, and were lying close together, shivering in the rain. The night seemed endless. A cold mist hung over the marshes.

A few trenches had been dug, south of the village of Mondement. Compared with those built later, they were shallow and crude, but their occupants had no fault to find with them; they could, at least, stretch their blankets across them for shelter.

At about five in the morning the dark fog lifted in the first light. As dawn broke the rain ceased. And, half an hour later, the shelling began once more; German and French guns kept up their infernal duel. Within a few minutes the shallow little trenches had been pounded and obliterated. At six o'clock, battalions of German assault troops were seen, through the mist, marching, unhurried, towards the village of Mondement. The French shells rained down upon the houses, the château and the church, but the Germans pressed on.

"In open order, advance!"

The shivering, hungry Moroccans emerged from the woods and jogged into the attack behind their officers; they would follow them anywhere; until the officers were no more. And what could they do then? They broke and drifted back; and were sent into the attack again.

The Germans had got into Mondement and were setting up their machine-guns there. Dozens of them. From the church, the château and the great farm close by came the ceaseless rattle and whine of bullets. There would soon be few Moroccans left. When, after each abortive attempt, they retired to the edge of the wood for a brief rest, the weary men fell asleep.

On the right of the marshes, also, the German attack had forestalled the offensive Foch had planned. By six-thirty, two divisions of the 11th Corps were already falling back. A curious incident occurred in this sector. The 268th Infantry, were seen retreating along the road towards Salon, accompanied by a number of civilian motor-cars. Inside were wounded men of the 268th, who had been hurriedly picked up before the regiment withdrew. The cars had, in fact, been "requisitioned" in Gourgançon by a private soldier, a reservist.

Thanks to this man's initiative, the cars were salvaged; and (above all) the wounded were brought back to safety.

"No," repeated Lieutenant-Colonel Lévy, "I simply cannot order these men to attack; it is quite impossible!"

He was commanding, not a regiment but the 103rd Brigade – a reservist unit – holding the line south of Linthes. On the previous night, he, too, had been ordered to attack, and he had made a tour of the line and seen the troops asleep in their bivouacs, looking more like corpses than living men. But they turned out when daylight came and lined up, although they seemed to be walking in their sleep. They had all been on half rations for the past two days. Lieutenant-Colonel Lévy called his officers together and said: "I want you to tell me, yes or no, whether you think these men are in a fit state to attack. I ask each of you to give me his opinion."

They were all agreed. The lieutenant-colonel reported to the divisional commander, and the attack was cancelled.

Unfortunately, neither the brigade nor the divisional commander could give orders to the Germans opposite, who were the Grenadiers of the Guards Division, von Bülow's left. The exhausted reservists of the 103rd Brigade were suddenly faced with these tough, strapping, regular soldiers who, twenty-four hours before, had pushed Foch's (9th) Army back by nearly eight miles. The Guards' attack on the 11th Corps was made at the exact spot chosen by Foch, the day before, for his flanking attack by the 42nd Division.

This division, a crack unit commanded by General Grossetti, was now marching from the western to the eastern end of the Army front, in accordance with Foch's plan. But, to his surprise, General Grossetti received a visit from a liaison officer, Captain Réquin, who had just witnessed the capture of Mondement by the Germans.

"If they consolidate their position at Mondement, mon Général, they will then move up on to the plateau and the German artillery will overlook the plain below. The 9th Army will be unable either to manoeuvre or even to disengage; and it will be wiped out. The French front will be cut in two; and that will mean total defeat; the end. You must somehow prevent the Germans debouching from Mondement!"

"Heavens above, man, make up your mind what you want!"

shouted Grossetti. "I can't march my men along to Fère-Champenoise and deal with Mondement as well!"

Someone said: "But the divisional artillery can, Sir. I can take my batteries into action on the Broyes plateau, wipe out Mondement and rejoin the division in its new positions."

The speaker was Colonel Boichut, a firm believer in close infantry-artillery co-operation (which he preferred to call "integration") and a remarkably clear-thinking, imaginative officer. He had already distinguished himself in action on several occasions, and was to become one of the most brilliant personalities at G.H.Q.; but owing to his non-conformist ideas, he was never allowed to occupy a high-ranking position.

The reduction of Mondement by Boichut's guns, proved, however, a longer operation that day than he had supposed, because the château was masked from view by the woods around it.

The men of the 5th Army, on Foch's left, had crawled out of their chilly, rain-soaked bivouacs and resumed their advance. No German shelling, no German attack. By six-o'clock the advance-guards of the 39th moving very cautiously forward, had reached Montmirail.

"Come on! Come on! They've gone! They left last night!"

Doors and windows opened everywhere. The Germans had cleared out, leaving only their wounded behind. Thirty minutes later General Mangin himself drove through the town. Men, women and children were grouped at the doors of their houses. The men doffed their hats, the women wept; so, too, did some of the men; perhaps because most of them were old.

North of Boissy-le-Repos the infantry were cautiously making their way up the slopes on the north bank of the Petit Morin, finger on trigger, searching every hazard, every spinney and bush. Not a soul to be seen. The whole countryside was strewn with debris the Germans had left behind them, now becoming a familiar sight: sacks filled with loot, linen, shoes, bric-à-brac and clocks. But – surprisingly – there was, also, food: bread, meat and tinned foods, although on both sides the troops had gone hungry for days. Where disorder and confusion prevail, such anomalies are not unusual. It was significant, too – and encouraging – to see so many abandoned German rifles.

Near Mondant a German army car was found, apparently waiting, on the side of the road. There was nobody inside, but the car was stacked with large-scale military staff maps, beautifully printed, "Made in Germany". French subalterns, captains, majors and even colonels, who, six weeks after mobilisation, were still without reliable maps, now eagerly seized upon these excellent maps of the French front, provided by the enemy.

There were dead horses in the fields and on the roads, and the air was foul as the men passed by. Dead Frenchmen, too, lay in the fields and dead Germans in shallow trenches. In a trench to the north of Bourbeton they saw the heads and shoulders of German soldiers apparently on the look-out above the parapet. But, after having fired several shots at them without effect, the French discovered they were dummies; beside them, on the floor of the trench, lay the bodies of dead Germans.

At his H.Q. in Villiers-Saint-Georges, Franchet d'Esperey was studying a report from a pilot-captain of the flying corps, who had just completed a flight over the 5th Army sector. To the right of it he had observed gun-flashes, smoke and shell-bursts, indicating the heavy fighting in which Foch's 9th Army was engaged. On the north bank of the Marne he had seen enemy columns marching north; and on his way back he had noticed (on his right) that the line of gun-flashes, smoke and shell-bursts had already receded. Franchet d'Esperey wondered if the 5th Army, in order to give full support to the 9th (Foch), was not making a definite turning movement eastwards? He must examine the situation more closely.

"Army H.Q. will move at once to Montmirail."

The able-bodied citizens of Montmirail were now engaged in digging enormous graves, some for dead horses, some for dead men. There were corpses everywhere; even in the narrow passages of the houses.

"On the left wing the Allied Armies, including units of the forward defence of Paris, are advancing steadily, from the banks of the Ourcq to Montmirail. The enemy is retiring in the direction of the Marne, between Meaux and Sézanne." The communiqué of September 8th had brought comfort and joy to every Parisian; their flickering hopes were reviving. Women, children and old people were streaming out towards the eastern and northern gates of the city, bombarding with questions every possible vehicle or person arriving there: the wounded, the "Territoriaux", the cyclists; even the *octroi* employees.

"My husband (or 'my son', or 'my father') is at the front. Have you come from there?"

Other groups crowded along the pavements (particularly in the rue La Fayette, where the famous taxi-procession had passed) "to see the prisoners coming in". I well remember my excitement at the idea of seeing prisoners arrive. In the minds of the spectators there was not only an impression of victory; there was also a morbid thirst for vengeance; and I can still hear grown-ups around me muttering threats of torture and other dread punishment. They (of course) did nothing of the sort; for one glance at the wretched captives sufficed; and, in any case, on that particular day they waited in vain, for no prisoners arrived.

The churches were crowded. At Saint-Etienne-du-Mont three thousand candles were lit around the shrine of Saint Geneviève, the Patron Saint of Paris, and a *tridium* was celebrated. Huge crowds of worshippers overflowed on to the square outside, and beyond, fervently singing the penitent's prayer: *Parce Domine*. During the silences the distant rumble of guns could still be heard in the north and east.

The successive stages of the battle of the Ourcq may, perhaps, be more easily followed in diagrammatic form. On September 6th the Army of Paris would appear as a slightly undulating line from north to south, with its tail just north of Meaux and its head near Betz. On the 7th this line becomes slightly tilted, its southern end having moved slightly east and its northern end, where the left wing was forced back, slightly west. Little change took place during the 8th; on the 9th the line takes a right-angle bend, the southern half having again moved slightly east, while the northern half becomes horizontal as the left wing of the 6th Army yields to the pressure of the German right.

The men of the 6th Army were very hungry and very tired; and now they were becoming impatient. "What the hell are the *Engliches* doing?" they asked. They had been told that their rôle was to hold on until the British arrived; the British Army was on its way up from the south and would take the Germans in the flank and rear.

"Perhaps they are attacking the German artillery already. You can see, the shelling is not so heavy."

It was true that, on the right of the front, the shelling was not so severe. The German heavy battery at Trocy, which had hammered the French assault-waves on the plateau the day before, was silent at last; and so were many others. The private soldier did not know, as yet, that it was the French artillery that had knocked them out, but the N.C.O.'s said: "They're done for, come on!" And they went on.

Trenches had to be attacked and captured, one by one. At Trocy and at Vareddes there were Germans still showing fight among the smoking ruins of houses and the shattered debris of their own guns. But the French were using only their bayonets now; even on those who put up their hands. (No use being squeamish, better have done with it.) These men, launched into yet another attack, were using up the last remaining vestiges of physical and moral stamina in their over-strained, half-starved bodies; their nerves were stretched to breaking-point. Once a position had been carried they would collapse, breathless; then ask: "What do we do now? Eat? If we don't, we're done for!"

The men who had captured Etrepilly, however, said very little. They found themselves looking at the smoking ruins of a very large steel hangar of which walls and roof had disappeared; but on the blackened floor were grim remains of two hundred and fifty German wounded, who had been lying on bales of straw when the shelling began.

The German batteries were busier on the left of the Army front, and it seemed that more and more German troops were being flung into the battle. They were pouring out of the woods along the Gribette river, out of Antilly and Betz, out of Montrolle wood; they were even debouching from the great forest of Villers-Cotterêts. These were von Kluck's 4th (Regular) Corps, the last remaining units brought up from the south to support his right wing. Their arrival on the scene was a bitter blow for the hard-pressed French infantry, for these 4th Corps regiments were advancing like swarms of ants, apparently

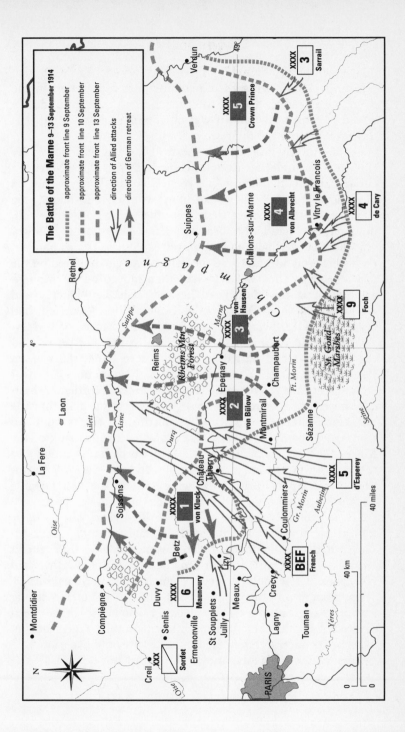

The Battle of the Marne 9–13 September 1914

········· approximate front line 9 September
– – – – approximate front line 10 September
▬ ▬ ▬ approximate front line 13 September
⇑ direction of Allied attacks
➡ direction of German retreat

undeterred by the French 75's. As they approached the French lines they would bring their machine-guns into action in the open, with deadly effect. If the French stood their ground they would be wiped out; and it was no consolation to be told that the British were on their way.

On the morning of the 9th the British Cavalry, followed by the 1st Corps under Sir Douglas Haig, had crossed the Marne at Charly and at Saulchery, between Château-Thierry and La Ferté-sous-Jouarre. They had met with no resistance; the Germans had not even destroyed the bridges. Further on, however, they had had to deal with a few batteries and infantry rearguards covering the German retreat. These troops had put up a sterner fight than those the British had encountered on the previous day. The 1st Corps had then moved on to the high ground along the main road between Château-Thierry and La Ferté. The 2nd Corps, under General Smith-Dorrien, had crossed the river lower down, at Nanteuil-sur-Marne and Méry.

The 3rd Corps, under General Allenby, had not yet crossed the Marne; it had halted on the southern bank, short of La Ferté-sous-Jouarre. The British right, having made a swift advance during the morning, had also received orders to halt. "It was essential (wrote French) "to my general plan that the 2nd Corps should not get too far north until the 1st and 3rd Corps were completely established on the further bank of the Marne."* No one knew why the 3rd Corps had halted; and the delay was the more regrettable because the 3rd Corps, that is to say, the British left wing, was in the best possible position to come quickly to the aid of the Army of Paris.

Great efforts were made, after the Allied victory in 1918, by official demonstrations of goodwill and mutual congratulation, to dispel the undoubted resentment caused by French's failure to bring swift support to the 6th Army. Feeling had run high. "The only criticism which may perhaps survive when present-day incomprehension and – it is not too strong a word – ingratitude due to lack of knowledge have been dissipated, is that the British suffered at this stage from an excessive prudence engendered by bitter previous experience."† Spears' comment is fair, and to the point. But he adds: "The

*Field-Marshal Sir John French, *op cit.*, p. 133.
†Major-General E. L. Spears, *op cit.*, p. 434.

fact remains, however, that the British Army crossed the Marne thirty hours ahead of any French infantry!" This, however, is incorrect. The 1st Zouave Regiment, in the 38th Division, was already covering Château-Thierry (on the north bank of the river) by the evening of September 9th; and a brief glance at the map will show that the Marne takes a sharp and pronounced turn southward after Château-Thierry to the point where the British crossed; furthermore, the British troops encountered little or no opposition until they reached the Marne.

Little is to be gained by reopening an out-dated controversy; but even today, when the battle of the Marne is mentioned, one may be certain that a voice will be raised in criticism of the *lenteur* of the British. The first part of Spears' reply is excellent; and I have already drawn attention to the reasons for French's excessive caution.

About twelve miles north of the British advance-guards the two cars with Hentsch and his assistants were travelling from east to west, having left von Bülow's H.Q. at Montmort at eight on the morning of September 9th. They were now on their way to von Kluck's H.Q. at Mareuil, five miles south-south-east of La Ferté Milon. Their speed had been reduced to a crawl.

The gap – the famous gap – facing the British Army and the left of the 5th Army was now hopelessly congested by traffic of every sort. Hundreds of horse-drawn Army vehicles filled the roads in either direction, moving at a snail's pace – or not at all – in a solid mass. Complete chaos reigned at every cross-roads. Drivers swore; or stood petrified under the lurid objurgations of their incensed N.C.O.'s; others got together, when their horses had collapsed from exhaustion, and pushed the now useless vehicle into the ditch. Wounded men would climb painfully out of their halted ambulance and thread their way, walking or hopping through the crowd. Detachments of cavalry, like visitors from another world, would leave the road and file slowly and silently across the fields, until the bottle-neck was passed.

Hentsch and his two cars jogged slowly on. Ambulances from the left wing of the 1st Army were making their way back to Fère-en-Tardenois, beçause "the British cavalry had been seen north-west of Château-Thierry". Hentsch, in the hope of avoiding the convoy, had turned north; but at Neuilly-Saint-Front and La Ferté-Milon he had run into more columns of ambulances, this time from von Kluck's right wing. "We have been fired on by French cavalry," they said.

Several times during the journey Hentsch had left his car to reprimand an offending driver or to question the leaders of convoys or cavalrymen. But now he had sunk back moodily into his corner and was silent. He was perhaps becoming more and more convinced – by the chaotic disorder around him and by the endless procession of ambulances – that retreat was the only solution.

Von Kluck's Chief of Staff was still General von Kuhl, the "remarkable personality with the eye of an eagle"; and it was he who received Hentsch when he arrived soon after midday on September 9th. Von Kuhl seemed in no way perturbed, and his opening comments on the situation of the 1st Army were, in fact, extremely optimistic.

"Have you not received a message this morning from the 2nd Army?" asked Hentsch.

"Yes, a radio at seven-thirty. General von Bülow reports a withdrawal by his right wing."

After a pause, von Kuhl went on: "There was a radio, also, from von Marwitz. His cavalry were present when some unit of the British Army crossed the Marne; they narrowly escaped being caught . . . . We had, therefore, to pull back slightly on the extreme left in order to avoid any danger of being attacked from the rear."

Von Kuhl, however, seemed in no way disturbed by this minor adjustment. "The French left is retreating on our front. We are now trying to turn their flank."

"Do you think we might begin our conference at once?" asked Hentsch.

"By all means; in my office. I will get Colonel Bergmann to join us."

Bergmann was the Deputy Chief of Staff. As soon as he came in the three men sat down side by side in front of a map of the 2nd Army front, spread out on the table. But Hentsch, without looking at the map, began by saying:

"It has taken us five hours to get from Montmort to here. Fifty miles. Do you realise what that means? The roads behind your left wing are in a state of chaos."

"Chaos, perhaps, is putting it rather strongly," said von Kuhl.

"Then let me tell you what we saw."

Hentsch then gave an accurate and vivid description of his journey. A silence followed. Then Hentsch got out of his chair, took a charcoal-pencil and began drawing lines on the map.

"Here is the line of retreat of the 2nd Army left. The whole Army is in an indescribable state of fatigue. Here are the British and 5th French armies marching into the gap. The 1st Army is now in grave danger. Even if you crush the left of the 6th Army opposite you, the remainder can always withdraw to the line of forts (which are in easy reach of their supplies in the entrenched camp) and hold out there for a long time. In the meantime, your flank will be driven in. That is the position; and you cannot alter it."

Hentsch went over to a large map on the wall. "The situation as a whole is not good. The 6th and 7th Armies have been brought to a halt in front of the line, Nancy-Epinal; the 5th has been checked at Verdun. Von Hausen is standing firm and even moving forward; but, on his right, von Bülow's army is now a shambles."

In regard to the dangerous situation on the 1st Army front, Hentsch's exposé was unanswerable; but it was inaccurate, so far as the rest of the front was concerned. He had not visited the advanced guard, nor even the front line of the 2nd Army; and yet he had unhesitantly described it as a shambles. Neither von Kuhl, however, nor his Deputy Chief of Staff had any knowledge of what was happening outside their own sector; and they were obviously impressed by the quiet, precise manner in which Hentsch had put his case.

"And what conclusions should one draw from all this?" asked von Kuhl.

"The Supreme Command considers that all the armies should be re-grouped as soon as possible; the 3rd to the north of Châlons, so as to join up with the 4th in the Verdun area at Clermont-en-Argonne; the 2nd and the 1st should withdraw in such a manner as to make their junction at Fismes."

Hentsch made a vague gesture towards the northern part of
the map: "A new army is being formed in the Saint-Quentin
area. We can then draw up a new plan of campaign, and
resume the offensive."

Von Kuhl and his deputy-chief again relapsed into silence
for a moment or two; then von Kuhl asked: "I take it these
decisions come from the Chief of the General Staff?"

"Yes," replied Hentsch. "In the present circumstances no
other course is open."

"Very good. I will at once give General von Kluck a full
report on our conversation and ask him for further orders."

These, perhaps, were not von Kuhl's exact words; but it
seems reasonably certain that he said something of the kind.
And it is at this point that we come to what may be called the
Mystery of Mareuil. Why was not von Kluck present at the
meeting?

According to certain German historians, von Kuhl "then
went to see the Army Commander". Another version ran:
"General von Kluck, who was near by, was then informed."
"Near by", perhaps, but where, exactly?

It is surely inadmissible that von Kluck should not have been
present at a meeting at which the future of his own army
was in question? It has been argued that: "The role of the
Chief of Staff is more important in the German than in the
French army. It was always he who collected the necessary
information and drew up suggestions for submission to his chief.
It was therefore, his personal responsibility – and his alone –
to conduct the meeting with Hentsch, etc." This may have
been true in principle and in regard to more or less routine
matters; but surely not on such an occasion as this? Hentsch
had already made personal contact with von Bülow, von Hausen
the Duke of Wurtemberg and even with the Crown Prince;
and it stands to reason that he should also have seen von Kluck.

The fact remains that no oral or written statement has ever
been made as to von Kluck's whereabouts on that particular
day. Several people must have known it, but they held their
peace, and von Kluck himself never disclosed the secret. There
is a touch of drama in this sudden disappearance of the leading
character at the very moment when Fate – in the person of
Lieutenant-Colonel Hentsch – was plunging the 1st Army into

the vast operation already set in motion by the withdrawal of von Bülow's right wing. Several possible reasons have been put forward to explain von Kluck's mysterious absence:

1. That he was deliberately hiding somewhere in his own H.Q., and did not wish to meet Hentsch, because he resented having been placed under von Bülow's command; or because he feared the wrath of G.H.Q.

2. That von Kluck was at the time regaling himself at lunch in some château or other, and therefore neglecting his duties as Army Commander.

3. That he was ill, and had delegated von Kuhl to act for him.

4. That he had been wounded the day before during a clash with French cavalry near La Ferté-Milon.

(3) and (4) seem barely plausible. If von Kluck had been wounded or ill, von Kuhl would have said so; and von Kluck, in fact, was seen to be in perfectly good health next day. I am inclined to favour (1). Von Kluck was probably thinking: "O.H.L. refuse to recognise my outstanding merit; and Hentsch can go to the devil, so far as I'm concerned." Or (possibly) "I took the risk of ignoring von Moltke's orders, and I've been caught out; but I refuse to accept criticism from Hentsch." Von Kluck's own account of the incident, however, merely confuses the issue still further: "Lieutenant-Colonel Hentsch, a senior officer from G.H.Q., arrived at about noon on September 9th, coming from 2nd Army H.Q. I was not informed of his visit, however, until after his somewhat hurried departure. This unfortunate misunderstanding might have been avoided if this officer had asked to see me personally; I was, in fact, at no great distance from my H.Q."

But, if this was so, why had von Kuhl said – or let it be understood – that he would report to his chief and ask for further orders? As Hentsch had not asked to be received by the Army Commander, von Kluck need only say (in effect) "let him get on with it", and nothing prevented him from showing his annoyance. No. Either von Kluck has no wish to see Hentsch; or he was prevented from doing so.

Looking again at the portrait of the old 1870 veteran, one is less and less inclined to accept the theory that he was accepting hospitality (in one form or another) at some neighbouring

château. This man was, clearly, neither an ascetic nor a dolt;
but I have discovered nothing in his private life to confirm
or refute such a suggestion. I prefer von Kluck as his portrait
reveals him, stolid and tough, not without a certain rugged
charm, a man who could keep his own secret.

No record exists of the exact time that elapsed before von
Kuhl came back with von Kluck's (alleged) reply, which was:
"The 1st Army cannot now change its direction east to make
its junction with the 2nd Army. The 1st Army will retire due
north, on to the Aisne, between Soissons and Compiègne."

The manoeuvre would still leave a large gap between the two
armies; but it would avert any immediate danger of envelopment.

"Your Majesty, the Chief of the General Staff awaits your
orders."

Emperor William made a gesture of assent, and the meeting
began at its usual hour. His two A.D.C.'s, Generals von
Plessen and von Lyncker, in uniforms almost rivalling the
splendour of their sovereign, had already arrived. Von Moltke's
plain blue tunic, unadorned with any decoration whatsoever,
seemed like a silent protest against all this finery. But for his air
of weary disillusionment, he might have been giving a lesson
in good manners to these popinjays.

The Emperor had noticed – perhaps – that his Chief of
General Staff was showing signs of strain. "Let us be seated,"
he said.

He was a poor listener, and this daily, orderly-room routine
bored him. The only voice pleasant to his ears was his own.
What he most enjoyed was making grandiloquent proclam-
ations to the troops. He had already delivered a rousing har-
angue to the men of the Imperial Crown Prince's Army, and
would have liked to repeat the performance – with Imperial
expressions of satisfaction – on September 7th on von Hausen's
front. "I should spend the night at Châlons" (he had suggested)
"and visit the 2nd Army H.Q. next day." "But, your Majesty,
that is impossible, your Majesty would be taking too great a
risk." And so he had been obliged to return to Luxembourg.
One of the penalties of greatness. And now he must listen to all
these reports.

"It would be advisable for the five armies on the right of the front to make a general withdrawal, in order to permit the 1st Army to rejoin forces with the 2nd . . . ."

In spite of his boredom, Emperor William had been startled. What? Withdraw five of his armies? But this would be a general retreat? Moltke, with weary persistance, was repeating the proposal; but the Emperor could stand no more:

"No, no, no! It is out of the question!"

He had risen to his feet (followed, at once, by the others) and was walking up and down the room, excitedly waving his arms. Turning to his A.D.C.'s he asked:

"Now gentlemen, what are *your* views?"

"Your Majesty is quite right. We must hold on to our present positions." (The glittering A.D.C.'s, if they wished to hold on to their own privileged positions, could hardly be expected to make any other reply.)

Moltke had been equally startled by the Emperor's No, no, no! for this was the first time since the beginning of the war that he had turned down any suggestion von Moltke had put before him. But, up to now, Moltke's suggestions had been concerned only with swift advances towards an imminent victory.

The Emperor, visibly annoyed, listened impatiently while von Molke put forward the reasons for withdrawal. He had now lost his air of listless weariness and was speaking with a certain animation, as if, indeed, this retreat were an exciting prospect.

"If General von Bülow ordered his army to retire without previously informing your Majesty, the reason was that withdrawal was absolutely necessary, and that he could not do otherwise. Your Majesty knows that General von Bülow is a most capable officer; one of the most experienced commanders in your Majesty's armies. This retreat is only a temporary measure; but is has now become inevitable!"

Moltke was becoming more and more excited. To their horrified amazement the A.D.C.'s suddenly noticed that the Chief of Staff, in the course of this vehement outburst (so different from his usual manner) had quite lost his head; for he had even dared to touch the Emperor's arm; to lay his hand upon the sleeve of Imperial Majesty! Von Moltke himself seemed embarrassed by his own audacity.

"No," repeated the Emperor. "We must have further information upon the situation of the armies on the right wing." And he moved away, sat down, alone, and said no more. The meeting was over.

Moltke had gone back to his H.Q. in the girl's school at Luxembourg and had shut himself in his office with Colonel Tappen. An officer brought a message to the door, but, on hearing the two men talking inside he had thought it wiser to leave them undisturbed. Von Moltke was speaking slowly, Tappen asking a question from time to time.

Von Moltke (one imagined) was saying that he had failed to obtain the Emperor's assent and that orders must now be sent to von Kluck and von Bülow to hold on in their present positions. In fact, he was doing nothing of the sort; von Moltke was dictating the draft of a general instruction ordering the withdrawal of the five armies covering the front between the Meuse and the Oise. He was deliberately acting against the Emperor's wishes, for he was quite convinced that, within a few hours, the appalling truth would be self-evident, proving him to be right.

"Things are going badly" he wrote, a little later, to his wife. "The fighting now in progress east of Paris will end to our disadvantage. One of our armies is forced to retire, and the others will follow. Whatever happens, I must take the consequences, and share my country's fate. In this great struggle we are destined to be crushed between East and West."

15

"DECISIVE VICTORY"

SPREAD OUT on the table was a map of the 9th Army front. Foch took some matches out of a box, broke one of them in two, and said:

"This half represents one division. The whole matches each represent army corps. Now watch carefully. I take the 42nd Division, which was here, at Broyes, and I move it; so."

The broken match moved over from the north-west to the south-east, near Linthes.

"This is where we took the worst knock; our front is bent inwards. You see the 42nd Division coming along? You see it, don't you, Ferrasson?"

Lieutenant Ferrasson was the youngest officer on the staff. One of his duties (and he excelled at it) was to entertain the Army Commander. After a long spell of hard work with Weygand (during which the attentive Weygand would give his own clarity and precision to his chief's brilliant, explosive, but disjointed monologue) Foch would send for young Ferrasson. "Come on, Ferrasson, come out for a walk." Unlike Joffre, Foch was by no means silent during these walks; he would talk endlessly on every kind of subject; history, philosophy, or political economy. But, for the moment, Ferrasson was watching the match sliding across the paper. The more the enemy advanced against the centre of the Army front, the more effective would be the blow against its flank; this was obvious.

"What do you think?"

"I'm sure it will work, Sir."

"Right. Let's go out for a walk."

And Foch talked on, apparently deaf to the terrific bombardment away to the north. An hour earlier, just before lunch, he had signed a proclamation to his troops: "According to information received by the 9th Army H.Q., the German

Army, after continuous marching and unremitting efforts
since the opening of the campaign, has now reached the extreme
limit of its resources. The vigorous offensive in which our
troops have been engaged for the past three days has caused
consternation in the enemy ranks, for they had been convinced
that we should offer no resistance. It is vitally important to
exploit the present situation. Everyone must be thoroughly
convinced that success comes to him who holds on the longest.
What is more, the news from the front line is excellent."

Foch was right. He had only to look at his own men to
realise that the German soldiers, who had marched just as far
and just as long as the French, were at the end of their tether.
And there could be no doubt whatever that the courage and
stamina of the French, when they turned and faced the enemy,
had taken the Germans completely by surprise. As to the news
from the front line, Foch was referring, no doubt, to the other
armies; for any ordinary soldier in the 9th Army could see for
himself that things were not going well.

"Very heavy losses. It is difficult to judge if the 9th Corps
(on the left of the Army front) can hold out until the 42nd
Division reaches its assault positions." So (in effect) read the
message just received by telephone from General Dubois. On
the right, General Eydoux, when Second-Lieutenant Tardieu
brought him yet another order to attack, had grimly snorted:
"What do you expect me to attack with? My own escort?"
(It was, in fact, the same General Eydoux who, the day before,
when his troops had already been severely buffeted, had
informed Foch by telephone that the positions lost would be
re-occupied "by fresh, well-disciplined troops".)

The critical point on the front was Mondement, from which
it was still feared the Germans might debouch in order to
occupy the plateau above. The Moroccan Division, under
General Humbert, were under orders to attack it once again,
with the help of the 77th Infantry, who had been withdrawn
from the line on the morning of the 8th and had spent the
night of the 8th/9th near St-Gond, in drenching rain and
squelching bivouacs. The description "fresh troops" was
certainly well-chosen.

As has already been said, the Château de Mondement was
masked from the French artillery by the woods around it.

The effect of the preliminary bombardment was for this reason disappointing. Nevertheless, Major Beaufort, wearing white gloves, "as was his custom on these occasions", raised his hand and shouted: "Forward, The Fifth! Pour la France!" A bugler beside him sounded the charge; and the men marched off in column of eight, as if on parade.

One company reached the foot of the walls, which the preliminary bombardment had breached at three places. Three only. There was no other way in. The problem facing the German machine-gunners barricaded inside was thus reduced to its simplest expression: they had only to keep the breaches well under fire. Any Frenchman who showed himself there was shot down. Meanwhile, the infantry, the Zouaves, and the Tirailleurs following them were being enfiladed from the large farm immediately west of the château. The attack had failed, and they had to withdraw to the shelter of the woods.

They had no sooner done so than an order arrived from General Humbert: "The Beaufort battalion will resume its attack on the château tonight." For the moment the Beaufort battalion was taking what cover it could at the foot of the walls, amidst the heaps of their dead lying in front of the three breaches. Anyone attempting to leave the precarious shelter of the walls was shot down as he entered the murderous zone of fire from the flank.

On Foch's left the 5th Army was continuing its advance, its right forcing back von Bülow's right, which, in fact, was already beginning its withdrawal. The officers had to order frequent halts, for their men grew quickly tired; but fatigue did not lower their morale, so long as they could be given sufficient rest. Near Marchais, General de Maud'huy (who was constantly on the move) passed the 49th and 18th Infantry regiments, halted beside the road. The men were in high spirits, laughing, joking and dressing themselves up in German helmets and haversacks. They had been detailed to pile up the German swords and rifles lying around. "Vive le Général!" they cried.

At about 13.30 Maud'huy received a message stating that Château-Thierry was apparently clear of Germans, or only lightly held. This was great news, for, once Château-Thierry was captured, the French could storm into the Ourcq valley and cut off von Kluck's retreat. The 18th Corps' orders, however, would have sent them too far north-east.

"Bring my car, at once," said Maud'huy. "To Army H.Q., Montmirail!"

The roads were congested with the supply columns following up the advancing troops. Maud'huy, with his head through the window, shouted at the drivers to let him pass. At one point, while he was edging his way past a load of steel girders, the inevitable happened; he was struck on the head; and on his arrival at Montmirail the Army H.Q. staff officers saw him stagger out of his car with blood trickling down his face.

"It's nothing at all," said Maud'huy. "Where is the General?"

Nevertheless, he was persuaded to have his wound dressed. Franchet d'Esperey was absent, but his Chief of Staff agreed: "Yes, march on Château-Thierry." The roads, however, were no less congested on the return journey. At one cross-roads the gendarmes, who had been striving (with little success) to disentangle a truly Gordian knot of traffic, suddenly heard a loud screech of brakes and saw a car turning out of the Nogent-l'Arthaud road. Then shots rang out. The person inside, firing his revolver out of the window, had an enormous bandage round his head.

"I am General Maud'huy! Clear this blasted mess out of my way!"

Three carts were duly tipped over into the ditch; and the general's car went through.

The cavalry detailed to enter Château-Thierry were forced to move, however, at a more leisurely pace. In the 20th Dragoons that morning, one hundred and fifty-three horses were found to be unfit for the road, even at a walk. No more than half the regiment could take part in the operation. The leading troopers legged and spurred their weary mounts into a trot as they crossed the first railway bridge; but a little later a burst of rifle-fire put several horses out of action; and the Dragoons dismounted.

These cavalrymen, who had been trained to fight only in the saddle, now had to take their carbines and assume the rôle of franc-tireurs, creeping through the outskirts of the town,

taking cover behind walls and in doorways. They were reinforced shortly after by a cyclist group, who also dismounted,
parking their machines beside the horses. Not one German was
to be seen. But German bullets were pitting the walls of houses,
and noisily shattering the windows. German machine-guns
set up a spluttering din. The fight was dragging on against an
invisible enemy; and the Dragoons and cyclists were making
little headway.

After a brief lull, the first French shell landed with a crash
in the town, and other salvoes came rumbling over; a few
houses went up in flames and burned fiercely. Very soon after
the German machine-guns had stopped firing, and the French
moved cautiously forward from house to house.

A mounted squadron of cavalry passed through at a walk,
making for the northern exit of the town. All firing had ceased.
But just beyond the gate that straddled the road the lances of a
group of German cavalry could be seen, barring the exit. These
Hussars, in the glossy uniform of the Imperial Guard, were now
lowering their lances . . . .

Captain Vidal stood in his stirrups and gave the order:
"Prepare to charge. Charge!"

The scene that followed seemed slightly unreal. Half trotting,
half walking, the exhausted animals jogged slowly forward,
their riders crouching low in the saddle, like knights at a
tourney, with lances down. There was a dull, head-on crash, a
confused mêlée, a few shots from the Germans; but they
quickly disengaged, wheeled their horses and made off, in a
clatter of galloping hoofs that raised dust from the road.

The two extremes of the French front were heavily engaged.
On the extreme right was General Sarrail's 3rd Army, extended
along a forty-mile front, holding on grimly to Verdun on the
one hand, and, on the other, putting up the stiffest possible
defence at the famous Revigny Gap, the bane of all French
generals since Dumouriez's* day. The men in this sector were
as tired and as sorely-tried as those on the left wing, where –
it was thought – the issue of the battle would be decided. The
truth was that the issue was being decided at every point on

*Charles-François Dumouriez (1739-1823). Famous general of the pre-
Revolutionary period.

the front. If the 3rd Army had given way, Joffre's entire front would have cracked, or would, at least, have been forced to retire; and Gallieni's cleverly-conceived attack on the German flank would have come to nought. The weather was still hot from Verdun to beyond Revigny, with heavy, low cloud; and the sultry air was foul with the sickening stench of battle.

The men of the 4th Army (de Langle de Cary) on the left of Sarrail's 3rd, had also to endure the same discomfort, when the wind was from the front; for they had been fighting for several days over the same ground. The left wing of this army was now attacking von Hausen's Saxons, in an effort to relieve the pressure on Foch. On the right, however, they were fighting a ding-dong battle, winning or losing a mile of ground in a series of attacks and counter-attacks that resembled the trench warfare of later years, but without trenches, which, military speaking, would now be thought nonsensical.

On the extreme left of the front the men fighting in the northern sector of the 6th Army (at right angles to the eastern sector) had no reason to imagine that the German High Command had ordered a withdrawal; for the moment they themselves were again being driven back. A number of regiments were now retiring along the main Paris to Soissons road, leaving Nanteuil ablaze behind them. Some isolated detachments who attempted to make a stand behind the railway embankment were surrounded and shot down.

The 38th Infantry, however, were now giving ground, inch by inch, in perfect order, under cross-fire from German machine-guns. As the ranks grew thinner the order came: "Close up!" The battalion was being led by the regimental commander, who, at 13.00 hours, had received verbal orders to retire.

"No written orders? Then I refuse. I must have something in writing."

He had waited two and a half hours; but no written order came. A few days later, however, "something in writing" was found on the body of one of the officers of the regiment, Lieutenant Salaün. The Germans had taken his képi, sword, revolver and field-glasses; but they had left his diary:

"September 9th. I am with a platoon of the 17th. Artillery duel. Opposite Betz. Weather fine. Aeroplanes. Woods on the left and troops moving about. 14.00 hours: my battalion is cut off; we are the last troops left, all the others have gone. *Nous sommes ici pour l'honneur.*"

In the eastern sector of the 6th Army (on a line running from north to south) the situation was less critical, but the men were almost collapsing from fatigue and would fall asleep, even under shell-fire. This was happening, in fact, along the whole front; and unless an attack was actually in progress or the men were in imminent danger of being hit by bullet or shell, most of them would fall asleep.

For this reason alone the march of the 42nd Division along the whole front of the 9th Army was a remarkable achievement. With General Grossetti and his escort leading, the battalions had marched in columns of eight; the artillery in sections abreast.

"It reminds one of Napoleon's "Square" battalions, Sir," said Captain Réquin.

A distant aeroplane, with black-cross markings, was the only modern note in a scene that might have been painted by Detaille.*

"Well," replied Grossetti, "we're going into battle; but I don't know where the enemy is. The 9th Corps has given way; the 11th Corps has vanished. In this formation we are at least in readiness for action at any time, anywhere."

Meanwhile, the officers who had been ordered to take the Château de Mondement ("whatever the cost") were trying to think of some method other than charging across the open with bugles blowing and officers wearing their white gloves. The Beaufort battalion, which had finally succeeded in withdrawing from its almost desperate plight at the foot of the château walls, had now re-formed in a clearing in the Mondement wood. Colonel Eon was briefing his officers.

"We make an approach-march to the edge of the wood, the 7th Company leading. A hundred yards behind us will be two guns, escorted by two companies. Lieutenant d'Ythurbide, who will act as advance-guard, will wave his cap when he thinks the time has come for the two guns to be unlimbered and manhandled into position. The guns will then open fire, and we shall await the result before giving the signal for the assault to begin."

Colonel Lestoquoi, commanding the 77th regiment of Zouaves and Tirailleurs, was also planning for a gun to come

*Edouard Detaille (1848–1912).

into action at four hundred yards' range in the avenue leading straight through the woods to the gates of the château. Another gun would be placed three hundred yards from the wall surrounding the park. These guns would, therefore, be firing at almost point-blank range and should practically destroy the château before the infantry were sent in. Such were the tactics now being introduced as a result of the appalling losses incurred during infantry attacks over open ground, without – or with ineffective – artillery support.

The guns opened up; the walls of the park and of the château itself began to crumble; enormous holes could be seen in the tower; the servants' quarters and outhouses were soon ablaze; and, one by one, the German machine-guns that had opened fire on the gunners were silenced.

The infantry rushed forward, in a sort of race for the château, which was won by the battalions led by Colonel Lestoquoi, who had ordered them to advance while the guns were still firing. "We had expected tough resistance, but, in fact, there was none." Many of the Germans had discreetly departed. The machine-gunners were found, dead or dying, lying beside what remained of their guns, half buried in rubble. The survivors were only too glad to surrender. In one of the passages was a grenadier, mortally wounded. His helmet bore the name of a battle in which, no doubt, his regiment had won distinction – "Waterloo".

Lieutenant-Colonel Weygand had left Foch's command post at Plancy with orders to "co-ordinate the operations of the 42nd Division with the 9th and 11th Corps". He may well have been wondering, as he drove along the road towards Linthelles, what remnants of the 9th and 11th Corps were still capable of co-operation of any sort. Groups of grim-faced, weary men were straggling back towards the rear, no officers nor N.C.O's amongst them.

"Where have you come from ?" – "We got lost." (Which may have been true.) "Why have you left the front line?" – "We had no ammunition left." (Which, in fact, was true.) It was significant, however, that the German infantry were making no attempt to exploit the situation. Weygand found General Dubois, the 9th Corps Commander, with his foot bandaged, sitting under an open shed.

"On the left of the front," said Weygand, "the battle's won. You must press forward. Put in everything you've got."

Dubois wearily shrugged his shoulders: "I've already done so. I've nothing left."

Pending the arrival of the 42nd Division, Weygand was, nevertheless, drawing up his plan. Seven divisions were to be detailed for the operation; on paper it looked impressive.

At 18.00 hours the 42nd Division – the spear-head of the attack – arrived at last in its front-line positions. It was already dusk. The evening mist from the marshes was drifting slowly over the countryside. Foch's orders had been: "Whatever time they arrive, attack!" The artillery opened fire.

Through their field-glasses unit commanders were observing the shell-bursts around Connantre, Sainte-Sophie and Nozet Farm. They could see very little. There was little likelihood of their seeing (as they had expected) enemy infantry lying flat on the ground, or taking cover behind the ruined houses. The reply from the German batteries was hesitant, spasmodic and ineffective. For most of the day this front had been a raging inferno of bullet and shell, with the German infantry relentlessly attacking the French lines; now it seemed half asleep.

The regiments of the 42nd Division began to move forward. In the centre was the 151st, between Linthes and Linthelles; on the right was the 94th, marching on Etang Farm and thence to Le Colombier; on the left was the 162nd, following the railway line, with the object of occupying Connantre from the north. All were advancing in battle order, in fading light. Colonel Trouchaud, commanding the 84th Brigade, sent a message to Grossetti: "It is so dark, I cannot see where I am going; I am marching by compass. The troops are very tired, and an ambush might be dangerous. Should we not postpone any further advance until the morning?"

"I will go and see him," said Grossetti to his staff officer. "No, no need for anyone to come with me. But, in half-an-hour's time, set fire to a straw-stack so that I can see my way back."

Grossetti set out across the fields, a sturdy figure against the night sky, quickly disappearing into the darkness. He was back within an hour.

"There is no sign of the enemy. We found nobody."

After its spectacular march across the front in "Napoleonic" formation this crack division had debouched into the void. As it happened, the brilliant maneouvre conceived by Foch had proved to be nothing more than an exercise with troops.

Nozet Farm, when the 68th arrived there, was found to be a massive building, dark and silent as the grave. No sign of life. At Corroy the men of the 93rd almost held their breath as they crept cautiously through the dead streets and past the shattered houses. But there, again, nothing was to be seen or heard, except an occasional, muttered curse as a soldier tripped over a dead body.

Meanwhile, Franchet d'Esperey, who had just returned from a tour through the entire area over which his army was now advancing, was reading over the proclamation already drafted by one of his staff officers.

"Soldiers,

On the historic battlefields of Montmirail, Vauchamps and Champaubert, which, one hundred years ago, witnessed the victories of our forefathers over Blücher's Prussians, your vigorous offensive has vanquished the German resistance. Firmly held in check on each wing, broken in the centre, the enemy is now retreating by forced marches towards the east and north."

All was now quiet on the front of the Army of Paris; but for most of its officers and men the sudden silence was somewhat disturbing. They knew nothing. An officer of the 14th Division, 7th Corps, wrote that night in his diary: "After five days and four nights of continuous fighting, decimated, exhausted and hungry, we lie down to sleep on the bare ground with nothing left but the will to give our lives tomorrow in carrying out the order given us: 'Hold on at all costs.' The officers and men of the 6th Army did not even know that the Germans had evacuated Betz, just in front of them. And the infantrymen of the 56th Division, who had occupied Trocy, thought that theirs was merely a local, temporary advance, an insignificant success, as short-lived as others they had won before. 'We thought the battle had been lost,' wrote Lieutenant Roussel of the 262nd."

And now dawn was just breaking; dawn on September 10th. Still the strange silence brooded everywhere. The Army of Paris was asleep in its bivouacs as French soldiers had slept so many years before, with its sentries on the go, its arms piled, the men asleep in every kind of posture. Some looked pathetically young, in spite of their grimy beards and the sufferings they had endured. The sky above the bivouacs grew paler now, dimly lighting trees, corn-stacks and strange, unhallowed things. It was near daylight, and lines and shapes grew clearer; the sleeping men roused and propped their heads, opening a drowsy eye.

Here was the countryside they knew so well; the everlasting earth where grass would grow, come what may. And dawn claimed its own as dawn had claimed its own since the beginning of time. Away to the east the pale blue sky was tinged with gold; no power on earth could check the rising sun. Here was another day and the stir and warmth of life itself. But, even as they wake, fear wakes, too, with its now familiar warning: "Take a good look at it all, my boy; for today may be your last." The gaunt ruins of shattered villages stand stark in the slanting sun; a grim reminder.

And yet, how quiet it was! A few shots in the far distance; nothing more; and why were the guns so silent? Was it a good sign? Or bad?

"En avant!" The squads and sections and regiments were on the road again, marching through the silent countryside, past the stubble and the corn-stacks and the fields of beet. But the pack still dragged heavy on the shoulders.

"The Germans have gone!" No one knew where the rumour came from; no one dared believe it; but it was true, it must be true, since they were marching on and there was nothing to stop them.

But, as the advance-guards reached the first villages on the road, their happy smiles vanished; shortly afterwards the entire 6th Army arrived on the scene of the battle they had fought and won.

Nanteuil was still burning. German dead lay sprawling in the streets. At Acy the door of the church was fouled by a great splash of blood; a dead mule lay beside it. On the straw-littered floor of the church at Vincy were bloodstained mattresses and soiled bandages; on the open harmonium a gruesome jar of reddened water; on the altar, empty bottles. The remains of a large farm in the middle of the village were still

smouldering amid a blackened mass of dead cattle lying
between the walls of what once had been a stable.

*   *   *

Lieutenant Richter, 75th Artillery Regiment, IVth (German)
Corps. "It was on September 9th, early in the afternoon, that a
liaison officer rode up and said: Move to new positions!

"When we had been given our route we suddenly knew the
bitter taste of defeat: we were to retire! The unhappy gunners
swore as they limbered up and moved off.

"We were marching north. No one knew where we were
going; not even the officers. We only knew that we were to
march north. On the plateau behind Trocy we passed through
the village of Vincy. Several of the corps ambulances were
standing there, abandoned. A depressing sight. What was to
happen to these unfortunate men, left there alone in a ruined
village? Some of the wounded were leaning out of the back of
the vehicles; as we went by one of them spat at us; I never
forgot that.

"We passed some batteries of the 74th and 40th artillery
regiments, still in action; they were staying behind to cover
the retreat. After that we moved on amidst innumerable
columns of infantry regiments in an inextricable confusion.
They formed a solid mass, overflowing on each side of the road.
The men walking in the fields could not keep up with the others,
and the regiments could not keep their men together. All the
men looked exhausted and unhappy. At sunset a staff car
arrived; and our battery-commander ran forward.

" 'Keep your heads,' said the officer. 'We are carrying out a
change of front, by orders from G.H.Q. Strategical reasons.'

"A strategical reason that was taking us farther and farther
from Paris seemed more like a bad joke to us. It was dark by
now, and we still were marching north. The men kept asking
us questions, and we did not know what to reply. All we could
do was to go on marching with them, in the icy cold mist that
was spreading everywhere. Above the mist the moon was
shining. Sometimes a car would pass us, and turn on its head-
lights for a few seconds. Not one of them slowed down, and no
one told us: 'You may halt.' The men and the horses seemed
to be walking in their sleep.

"At two in the morning we arrived in a town. I heard some voices in the dark, saying: 'It's Villiers-Cotterêts'. There we met some troops of the 9th Corps:

"We have taken ten thousand prisoners and fifty guns. And now we are ordered to retire! And they call that 'strategy'! "

"Even the soldiers grumbled. And we went on further and further north. The horses crawled and stumbled along, looking even more wretched than the men.

"When daylight came, we found ourselves marching under the cold, grey sky of northern France. We went through ruined, deserted villages. A halt was called at five in the morning on the road from Villers-Cotterêts to Soissons. We dropped down on the roadside and slept on the bare, stony ground. But we slept badly. The march on Paris seemed very far away! We realised we were moving towards some new battlefield; and more fighting."

*   *   *

The Army of Paris, continuing its advance, was now moving on to ground where the air was still foul with the sickening aftermath of war. Under the clear September sky the roads and fields were littered impartially with French Lebels and German Mausers, French képis and German helmets. The men looked around them at the hundreds of spent cartridges glistening in the sun; at the yellow wicker shell-covers and the blue shells inside. Tempting "souvenirs" some thought. Dirty paper, rags, empty bottles, blackened dixies, mess tins and rubbish of every description lay all around; as if some giant dust-bin had been emptied over the land. Here, indeed, was the dark side of the war of bugles and drums.

Dead horses lay in dreadful, fetid decay along the roadside. On the grass and stubble were hundreds of dead men, some in red trousers, some in German *feld-grau*. "It was the increased man-power resulting from the introduction of the three-year period of military service" (prior to 1914) "that made the victory of the Marne possible." So wrote General Béthouart, later.

This grim comment on the value of manpower was true, not only of the battle of the Marne, but also of every other battle of the Great War. When, in Normandy, in 1944, infantry were held up by a nest of enemy resistance the leading patrol could quickly report to the Tactical Air Force: "Village at — farm at — Square 233." Within a few minutes the place would be destroyed, and the infantry would move on. In 1914, however, aerial bombardment was, as yet, unknown; but the Germans were well equipped with heavy artillery, whereas the French had, practically, none. French strength lay in its manpower: a million bayonets. The "75", although, undoubtedly, a remarkable weapon, was no substitute for heavy guns and howitzers.

It was true, also, in 1944, that, as German snipers were trained to pick off Allied officers, orders were issued – in certain units – for officers' badges of rank to be concealed and for officers to carry rifles. In September 1914, however, a pair of white gloves would be found in almost every French officer's kit.

"Lie down, Sir, lie down!"

"Lie down? Certainly not. A French officer never lies down."

This was, indeed, a different kind of warfare. Let me quote, again, the figures of French casualties for the months of August and September, 1914: 329,000 killed, died of wounds, wounded or made prisoner. The French losses in two months amounted to almost one-sixth of their total losses during the war.

Such was the price paid for a victory that – for the time being at least – had removed the threat of German hegemony in Europe. The French were unaware, as yet, that a great battle had been won. The official communiqué, dated September 9th at 23.00 hours and published in the newspapers next morning, even suggested – especially to those who (by now) were beginning to read between the lines – the possibility of further withdrawal: "On the left wing, repeated German efforts to dislodge French troops holding the right bank of the Ourcq were unsuccessful." This unfortunate impression was strengthened later by the fact that, in the evening papers, the space usually occupied by the afternoon communiqué was left blank. People began to look gloomy once more. Their load of anxiety had been lifted for a brief moment; now it seemed as heavy as ever.

But at six o'clock that evening, an army car, with a tattered German flag stuck out of the window, drove at full speed along the boulevards. It seemed a good omen; and hope revived. But how often this had happened already! Who would have guessed that, for four years, life was to be a succession of high hopes and bitter disappointment? Not until next morning was the great news finally released: "On the left wing, the Anglo-French troops have crossed the Marne between La Ferté-sous-Jouarre, Charly and Château-Thierry in pursuit of the retreating enemy." The staff at G.H.Q., fearful perhaps of some last-minute reversal of fortune, were deliberately slow in announcing a success.

In another respect, High Command were now faced with a quite novel problem, particularly for men who had been nurtured in the historical tradition. This new-born victory was (as yet) without a name; but the vast extent of the battle-ground offered a wide choice. Joffre, for all his Republican – and, presumably, anti-clerical – sympathies, seemed to think that the child should be formally baptised.

"What name shall we give this victory of ours?"

" 'The Catalaunian Fields',"* suggested Berthelot. "A new Attila has now been vanquished there."

Joffre, with his usual good sense, feared that the somewhat obscure allusion might (as he said) "be lost on many". Belin then proposed: "Paris – Verdun", but that was considered too evocative of a cycle-race. General Gamelin claimed, later, that it was he who suggested: "La Marne", and that Joffre at once concurred. "The Battle of the Marne" (he said) "has ended in a decisive victory."

Looking back, I seem to remember that the name made no deep, popular appeal at the time; its significance was less quickly understood than that of Verdun, for example, later. But, as time went on, its immense importance became more fully recognised; it became a sign, a milestone on the road of history. We children would sit round the table, listening, I remember, to the women talking as they knitted, now, for the soldiers; and their talk was of another battle that had already lasted many days: the battle of the Aisne. The war, alas, dragged on . . .

*In A.D. 451 a coalition of Romans, Franks and Visigoths liberated Gaul from Attila's Huns on the plains between Châlons-sur-Marne and Troyes.

INDEX

Acy, 247
Aisne, Battle of the, 251
Alexandre, Colonel (later General), 61, 115
Allenby, General, 228
Alsace, 14, 21–22, 53, 54, 147, 168
Amiens, 50, 51, 84
Antwerp, 40
Ardennes, The, 20, 26, 36–37, 57, 77
Artillery, French, 194
Auboncourt, 86
Augusta Regiment (French), 167
Auvelais, 21

Bar-sur-Aube, 101, 104, 108, 120, 124, 130
Baur, Dr, 162
Beaufort, Major, 239, 243
Belfort, 19
Belgium, 14, 15, 17, 19, 20, 22, 23, 28, 38, 39, 49, 57
Belin, General, 43, 44, 47, 116, 126, 128, 251
Bergmann, Colonel, 230
Berthelot, General, 43, 47, 55, 115, 116, 121, 126, 251
Béthouart, General, 249
Betz, 195, 225, 226, 227, 242
Blondlat Brigade, 160–162, 163, 166
Boichut, Colonel, 223
Bordeaux, 80–81, 97
Bourdeau, Major, 105, 106
British Army, The, 26, 41, 60, 68, 78, 118, 150, 153, 204, 205, 217, 225–226, 228, 229, 230
British Regiments:
    9th Lancers, 204
    18th Hussars, 204
Broussilov, General, 67

Broyes, 223
Brussels, 14, 40
von Bülow, General, 26, 36, 41, 84, 85–86, 91, 93, 94, 151, 155, 167, 187, 202, 209, 213, 216–219, 222, 230, 235
von Bülow, Prince Bernhard, 36

Cambrai, 26
Carre, Major Henri, 171
de Castelnau, General, 48, 49, 58, 59, 168, 195, 207
Casualties of the Battle, 250
Cavalry, British, 78, 87, 89
Cavalry, French, 24
Cavalry Corps, 1st., 23, 24
Chambry, 148, 152, 193
Chapron, M., 43, 44
Charleroi, 14, 15, 21, 26, 36, 58, 60, 61, 141–142, 156, 185
Chasseurs, Moroccan, 133, 134, 136, 149
Château-Thierry, 84, 88, 94, 95, 106, 197, 228, 229, 230, 239–240, 251
Châtillon-sur-Seine, 132, 153, 206
Chaulet, Colonel, 152
Churchill, Sir Winston, 47, 68, 128–129
Clergerie, General, 100, 104–105, 106, 107, 113, 114, 116, 117, 118
Coblenz, 26
de Colbert, Captain, 76, 77
Compiègne, 64, 68, 69, 84, 87
Congy, 160, 161, 162, 166
Conneau, General, 126, 204
de la Cornillière, Lieutenant, 137, 139
Cossacks, 14
Coulommiers, 214
Courgivaux, 153, 154, 184
Crépy-en-Valois, 55, 112
Cros Regiment, 166

Crown Prince of Germany, The, 26, 35–36, 85, 90, 91, 93, 168, 207, 214, 216, 234
Cuirassiers, French, 11, 24, 177

Defforges, General, 63
Dinant, 38, 57
Ditte, General, 133, 160
von Dommes, Colonel, 208–211
Dragoons, French, 24, 176–177, 204, 240
Dubail, General, 46, 58, 59, 168, 206, 207
Dubois, General, 160, 161, 166, 199, 238, 244–245
Dubujadoux, Lieut.-Colonel, 152

Estienne, Colonel, 146
Emperor Franz Regiment, 167
Ethe (near Virton), 20, 21
Etrepilly, 196, 226
Eydoux, General, 190–192, 199, 238

Faure, Mme, 53
Félineau, General, 20
Ferrasson, Lieutenant, 237
Foch, General, 48, 59, 60, 70, 108, 125, 129, 142, 158–159, 160, 163, 166, 186, 187, 190, 191–192, 195, 196, 199, 201–203, 206, 210, 222, 224, 237, et seq.
Foerster (German military critic), 33
Fralon, Major, 166
Franchet d'Esperey, General, 62, 64, 70, 103–104, 117, 125, 126–127, 129, 130, 153, 158, 185, 186, 191–192, 202, 210, 224
Fréchet (interpreter), 105
French, Sir John, 64–70, 103, 117, 118, 119, 120, 125, 127, 130–132, 134, 153, 205–206, 217, 228, 229

Gagny, 181, 182
de Galbert, Major, 56, 63, 130, 131
Gallieni, General, 49, 52, 79, 81, 97–132, 153, 171-2, 181, 195, 196, 242

Gamelin, Major (later General), 43, 48, 56, 63, 114, 126, 128, 203, 251
Girodon, Colonel, 105, 106
Givet, 57, 58
Grand Marin, River, 204, 205
de Grandmaison, Colonel, 18–19, 51, 52, 159
Grey, Sir Edward, 33, 34
Grossetti, General, 203, 222–223, 243, 245
Guards Army Corps (French), 167, 198–207
Guérin, Captain, 72, 73, 136, 137, 139
Guise, 61, 63, 64, 69, 77, 84, 91, 102, 156

Hache, General, 139, 141
Haig, Sir Douglas, 228
Haeseler, Field Marshal Count, 41–42
Harloff, Lieut. Wilhelm, 197
von Hausen, General, 36, 84, 85, 87, 90, 91, 93, 94, 151, 155, 168, 187, 202, 206, 211, 214, 216, 234, 242
de Hautecloque, General, 20
von Heeringen, General, 26, 35
Hély d'Oissel, General, 62, 63
Hentsch, Lieut.-Col., 208–211, 212, 213, 214, 215–216, 217–219, 229, 230–233
Herrick, Myron T., 97–98
Highland Regiments, 78
Hindenburg, General von, 29–30, 94
Hirson (Aisne), 19
Huguet, Colonel, 120, 124–125, 130
Humbert, General, 160, 161, 162, 238, 239
Hussars, The 12th, 20

Infantry Regiment (First Tirailleurs), 21
Infantry Regiment, 69th (German), 34
Infantry Regiment, 103rd (French), 20
Irish Guards, The, 78

Jacob, M., 161–162
Joffre, General, 19, 22, 24, 43–53, 56–70, 78–79, 84, 98, 99, 101–104, 108, 109–132, 134, 149, 153, 156, 158, 195, 196, 201, 203, 206, 207, 209, 210, 211, 216, 218, 242, 251

Kaiser, The German, 20, 26, 30, 32, 33–34, 35, 41, 42, 85, 234–236
Kitchener, Lord, 68, 119
von Kluck, General, 15, 26, 36, 40–41, 84, 85–86, 90, 91–96, 98, 99, 105, 106, 114, 116, 126, 134, 140–141, 148, 149–155, 185, 187, 192, 194–195, 203, 208, 209, 213, 217–218, 226, 230–236, 240
von Kuhl, General, 210, 230–233
Kutscher, Captain, 198

La Chambre, Lieut., 172
La Fère-Champenoise, 202
La Ferté-sous-Jouarre, 214, 228, 251
Lamaze, General, 134
Langle de Cary, General, 58, 59, 70, 158, 168, 191, 206, 242
Lanrezac, General, 36, 56–70, 77, 102–104
Laon, 62, 64
Laude, General, 171, 178, 179
Lauenstein, General, 217, 218, 219
Lavedan, Henri, 15
Lebas, General, 49
Le Cateau, 41, 67
Lefas, Lieut., 172, 174–179, 183
Legrand, Sgt.-Major, 137–138
Lenharrée, 188, 190, 198
Le Plessis, 179–180
Lestoquoi, Colonel, 243–244
Lévy, Lieut.-Col., 222
Lichnovsky, Prince, 35
Liége, 23, 38, 40, 57, 177
Lille, 15, 28 49
Linthelles, 244, 245
Linthes, 222, 237, 245
Lorraine, 14, 26, 208, 209, 210
Louvain, 14
Luxembourg, 26, 27, 38, 83, 155, 208, 216, 234

Mangin, General, 140, 141, 142, 153, 154, 186, 223
Marne, River, and Battle of the Marne, 43 *et seq.*, 199 (for so-called "Miracle of the Marne" see p. 141)
Marr Johnson, Lieut.-Colonel, 69
von Marwitz, General, 208, 212, 214, 230
de Maud'huy, General, 146–147, 186, 239, 240

Maunoury, General, 51, 59, 60, 79, 98, 99, 102, 109, 113, 114, 116–117, 118, 128, 134, 148, 151, 153, 168, 171, 191, 195, 210
Meaux, 89, 92, 109, 112, 113, 114, 129, 148, 168, 178, 224, 227
Melun, 117, 118, 125, 127, 130, 131, 153
Messimy (French War-Minister), 24, 79
Metz, 59, 90, 94, 147, 207
Meurthe, River, 35
Meuse, River, 23, 35, 36, 55, 57, 66, 144, 207, 236
Mézières, 15, 77
Michel, General, 52
Millard, Abbé, 157
Millerand (French Minister), 79, 81–82, 101, 102
von Moltke, General Helmuth, 26, 29–30, 32, 33–34, 36, 83–96, 149, 155–156, 208–219, 233, 234–236
von Moltke, Marshal, 27, 29, 30, 91, 215
Mondement, 161–162, 221, 222–223, 238, 243
Mons, 26, 41
Montceaux-les-Châtaigniers, 143
Montceaux-les-Provins, 145–147, 148, 153, 184
Montmirail, 151, 185, 223, 224, 240, 246
Montmort, 216, 217, 229
Morains-le-Petit, 167, 168
Moroccan Division, 160–161, 162, 167, 220–221, 238
Mulhouse, 14
Murray, Field-Marshal Sir Archibald, 64, 69, 118–119, 129, 132

Namur, 22, 48, 57
Nancy, 35, 58, 59, 208, 210, 214
Nanteuil, 173, 242, 247
Néry, 87, 89
Nivelle, Colonel, 194

Oise, River, 63, 70, 84, 88, 89, 112, 122, 236
Our, River, 116, 134
Ourcq, River, 151, 169, 194, 204, 209, 210, 224, 225, 240, 250

Paris, 27, 28, 79, 80–82, 87, 92, 97–101, 169, 225
de Partouneaux, Major, 115
Patton, General, 144
Pau, 52
Péguy, Charles, 53–55, 71–74, 121–122, 123, 124, 133–142, 148, 152
Pellé, Colonel, 117
Penchard, 133, 134, 136, 148
Péronne, 15, 63
Pétain, Marshal, 140, 141, 142, 144–146, 154
Petit Morin, River, 157, 185, 204, 205, 209, 223
Poincaré, President, 56, 62, 79
Poirier Crest, 167, 200
Pont, Colonel, 114, 115

REGIMENTS (see also under Chasseurs Cuirassiers, Dragoons, Zouaves, etc.; also under BRITISH ARMY)

FRENCH:—
 Corps, 3rd, 64, 184
   9th, 160, 166, 184
   10th, 64, 153
   11th, 192, 221
   12th, 108
   18th, 184
   (Cavalry) 24, 99, 176
 Divisions, 6th, 146
   7th, 171, 183
   14th, 246
   35th (Bordeaux), 147
   42nd, 244, 245
   45th (Algerian) 99, 113, 128
   55th, 54, 55, 121
 Dragoons, 17, 24, 80, 176, 177
 Hussars, 12th, 20, 24
 Infantry, 19th, 188
   32nd, 189
   38th, 242
   65th, 167, 168
   69th, 34
   73rd, 154
   77th, 163, 238
   103rd, 20, 179, 181
 Infantry, 116th, 188
   123rd, 145
   268th, 221

Marines, 99
Moroccan Brigade, 133–142, 149, 160, 163, 166, 238
Reserve Battalion, 276th, 54, 71, 72, 121–124, 134–142
Tirailleurs (African Infantry), 21, 239

GERMAN:—
 Artillery, 75th, 248
 Dragoons, 89
 Grenadiers, 222
 Saxons, 37, 38, 86, 87
 Uhlans, 23, 54, 80, 89
 Wurtembergers, 20, 21, 35, 85, 216

Réquin, Captain, 203, 222, 243
Revigny Gap, 168, 207, 241
Rheims, 50, 69, 88, 151
Rhine, River, 19
Richter, Captain, 196, 199
Richter, Lieut., 248
von Richthofen, General, 208–209
Roye, 55, 71
Ruffey, General, 58, 79
Ruprecht, of Bavaria, Prince, 26, 35, 85, 210, 213–214
Russian Army, The, 27, 67, 94

Saint-Gond, 157–169, 186, 187, 198, 220, 238
Saint-Quentin, 61, 63, 64
Saint-Soupplets, 148, 152, 195
Salaün, Lieut., 242
Sambre, River, 26, 36, 58, 144
Sarrail, General, 79, 168, 206–207, 241
von Schlieffen, General, 27–28, 29, 32, 48
Sedan, 36, 40, 100
Seine, River, 112, 115, 119, 120
Semlis, 88, 105, 112, 122–123
de Serre, Lieut., 164–165
Sézanne, 101, 103, 108, 158, 166, 224
Smith-Dorrien, General, 228
Soissons, 59, 106, 151, 249
Somme, River, 13, 15
Sordet, General, 23, 24, 99, 176
Spears, Major-General (quoted), 45, 64, 104, 132, 148, 228–229

Tappen, Lieut.-Colonel, 34, 85, 89, 91, 93, 155–156, 208–211, 236

Tardieu, Lieut. André, 191, 192, 203, 238

Taxis of Paris, 170–183, 225

Togo, Admiral, 126

de Trentinian, General, 20

Tricot, 71

Trouchaud, Colonel, 245

Troyes, 164, 165, 171

Tuchman, Barbara (quoted), 66

Turcos, French, 196

Uhlans (German cavalry), 23, 54, 80, 89, 122–123, 184

d'Urbals, Major, 193

Valabrègue, General, 66, 141

• Verdun, 35, 58, 168, 206–207, 241, 251

Vidal, Captain, 241

Villeroy, 134, 135, 136

Vincy, 247, 248

Vitry-le-François, 43, 44, 46, 53, 67, 69, 101, 156

Viviani, René, 19

Vosges, 13, 15, 26, 207

Waldersee, 27

von Werder, Lieut.-Colonel, 156

Weygand, Colonel (later General), 142, 159–160, 166, 203, 237, 244

Wilson, General, 69, 127, 129, 132

Wirth, Captain, 197

Wurtemberg, Duke of, 26, 35, 85, 91, 93, 168, 187, 211, 216

Wurtemberger Regiment, 20, 21

Zarapoff, Captain, 164

Zouaves, The, 21, 149, 152, 193–194, 229, 239